339.20973
L579d
1998

AGM9577-1

SE

THE NEW DOLLARS AND DREAMS

American Incomes and Economic Change

FRANK LEVY

THE RUSSELL SAGE FOUNDATION • NEW YORK

MAY 1 2 1999

The Russell Sage Foundation

The Russell Sage Foundation, one of the oldest of America's general purpose foundations, was established in 1907 by Mrs. Margaret Olivia Sage for "the improvement of social and living conditions in the United States." The Foundation seeks to fulfill this mandate by fostering the development and dissemination of knowledge about the country's political, social, and economic problems. While the Foundation endeavors to assure the accuracy and objectivity of each book it publishes, the conclusions and interpretations in Russell Sage Foundation publications are those of the authors and not of the Foundation, its Trustees, or its staff. Publication by Russell Sage, therefore, does not imply Foundation endorsement.

Library of Congress Cataloging-in-Publication Data
Levy, Frank, 1941–
    The new dollars and dreams : American incomes and economic change /
    Frank Levy.
        p.   cm.
        Completely rev. ed. of: Dollars and dreams. 1988.
        Includes bibliographical references and index.
        ISBN 0-87154-514-4 (hardcover). — ISBN 0-87154-515-2 (pbk.)
        1. Income distribution—United States.   2. Income—United States.
        3. United States—Economic conditions—1981–   I. Levy, Frank, 1941–
        Dollars and dreams.   II. Title.
    JHC110.I5L47 1998   98-20635
    339.2'0973—dc21   CIP

RUSSELL SAGE FOUNDATION
112 East 64th Street, New York, New York 10021
10 9 8 7 6 5 4 3 2 1

In memory of Ray

For Floss, Dave and Marin,
and most of all
for Kathy

Contents

Foreword

To someone who is informed but not a professional, there is nothing more maddening than trying to make sense out of the debate on the state of the American economy. How rosy is the picture? How concerned should we be about the rise in inequality? Did things used to be better for the average American than they are now? Are all the good jobs going overseas? Can the government do anything that would help people move up economically? On all of these questions, and many more, one encounters a welter of conflicting claims, based on competing and supposedly scientific studies that heavily reflect the ideological biases of the people making them. It is almost impossible to figure out where the truth lies. Frank Levy now rides to the rescue with *The New Dollars and Dreams*, which is a clear, comprehensive, concise, and intellectually honest history of the American economy during the second half of the twentieth century. The original *Dollars and Dreams*, published in 1987, mainly concerned itself with the third quarter of the century. This new work brings Levy's argument up to the present and reflects the important new work he has done on education.

The first half of Levy's story, which will be familiar to readers of *Dollars and Dreams*, is this: At the end of the World War II, most Americans still had a way of life that was essentially that of the Great Depression. The next twenty-five years revolutionized ordinary American life. Rapid growth in productivity generated substantial increases in prosperity at every economic level. People bought houses and appliances, sent their children to college, moved around the country more than they used to do—even substantially upgraded the nutritional value of their diets.

Then, in the early 1970s, the American economy abruptly and unexpectedly stopped being so bountiful. Growth in productivity stalled, and incomes stopped growing. Inflation rose dramatically until the end of the decade, when Paul Volcker of the Federal Reserve halted it at the price of a severe recession that greatly increased unemployment. By that time, people's faith in continued economic progress from generation to generation had severely eroded, and a major fault line had opened up in the American population.

One of Levy's main contributions to our understanding is demonstrating that the most important economic division is not between races, or genders, or economic sectors, but between the college-educated and the noncollege-educated. The former group keeps pulling further and further ahead of the latter. When the economy is growing, as is the case now, the benefits go disproportionately to the well-educated people at the top of the income distribution. During the post–World War II boom nearly everybody did better. Today, not only are the less-educated falling behind, so are female-headed families, the middle of the country, and the central cities. Levy ends by worrying that we may be seeing the emergence of the kind of hard class system that has never existed in this country.

Liberal economists have a reputation for hubris—for believing they can use government as an all-powerful instrument to fix any economic problem that arises. Levy is not that kind of liberal economist. He does not pretend that the constant churn in the American economy, as companies, industries, and regions rise and fall, can be avoided. He does insistently reject the view that wealth, poverty, and all other economic realities are products of inexorable natural forces, impervious to the effects of government. Government substantially affects the rates of inflation and unemployment. Government has nearly eliminated poverty among the elderly. Today, Levy insists, government can do a much better job of providing economic opportunity to all and of cushioning the severest blows suffered by the victims of economic change.

What people in the early stages of life need most from government, and cannot be sure of getting from any other source, is a public education that genuinely equips them with the skills that the current economy demands. What older people need is access to health care, if they do not have it, and protection against poverty, if things just have not worked out for them. These are needs that are not going to be met by prosperity alone, without any government role.

Frank Levy convinces us that it will not do to say that the American economy is working magnificently for everybody, or that any intervention by government would be foolhardy. In that sense *The New Dollars and Dreams* is not only a clear-eyed explanation of economic trends, it is a calm call to action as well.

NICHOLAS LEMANN
Correspondent, *The Atlantic Monthly*

Acknowledgments

The New Dollars and Dreams grew out of my 1987 book, *Dollars and Dreams*. In the years since that book was published, the economy has changed, and I hope I have learned more about the economy. Some parts of this book are taken directly from the earlier book—for example, a description of the economy in the 1950s. Other parts of the book are new, including some new interpretations of old facts.

In the earlier book, I concentrated on the post-1973 slowdown in productivity and income growth. When I was writing, that slowdown had been clear in the data, but I believed it could be used to better advantage in explaining such widely discussed questions as whether the middle class was vanishing. I did not give as much attention to income inequality. Writing in the mid-1980s, I thought increased inequality was being driven by the 1980 to 1982 blue-collar recession, and the trend would reverse as the economy recovered. I was wrong, and income inequality receives more attention in this book.

This book would have not been written without the help of many people. My wife Katherine Swartz, read the draft manuscript and offered extensive comments. Those two acts comprise the tiniest fraction of what she has given me. With luck, some of it appears in these pages. I am indebted to Dave and Marin Levy, adults now really, who have taught me a great deal in a short time. My colleague Richard Murnane contributed to the book through his comments on the manuscript and through our continuing conversation about economics, which has lasted for ten years. Gordon Berlin, Reynolds Farley, Eric Wanner, Joyce Zickler, and an anonymous reviewer each gave detailed comments on the manuscript that helped to reshape the book's final draft. Sue Dynarski, a Massachusetts Institute of Technology (MIT) graduate student, carefully read an almost final draft and corrected many errors.

Other friends and colleagues read pieces of the manuscript or took the time to help me understand particular issues. They include Jodie

Allen, Eugene Bardach, Ernie Cortes, Sheldon Danziger, Mac Destler, Tom Edsell, William Gale, Darius Gaskins, Peter Gottschalk, Bob Hartman, Tom Kane, Arthur Kennickell, Nick Lemann, Jim Poterba, Dani Rodrik, Dan Rose, Frank Sammartino, Lou Uchitelle, David Warsh, and David Wessel.

Creating the numbers, tables, and graphs for this book took enormous effort. Patrick Wang, a recent graduate of MIT, did all the work for the draft manuscript with great skill and good humor. David Autor of Harvard University and Christopher Mazingo of MIT prepared the data for the book's final draft, updating Patrick's numbers through 1996 and calculating some new ones. They worked with great care under substantial time pressure. Jennifer Johnson of MIT applied considerable skill to the design of most of the book's maps. Lisa Neidert and Alfred Anderson of Public Data Queries, Inc., did a series of tabulations on the 1949 census on very short notice.

I have also benefited from the intellectual support of my colleagues at MIT. Singling out individuals is not altogether accurate, but I want to mention several names who made my move here much easier: Langley Keyes, Richard Lester, Paul Osterman, Judith Tendler, and the participants in the Department of Economics Public Finance Lunch. They each have taught me a lot, not all of it economics.

Financial support came from the Russell Sage Foundation, a grant from the Alfred P. Sloan Foundation to MIT's Industrial Performance Center, and the generosity of Dan and Joanna Rose who fund the Rose Chair in Urban Economics at MIT.

Finally, this book would not have seen the light of day without the patient support of David Haproff and Suzanne Nichols, respectively the director of publications and the production manager at the Russell Sage Foundation. Every author should be so lucky as to work with people like these.

Despite the help of all these people, this book is certain to have remaining errors and the errors are mine.

Since this book grew out of the earlier *Dollars and Dreams*, I am taking the liberty of including the acknowledgments for that earlier book.

My greatest debt is to my family. My wife Kathy and my children Dave and Marin have seen me through three years of writing. They put up with enormous aggravations. I owe them a great deal. Major financial support for *Dollars and Dreams* came from the Alfred P. Sloan Foundation and the Russell Sage Foundation, through the National Committee for Research on the 1980 census. Their generosity gave me the time to explore the income distribution at my own leisurely pace. Along with their funding came a superb group of reviewers—Victor Fuchs, Gordon Green, Jim Morgan, David Sills, and Charles Westoff—whose comments on an earlier draft made my job much easier. The Russell Sage Foundation also provided Priscilla Lewis, an editor with the patience of Job.

Moral support came from my colleagues at the University of Maryland's School of Public Affairs. In-kind support came from several other university units: The Computer Science Center of the Division of Behavioral and Social Sciences, and the Provost's Office of the Division of Behavioral and Social Sciences. Other support came from the U.S. Bureau of the Census and a Ford Foundation grant to the Urban Institute.

Three people were indispensable, Richard Michel of the Urban Institute is the origin of some of the ideas in this book, and all of the book's ideas were discussed with him in great length. Joung-Young Lee, now at the University of Inchon, provided research and programming assistance with an enormous can-do spirit. Rosemary Blunck of the University of Maryland's School of Public Affairs kept her sanity and mine through revision after revision as I was learning about my subject.

Equally indispensable were two libraries: The McKeldin Social Science Library at the University of Maryland and the Urban Institute library. In those rare instances where I could not find what I needed on their shelves, the library staff would quickly get it for me.

After I finished the first draft, a number of friends and colleagues commented on all or part of the manuscript. Still others took the time to educate me on particular topics where my understanding was weak. After all the writing—surely one of the loneliest vocations—all the comments and conversation proved a very welcome change. Thanks go to Henry Aaron, Jodie Allen, Gordon Berlin, Suzanne Bianchi, David Bloom, Barry Bosworth, Gary Burtless, Sam Ehrenhalt, Frank Furstenberg, Boyd Gibbons, Charles Hulten, Florence and Raphael Levy, Larry Long, Maureen McLaughlin, Tom Mueller, Patricia Ruggles, Paul Ryscavage, Allen Schick, Eugene Smolensky, Barbara and Clifford Swartz, Kathy Swartz, David Truman, Bruce Vavrichek, and Ed Welniak.

Final thanks go to Gene Bardach, Richard Easterlin, Marty Levin, Sandy Muir, Jim Tobin, and Aaron Wildavsky, who, in different ways, expanded my sense of what an economist can do.

FRANK LEVY

CHAPTER I

A Half Century of Incomes

W RITING about an economy is like writing about a river. The backdrop is the motion, a constant evolution with no beginning or end. The stories mix human effort and impersonal forces, sometimes working together, sometimes in opposition.

The chapters that follow trace the development of American incomes from the end of World War II through the late 1990s. During this time, our broadest economic goals have remained unchanged: a shared prosperity, the opportunity to progress over a career, the opportunity for our children to do better than we have done. In some decades, the economy has largely delivered these goals. In other decades, it has failed in different ways. When it fails, we develop policies to improve the economy's performance. Since the economy is constantly evolving, we solve existing problems, new problems surface, and the story continues.

The 1998 economy is a case in point. As this book was being finished in the spring of 1998, the nation was finishing the second decade of an experiment in free market economics to accelerate economic growth. The economy has always had markets, of course. Over time, better transportation and communication strengthened competition by knitting local U.S. markets into national markets and then into global markets. We also made conscious choices. Through the court-mandated deregulation of telephones, Jimmy Carter's deregulation of airlines, railroads, and trucking, and most powerfully, Ronald Reagan's philosophy of limited government, we embraced free markets as our main economic strategy much as we embraced Keynesian economics as our main strategy in the 1960s.

Three Economic Stories

How well has the free market experiment succeeded? The question has no single answer. In the summer of 1998, we could see three dif-

1

ferent economic stories. The most visible economic variables—inflation, unemployment, the government deficit—had all improved dramatically. Unemployment stood below 4.5 percent, the lowest in twenty-five years. Despite extremely tight labor markets, inflation was running at a very modest 2 percent per year. Interest rates were low. The government budget deficit—alarmingly large a decade ago—had temporarily vanished. Consumer confidence and U.S. stock markets were at record highs. All this was part of a business cycle peak—too sweet to last indefinitely—but it was a remarkable achievement.

A second story was the slow growth of average wages. From the close of World War II through 1973, average wages, adjusted for inflation, grew at 2 to 3 percent per year. Rapid wage growth was the basis of a mass upward mobility in which most workers saw big income gains over their careers. After 1973, average wage growth slowed dramatically. It remained slow even in the buoyant economy of the late 1990s.*

The third story was the high level of income inequality, a measure that has traced a long arc through this century. In the 1920s, the richest 5 percent of all families received about 30 percent of all family income.[1] Then, toward the end of the Great Depression, income inequality began a long decline. U.S. Census statistics, which understate the very highest incomes,† report that the income share of the richest 5 percent of families fell to 17.5 percent by 1947 and to 15.6 percent in 1969. Inequality stabilized through the mid-1970s but then began to grow. The income share of the richest 5 percent of families rose to 17.9 percent in 1989, and 20.3 percent in 1996—larger than in 1947. To put the matter in different terms, the top one-half percent of federal tax returns—about 560,000 returns out of 116 million—now report almost 11 percent of all adjusted gross income (AGI) tabulated by the Internal Revenue Service.‡

When you stand too close to this economy, you get a distorted picture. Think about recent sound bites: "The New Economy"; "An

---

* From April 1997 through March 1998, one measure of hourly wages grew by a respectable 2 percent, adjusted for inflation, but this growth occurred in a labor market that most people judge too tight to sustain.

† Census statistics understate the highest money incomes by not counting income from capital gains and by not counting incomes over fixed reporting limits. In 1996, individual earnings above $1,000,000 were rounded down to $1,000,000 in census inequality calculations. Generally, similar limits apply to family and household incomes. These limits currently affect 75,000 to 100,000 households out of 100 million households.

‡ In the mid-1990s, there were about 100 million households versus 116 million tax returns but the two populations differ in important respects. Some households file multiple returns. Other households file no tax returns since their income is too low to require payment of federal income taxes—Jim Poterba, personal communication, (1998).

Economy As Good As It Gets"; "A Polarized Economy"; "An Information Economy"; "An Entrepreneurial Economy"; "A Downsized Economy." No one of these phrases tells the story because all of them are more or less true.

When you take a step back and see today's economy in historical perspective, certain facts become clear. In the first quarter-century after World War II—from 1946 to 1973—the economy grew very rapidly and achieved most of the nation's economic goals. In the quarter-century since 1973, the economy's performance has been much weaker. For reasons we will discuss—reasons largely beyond the reach of policy—average wage growth slowed sharply after the early 1970s. As a consequence, many of today's older workers have not seen significant income gains over their careers. If slow average wage growth continues, many young workers—particularly those who have not attended college—will not earn as much as their parents earned.

The conflicting trends we see around us mean that the economy *may* be entering a period in which it can once again generate broadly rising incomes. Whether or not the turning point occurs depends on three factors. One is the growth rate of labor productivity, the increase in output per hour of work. The second is the economy's level of skill bias, the degree to which new production processes, including expanded trade, favor better educated workers over less educated workers. The third is the quality of the nation's equalizing institutions: public and private education, the welfare state, unions, international trade regulations, and the other political structures that blunt the most extreme market outcomes and try to ensure that most people benefit from economic growth.

To anchor the discussion, I will focus on the evolution of the U.S. income distribution. The income distribution is a mirror of economic life and I will look less at the distribution's statistics than at the stories that explain the statistics—stories about people, places, industries, and jobs. The three abstract factors—productivity growth, skill bias, and equalizing institutions—will help tie the stories together. For example, in the 1950s the continuing mechanization of agriculture both made farming more efficient and displaced large numbers of farm laborers. Often, however, farm laborers could get on a bus to a city where they could find factory jobs at higher pay.* In other words, the 1950s economy was not skill-biased: Low-skilled workers displaced in one industry could get good jobs in another industry and so incomes automatically grew throughout the distribution.

---

* Kevin Murphy (personal communication in 1993) points out that this was particularly true for blacks. Many of the agricultural jobs held by blacks in the 1940s were ultimately eliminated by mechanization. Yet black incomes rose substantially over the next thirty years as black men and women moved into other industries.

Today, the economy favors the better educated over the less educated. When computerization or international trade displaces a semiskilled worker, the move to a good job means acquiring the training to become a computer repairman or laboratory technician, a much harder move than getting on a bus. If these changes were occurring when productivity and the economy's wage level were growing rapidly, the skill bias would create a benign inequality in which less-educated workers got a little richer and well-educated workers got much richer. Until very recently, productivity and the economy's average wage have grown slowly and so many less-educated workers have taken absolute income losses.*

We cannot legislate the rate of productivity growth and we cannot legislate the level of skill bias in technological change and trade. That is why equalizing institutions are important. One of these institutions—quality education—is currently as popular as motherhood. Other institutions including unions and much of the welfare state are frequently described as ideas whose times have passed, obstacles to individual freedom and well-functioning markets. Today, when the unemployment rate is 4.5 percent, arguing against these institutions is provocative chatter. In the longer run, it is dangerous nonsense. People will not continue to support free market policies if they believe only others benefit. John Gray, a conservative political philosopher who would disagree with much in this book, makes the point well:

> [The philosophy of unfettered markets] maintains that only a regime of common rules, perhaps embodying a shared conception of rights, is required for the stability of market institutions and of a liberal civil society. This species of *liberal legalism* overlooks, or denies that market institutions will not be politically stable—at any rate when they are combined with democratic institutions—if they do not accord with widespread conceptions of fairness, if they violate other important cultural norms, or if they have too destructive an effect on established expectations.[2]

The Plan of the Book

The history that follows is divided into five parts. Chapters 2 and 3 contain an economic overview of the last fifty years. Chapter 2 describes the economy as it was immediately after World War II. Chapter 3 tells the economic story of the last five decades. The story

---

* During 1996 to 1997, productivity growth averaged 1.6 percent per year versus 1 percent per year over the previous two decades and 2 to 3 percent per year between 1947 and 1973. In chapter 8, I discuss the consequences if this higher rate is sustained.

centers on changes in labor productivity and changes in the average family's income—related topics. Since economic history is more than economics, noneconomic factors make appearances as well: politics, demography, the Civil Rights Revolution, and women's drive for equality.

Chapters 4 and 5 begin a discussion of inequality by focusing on the labor market and the distribution of earnings. Chapter 4 examines the economy's shift to a service society, and the argument that this shift is responsible for both rising inequality and a slowdown in growth. While there is some truth here, much of the argument is a case of mistaken identity. The real culprit in "deindustrialization" is a surge in skill bias that reduced opportunities for less-educated labor in all industries beginning in the early 1980s.

Chapter 5 looks inside manufacturing and services to examine the changing nature of work and pay. The chapter traces the evolution of the occupational distribution for both the whole economy and for different groups of workers—black women, white men, and so on. Using these data, I will assess three overlapping pictures of today's labor market. One is that today's economy has difficulty producing good jobs—stable work at good pay. The second is that earnings inequality is now tightly tied to genetic intelligence and is beyond the reach of policy. The third is that the labor market has become a winner-take-all market with most income gains concentrated among a very few individuals.

In chapter 6, I examine how income varies across geography and how these variations have changed over time. Over fifty years, the growth of national markets has made the nation's regions more alike while differences within regions—cities versus suburbs—have grown larger.

Chapter 7 describes changing living arrangements and the welfare state, a second pair of related topics. The welfare state, a major equalizing institution, has been based on a fairly constant set of assumptions for sixty years. Over the same sixty years, both living arrangements and the economy have changed substantially, with some of the changed living arrangements induced by welfare state programs. A constant welfare state in a changing world has created the current imperative for reform. It is straightforward to design reforms that either encourage individual initiative or ensure a decent income. The trick—a trick we have not mastered—is in constructing reforms that do both.

In chapter 8, I use the perspective of the previous chapters to reassess today's economy and sketch the policies we need if we are to continue to progress as a nation.

Notes on the Data

When my previous book, *Dollars and Dreams*, was published in 1987, it began with a statistical review of trends in average family and household incomes* and income inequality. Statistics on income and wealth are more familiar today, and so these statistics along with a definition of the gini coefficient—a standard measure of inequality—are now included as the appendix.

Two statistical issues deserve mention here, beginning with my sources. The bulk of the statistics in this volume come from the decennial census and the monthly *Current Population Survey*, both collected by the U.S. Bureau of the Census. These are the main income data available for historical studies,[3] but they contain some limitations. Most important, the census defines income as pre-tax money receipts, excluding capital gains. This definition misses the value of non-money income like Medicare and employer-provided health insurance. It misses the bite that taxes take from income. By excluding capital gains, it understates some incomes toward the top of the distribution. The appendix contains some examples of the differences made by these limitations. For most of what I discuss, the differences are not a problem. Where census statistics are inadequate for my purposes, I will supplement them with other data.

The second point involves the choice of a price index to adjust for inflation. This book traces the purchasing power of incomes and wages over the last fifty years. To do this, I must use a price index to translate historical dollar amounts into today's dollars. In recent years, a variety of reports have argued that standard government price indices—for example, the consumer price index (CPI)—overstate inflation.[4]

Unless otherwise noted, historical dollar amounts will be converted to 1997 dollars using the Bureau of Labor Statistics' chain-weighted personal consumption expenditure (PCE) deflator.† Observers agree that among government price indices, this recently revised index does the best job of measuring the inflation faced by the

---

* In U.S. census data, a family is defined as a living unit inhabited by two or more people related by blood, marriage, or adoption. A household is simply an occupied living unit. Thus all families live in households but households also include persons living alone, unrelated roommates, and so on.

† An exception is the use of official federal poverty statistics. These statistics are based on the federal poverty standard, which is annually adjusted for inflation using the consumer price index.

typical consumer over the last five decades.* When I discuss changes in "real" income or "real" wages, I am referring to changes over time in dollar amounts that have first been corrected for inflation using this index.

---

* Note that the choice of an inflation index does shape history. Statistics based on the chain-weighted PCE rather than the CPI will show less inflation between World War II and the present, greater gains of purchasing power over the same period, and a picture of the late 1940s which shows us poorer than we might believe. This last point follows from the fact that our history takes the purchasing power of today's dollar as a fixed reference point. If the growth of purchasing power since World War II was larger than we had previously estimated, it follows that purchasing power in the late 1940s must have been smaller than we had estimated.

CHAPTER 2

Beginning Again: The U.S. Economy in the Late 1940s

O SOME of us, 1947 was not so long ago. World War II had ended, wartime rationing had been lifted, F. D. R. had died, and Harry Truman was president. It is a time that merges in the memory with the 1950s and early 1960s. Between 1947 and 1960, however, the nation covered enormous ground. In this chapter, we begin our story by describing the economy and the income distribution as they looked in the late 1940s.

Income and Consumption

Depending on the times, we measure our incomes against any of three standards: subsistence, other people's incomes,* or incomes of the recent past. In the late 1940s, our incomes were defined by the Great Depression and World War II. On the eve of the Great Depression, in 1929, the typical family had income of $13,900 (throughout the book, dollar figures are 1997 dollars unless otherwise noted).[1] By 1935 to 1936 this average income had declined by almost one-third, and unemployment was running at almost 25 percent. The economy slowly moved into recovery, and by 1940 incomes had almost regained their 1929 levels.

America's entry into World War II completed the return to full employment, but financing the war required high taxes and rationing of output so that income could not be spent. In 1946 the typical family earned about one-third more than it had in 1929, but spent no more

---

* For example, during much of the postwar period public opinion polls showed that a relatively constant proportion of the U.S. population described themselves as happy, even though real incomes rose steadily. In an ingenious article, Richard Easterlin (1974) explains this stability by applying the economist James Dussenburry's relative income hypothesis. In this hypothesis, one views one's income in relation to the incomes of others, rather than in absolute terms.

on consumption. With this as a backdrop, the 1947 economy looked good. Median family income stood at $19,500, and the economy was quickly converting to peacetime production.[2]

In one sense, $19,500 overstated actual well-being. Normally a family consumes both nondurable goods, such as food and vacations, and a portion of previously purchased durable goods, such as homes, cars, and appliances. The depression and the war together, however, had caused the production of durable goods to stagnate, and so consumption of durables was low.

Consider automobiles. During the 1920s, the number of automobiles on the road had increased by fourteen million, but through all of the 1930s only three million more were purchased. What should have been a booming market held steady at a little under one car for every three adults.[3] (Today the figure is about three cars for every four adults.)

Housing showed similar stagnation. Over the 1930s, population had grown by 9 million to 131 million, but the number of owner-occupied homes had increased by only 1 million. The proportion of householders who owned their own homes had declined from 48 percent to 44 percent[4] (compared with 66 percent today), and within these units there was substantial doubling up:

- One family in fourteen lived in a household headed by another family or person, usually a relative.

- Seven unmarried adults in ten lived with other adults or families.

- About one-quarter of the over-sixty-five population (2.8 million persons) lived in households headed by their children.[5]

By today's standards, these arrangements were very cramped, although they were more normal by prewar standards. As with automobiles, a potentially flourishing market for living space and privacy had been held in suspension for sixteen years.

Because few new homes had been built, the nation's housing stock was slow to modernize and the average house of the mid-1940s offered far fewer amenities than we now take for granted. One-third had no running water, two-fifths had no flush toilets, three-fifths had no central heat, and four-fifths were heated by coal or wood. About half did not have electric refrigerators, while one-seventh did not have radios. Television and air conditioning were largely unknown.[6]

Diets also fell below today's standards, particularly in the consumption of meat. At the end of the war, we were eating sixty-two pounds of red meat per person per year, about half of what we eat today. Our consumption of chicken and turkey was about one-quarter (seventeen pounds per person per year) of what it is today.[7] Those who approve of less red meat would find other things to like. Fruit and vegetable consumption was about what it is today, and we were eating less butter, margarine, and lard. On the whole, however, the 1947 diet was what we would now call stark.

Equally stark by today's standards was access to public health and medical care. In 1949, the nation saw 42,000 new cases of polio. Among children of all races, the infant mortality rate was 31.3 per 1,000 live births: today it is 8.5. Among black children, it was 47.3: today it is 14.4. Life expectancy at birth was 67.7 years, 8.1 years shorter than today.[8]

The Great Depression and World War II were over, but for many families the middle class was not yet within reach. Public opinion polls underlined the point. In the early 1950s, only 37 percent of the public described itself as middle-class, while 59 percent described itself as working-class.[9]

The Industrial Structure

With the enormous demands of war production, it is natural to think of the 1940s as a time when manufacturing was king. It was king to an extent, but a healthy economy is always changing: agriculture was still an important employer, while services were growing rapidly.

The distribution of output and employment by industry is given in table 2.1, which shows the surprisingly large service sector. By the end of World War II, service-producing industries (including the government) accounted for more than half of both total output and total hours of employment. A look at the list of service industries explains why. Most service professions have been with us for some time: doctors, teachers, auto mechanics, utility workers, sales clerks, warehousemen. While some of these services are directly consumed by individuals, many others are consumed by business in the manufacture of goods. Later in our story we discuss the tendency of services to "follow" goods production.

If the late 1940s industrial base had one foot in the future, it was also tied to the past. The 1880 census is the last one showing that more than half the labor force worked in agriculture. Over time, the entire population could be fed through the efforts of a declining share of the labor force because of the rapid growth in output per agricultural worker (labor productivity in agriculture). Nevertheless, in 1947 agriculture still accounted for 12 percent of all hours of employment in the economy.

Between the past and the future were the traditional goods-pro-

Table 2.1 The Industrial Base, 1947

Industry	Percentage of All National Output Produced in the Industry	Percentage of All Hours of Employment Generated in the Industry
Agriculture	9%	12%
Goods-producing		
Mining	3	2
Construction	4	5
Manufacturing	29	28
Service-producing		
Transportation, communication, and public utilities	9	7
Wholesale trade	7	5
Retail trade	12	15
Finance, insurance, and real estate	10	3
Services	9	13
Government	8	12
Total	100%	100%

Sources: U.S. Department of Commerce, Bureau of Economic Analysis, (1981) tables 6.1 and 6.11B.
Note: National output equals gross domestic product.

ducing industries: manufacturing, mining, and construction. Together they accounted for about one-third of all hours of employment.

Economic Geography

In 1947 an educated guess would have placed a monument marking the economy's center of activity someplace in central Indiana. Three regions—New England, the Mid-Atlantic (New York through Pennsylvania), and the Great Lakes—accounted for fully one-half of the U.S. population (figure 2.1). The Pacific Coast (California through Washington) had doubled its population since 1920, and its rate of growth was much faster than that of the rest of the country, but its growth had begun from a relatively small base; the region was still home to only one person in ten.

The nation's center of *population* was further west and south—somewhere in southern Illinois[10]—but in economic terms, the northern tilt of population was reinforced by a similar tilt in incomes. The

Figure 2.1   Population Density Across U.S. Regions, 1949

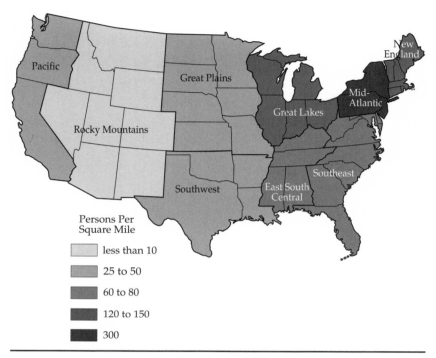

Source: U.S. Department of Commerce, Bureau of the Census (1950).

Southeast and East-South-Central regions—states running from Maryland and Florida through Arkansas and Louisiana—was dominated by low-wage agriculture. The 1949 median family income in, say, North Carolina averaged $13,100, far below the national average. A portion of this gap reflected a lower southern cost of living.[11] More important were the extremely low incomes of southern black families locked by segregation into agriculture and other low-wage work. Their incomes were part of a larger whole in which the South was an economically depressed region. In the 1949 census, white family incomes in Georgia averaged only $13,200, while in New York and California *all* families averaged $22,000. These low southern incomes further pushed the national economic balance toward the North.

Outside the South, regional income differences were smaller, but these regions, too, were separated by expensive travel and communication. There was no interstate highway system or jet passenger planes. Long distance telephone calls were a luxury. Most families used them only to announce a birth or death. Not everything was

Figure 2.2   Median Family Income Across U.S. Regions, 1949 (1997 Dollars)

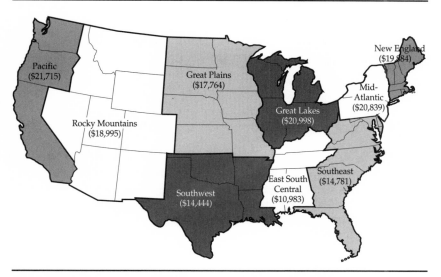

Source: U.S. Department of Commerce, Bureau of the Census (1950).

regionalized. Across the country, people could listen to network radio shows (*Jack Benny*), read the same weekly magazines (*The Saturday Evening Post*), and shop by mail from the Sears and Roebuck and Montgomery Ward catalogs. On balance, however, economic activity took place in a set of separate geographic areas without competition from neighboring areas, much less foreign countries, toll-free telephone numbers, or web sites.

The gap between the South and the rest of the country was the largest distinction in the geography of income. By contrast, city-suburban income differences were modest. It was not so much that suburbs were poor, but that much of the urban middle class still lived in central cities. The Great Depression and World War II had undermined the market for new housing and new cars; in geographical terms, this was equivalent to depressing suburban growth. The war had also strengthened central cities through emergency production needs. Because time had been so short, much war production took place in converted existing facilities in cities.[12]

In 1947, then, central cities were economically viable. They contained one-third of the nation's population. (Another fifth lived in the suburbs.) The ten largest cities held two and a half million manufacturing production jobs, 20 percent of all such jobs in the country.[13] The census first tabulated separate city and suburban incomes for 1959. In that year, median family income among central-city families was $29,100 (in 1997 dollars), only 12 percent less than median family income in the suburbs, and $2,300 above the national average for all families.[14]

The Labor Force and Occupations and Earnings

In 1947 white men accounted for about two-thirds of the labor force. This proportion is large, but the group's importance was even larger because the other major labor-force groups—white women, black men, and black women—were concentrated by custom and legal segregation into a limited number of occupations.

These white men were experienced workers. There had been no 1920s baby boom to yield large numbers of young workers twenty years later, and Social Security and private pensions were not sufficiently developed to permit large-scale retirement among older workers.[15] Sixty percent of white male workers were over age thirty-five, and among white men over age sixty-five, one-half still worked, compared with about one-sixth today. While the men were experienced, they did not have much formal education. Two-thirds had not finished high school, while only one-eighth had some college. Beneath these averages were clear differences by age: white men in their late twenties averaged twelve and a half years of education, while white men in their late forties averaged nine years. The better education of young men compressed the usual pattern in which income increases with age (and experience). In 1947 the average income gap between thirty-year-old and forty-year-old white men was 7 percent. By the late 1960s, when forty-year-old men were relatively better educated, the gap had opened to 13 percent.

To describe white men's occupational structure, it is useful to think of five occupational groups:

1. *Professional and managerial workers:* managers, administrators, scientists, teachers, lawyers, doctors, ministers

2. *Other white-collar workers:* sales clerks, clerical workers, technicians

3. *Blue-collar workers:* craftsmen, precision workers, machine and equipment operators, laborers, handlers

4. *Service workers:* cooks, custodians, barbers, beauticians, protective service workers, including police and firefighters

5. *Farmers and workers in farm-related occupations*

Note that most service workers are employed in the service *sector,* but the service sector also contains many blue-collar workers (auto mechanics, telephone repair persons) as well as professional and managerial workers (doctors, lawyers, managers).

Table 2.2   Occupational Distribution, 1949

	White Men	Black Men	White Women	Black Women
Number of Workers (in millions)	39.9	4.3	13.3	2.0
Occupational distribution (percent)				
Managerial, administrative, and professional workers	17%	4%	14%	6%
Other white collar	15	6	48	7
Blue-collar workers	47	49	23	18
Service workers	6	13	14	59
Farmers and farm-related workers	13	26	1	10
Total	100%	100%	100%	100%

Source: Author's tabulations of the 1950 Census Public Use Microdata Sample files.
Note: Totals do not always add up to 100 percent because persons in the armed forces are excluded and due to rounding.

By this typology, white men's work was a blue-collar affair. In a random sample of one hundred white men, forty-seven would have been craftsmen, machine operators, laborers, and other blue-collar workers. Thirty-two would have been white-collar workers (with half in management and the professions). Thirteen would have been farmers, six would have been service workers, and two would have been in the military (table 2.2).

These men would have averaged $16,800 in annual earnings, an average that obscures several variations. One was age. In any single year, older men had higher earnings up through men in their early forties, after which earnings declined.* Far larger were variations by occupation. While all white men averaged $16,800, white male farmers averaged $8,900, and white male doctors averaged over $30,000.

Compared with white men, black men in the late 1940s were in a very weak position from which they were slowly emerging. Ten years earlier, on the eve of World War II, half of all black men had worked in the rural South—the Southeast, East South Central, and the Southwest—while another quarter lived in southern cities.[16] Only one-third had gone beyond the seventh grade (compared with three-quarters of white men). Their incomes, nationwide, averaged $5,000, less than half of white men's average income. This weak position was reinforced by both legal and informal discrimination.

The demands of war production had opened up manufacturing jobs for blacks and encouraged migration out of the South, largely to

---

* Again, these figures reflect earnings patterns in a single year. As an individual moves through time, he or she is affected both by these patterns and by productivity growth, which may be raising wages for all workers throughout the economy. We discuss this point in more detail in chapter 4.

northern and midwestern cities. Black migration was also forced by the mechanization of southern agriculture, which eliminated farm laboring jobs. By the end of the 1950s, fully one-third of the southern black population would have moved to other regions. In 1947, however, the migration was still in progress, and one-quarter of all black men were still concentrated in southern agriculture.[17] Those not in agriculture were in low-level blue-collar occupations and in personal service work, while only 10 percent held white-collar jobs (table 2.2). Nonetheless, the migration through the late 1940s had been sufficient to raise black men's average income to $8,400, or about half the average for white men.[18]

For white women, it is easy to imagine the late 1940s as a period of regression: the wartime labor shortage was easing and "Rosie the Riveter" was going back to the kitchen. There is some truth here, but only some. During the war, women's labor-force participation—the proportion of all women over age fourteen who were working or looking for work—peaked at 35 percent in 1944. That participation rate was high for its time, but it was far lower than today's 58 percent. At the war's end, it declined only modestly to about 31 percent in the early postwar years.

This 31 percent figure was an average of participation rates that declined by age and reflected a straightforward pattern. White women worked until they married; then they stopped. Labor-force participation rates of single white women in their twenties, thirties, and forties were about 80 percent. For married women in their twenties, thirties, and forties, rates were 20 to 25 percent, and few women returned to work even after their children had grown. Statistics suggest that working women had about one and a half more years of schooling than working men, but this difference reflected the fact that most working women were young women who had more schooling, on average, than older women.[19]

When white women did participate in the labor force, they worked in a relatively small number of occupations. One-third worked in administrative support jobs as secretaries, clerks, or receptionists. Another fifth worked as machine operators, largely in garment manufacturing and textiles. These two occupations—together with sales, teaching, nursing, and various personal services (cooks, waitresses, beauticians)—accounted for three-quarters of all white women's jobs (table 2.2).

Comparing women's and men's earnings must be done with some care. Most women worked less than full-time, and so meaningful comparisons are restricted to men and women who were year-round, full-time workers. Statistics for 1955 suggest that full-time white women workers averaged about $15,500 in income, 65 percent of the average income of white men who worked full-time.[20]

Unlike white women, black women had always worked in large numbers. In 1947 their labor-force participation rate averaged 50 percent across all age groups (compared with 31 percent for white women), and they were less likely than white women to leave the labor force when they married and had children.[21] In the labor market, they shared many of the disadvantages of black men: geographic concentration in the South, an average of seven years of schooling, and official and informal discrimination.

These disadvantages were reflected in black women's jobs. In 1949 two-fifths of black women worked as household domestics, and another fifth worked in cafeterias, as custodians, and in personal service jobs. Low-rung occupations translated into low earnings. In the mid-1950s, black women who worked full-time averaged $7,900 in income, about half as much as white women.

Black-white distinctions were not society's only dividing line. Ethnic and religious divisions were important as well. Compared to earlier decades, however, most of the population was native-born. Immigration had surged in the early part of the century but fell dramatically during the Great Depression and World War II. In 1950, 6.9 percent of the population was foreign-born, compared with 13.2 percent in 1920 and nearly 10 percent today.

Family Structure and the Government

Describing family structures in 1947 as traditional would be an understatement. Few unmarried people could afford to live alone, and 94 percent of the population lived in families. With depression and war over, families suddenly formed much earlier: half of all men married by age twenty-three, and half of all women married by twenty-one. In the middle of the Great Depression, the average age of marriage for each had been a year higher.* Among all families, 80 percent had both a husband and wife under age sixty-five, and in most of these husband-wife families the wife did not work.

The number of independent elderly families was relatively small (table 2.3). This partially reflected the low life expectancy,† but it also

---

* In the longer view, all of these numbers represented long-term declines from the beginning of the century, when half of all men were married by age twenty-six, and half of all women were married by age twenty-two. After 1970 the numbers began to climb again, so that today half of all men are married by age twenty-seven, while half of all women are married by age twenty-four and a half.

† Life expectancy is shorthand for a more complicated set of statistics. In terms of total life expectancy, the greatest postwar gains have come from declines in infant mortality. Nevertheless, the more relevant statistics—for example, the additional life expectancy of a man who was forty years old in 1922 (and so would be sixty-five in 1947) versus the additional life expectancy of a man who was forty in 1960—also show increases.

Table 2.3   Family Structures, 1949

Age	White	Black[a]	All[a]
Families (percent)[b]			
Head aged sixty-five or over	13%	10%	12%
Husband-wife family under sixty-five			
Wife works	16	23	18
Wife does not work	65	52	60
Female-headed family under age sixty-five	6	15	10
Total	100%	100%	100%
Unrelated individuals (percent)			
Persons aged sixty-five or over	14%	6%	13%
Males			
Aged thirty-five to sixty-four	26	25	26
Aged thirty-four or under	25	28	26
Females			
Aged thirty-five to sixty-four	18	19	19
Aged thirty-four or under	16	20	16
Total	100%	100%	100%

Source: U.S. Department of Commerce, Bureau of the Census (1950).
[a]Includes other nonwhite races.
[b]Based on a total of 38.5 million families, comprising 139 million persons.

reflected the large number of older parents who lived in their children's homes.

The number of families headed by a woman under age sixty-five was also small, though there were important differences by race. Among all white families under age sixty-five, one in fifteen was headed by a woman. The corresponding proportion among black families was one in seven.

Not all of these black female-headed families lived in central cities. Nevertheless, the relatively high number of urban black families headed by women had been a problem for some time. In 1899 W. E. B. Du Bois described the large numbers of such black families in Philadelphia's poor Seventh Ward. Many of these women described themselves as widows, but Du Bois's description is more ambiguous.

> The economic difficulties arise continually among young women and servant girls; away from home and oppressed by the peculiar lonesomeness of a great city, they form chance acquaintances here and there, thoughtlessly marry and soon find they cannot alone support a family; then comes a struggle which generally results in the wife's turning laundress, but often results in desertion or voluntary separation.
>
> The great number of widows is noticeable. The conditions of life for men are much harder than for women and they consequently have a much higher death rate. Unacknowledged desertion and separation

also increases this total. Then, too, a large number of these widows are simply unmarried mothers and represent the unchastity of a large number of women.[22]

Over time, children born out of wedlock and families headed by women (overlapping but separate concepts) would become an increasing source of income inequality among blacks and among whites as well. We trace their development in the chapters that follow.

If female-headed families were significant among blacks, they were still rare in the population as a whole. This fact, together with the high labor-force participation of older workers, meant that almost all U.S. families (95 percent) had at least one member who worked all or part of the year. Among all families, earnings—including wages, salaries, and income from self-employment—constituted about 90 percent of all money income reported by the census. Dividends, interest, rents, and government payments comprised the remaining 10 percent.[23]

The situation today is quite different. Earnings now make up about 80 percent of all census income (rather than 90 percent), while more than 10 percent of income comes from government payments alone.[24] In 1947 government payments were limited but then, as now, payments came through two kinds of programs. One was a set of social insurance programs, including Social Security and unemployment insurance, to which wage earners directly contributed. The other was a set of means-tested programs, including Aid to Dependent Children (later AFDC) and county relief, which were aimed specifically at the poor and funded from general tax revenues.

In 1947 many social insurance programs were still in their infancy. Relatively few persons had paid into Social Security long enough to qualify for benefits, so that in 1950 the program paid benefits to two million persons over age sixty-five, only one-sixth of the over-sixty-five population.[25] Many of today's social insurance programs, such as Medicare, simply did not exist. As a result, elderly families, whether or not they lived independently, typically had low incomes.

Antipoverty programs were similarly quite small. Food stamps and Medicaid would not be established for another twenty years, while Aid to Dependent Children paid benefits to six-hundred thousand families—about one in forty families with children.[26]

A small welfare state could be financed with small domestic government expenditures, and in the lull between World War II and the Korean War defense expenditures were small as well. With government expenditures so low, taxes were correspondingly low. A family with the median income ($19,500) paid federal income taxes and Social Security payroll taxes totaling about 7 percent of income, while state and local taxes (sales taxes, property taxes) added about 3.5 per-

Table 2.4 Composition of the Family Income Distribution by Type of Family and Occupation of Family Head, 1949 and 1996

	1st Quintile (Poorest)		2nd Quintile		3rd Quintile		4th Quintile		5th Quintile (Richest)	
	1949	1996	1949	1996	1949	1996	1949	1996	1949	1996
Upper income limit of quintile (1997 dollars)[a]	$9,900	$20,100	$16,900	$35,000	$22,900	$52,100	$32,300	$76,800	n.a.	n.a.
Family type										
Family head (male or female) aged>sixty-five and over	25%	22%	11%	25%	7%	17%	6%	10%	8%	9%
Husband-wife family head aged thirty-five to sixty-four	42	19	48	31	61	48	58	63	71	76
Husband-wife family head aged<thirty-four	18	10	33	19	28	20	32	18	17	11
Female head aged<sixty-five	15	42	8	19	4	11	4	6	3	3
Male head aged<sixty-five with no spouse	n.a.	7	n.a.	6	n.a.	5	n.a.	4	n.a.	2
Totals	100%	100%	100%	100%	100%	100%	100%	100%	100%	100%
Occupation of family head										
Professional and managerial	7%	5%	11%	11%	12%	19%	20%	29%	36%	52%
Other white collar	3	13	9	17	10	18	12	20	12	20
Blue collar	15	16	39	28	41	34	46	32	34	17
Service and agriculture	37	18	16	15	17	12	12	9	10	5
Head does not work	38	48	25	29	20	17	9	9	8	6
Totals	100%	100%	100%	100%	100%	100%	100%	100%	100%	100%
Percent of working wives in husband-wife families	15%	27%	19%	50%	20%	68%	25%	80%	32%	81%
Percent of families with at least one working member	75%	62%	92%	82%	98%	92%	99%	96%	99%	97%

Sources: U.S. Department of Commerce, Bureau of the Census (1975b), and tabulations of the 1950 Decennial Census Public Use Microdata Sample files and the March 1997 Current Population Survey

Note: Columns may not add to 100 percent due to rounding. n.a. refers to information that is not available.

[a]The upper limit of the first quintile is also the lower limit of the second quintile, and so on across quintiles.

cent more. The resulting tax burden—10.5 percent—was less than half of what it is today.[27]

Then and Now: The Income Distribution in 1949 and 1996

We summarize our discussion of the late 1940s by comparing the content of the family income distributions in 1949 and 1996.[28] These statistics are not the stuff of daily conversation, but they can be understood through two comparisons: comparisons among families at different income levels in the same year; and comparisons of income distributions in different years.

Table 2.4 divides both the 1949 and 1996 family income distributions into five groups—quintiles, as they are called—where each quintile contains one-fifth of the nation's families in the year. The first quintile of the 1949 distribution contained the poorest one-fifth of families in 1949; the fifth quintile of the 1949 distribution contained the richest one-fifth of families in 1949, and so on.

To be in the first quintile in 1949, a family's income had to have been less than $9,900 (in $1997). By census estimation, these first quintile families received a total 4.5 percent of all income going to families, and they differed in several dimensions from other families higher in the distribution.

A major difference was family type: Two-fifths of families in the first quintile were either elderly or one of the small number of younger families headed by a single woman. Despite the preponderance of elderly and female-headed families, retirement was rare and welfare was limited so that work was common. Nearly two-thirds of all families in the quintile had a household head who worked, and three quarters of all families in the quintile had at least one worker, usually in farming (with its low cash incomes)[29] or in personal service work.

A byproduct of the low position of the elderly was the relatively high position of children. While the bottom quintile contained 20 percent of families (by construction), it contained only 15 percent of the nation's children (table 2.5), though this figure included nearly half of all black children. Children's good position in the distribution reflected both the number of low-income elderly and the baby boom in the middle class.

In terms of residence, this bottom quintile in 1949 was heavily skewed toward the low-wage South and contained a quarter of all white families and half of all black families who lived in the Southeast and East-South-Central regions. Conversely, it contained relatively few central city families from any region, reflecting both low rural incomes and central cities' strong economies.

Table 2.5   Distribution of Selected Groups Across the Quintiles of the Family
Income Distribution: 1949 and 1996

Characteristic	1st Quintile (Poorest)	2nd Quintile	3rd Quintile	4th Quintile	5th Quintile (Richest)	Totals (Percent)
Family heads aged>sixty-five						
1949	44%	19%	13%	11%	12%	100%
1996	28	31	19	11	11	100%
Black families						
1949	36	32	24	5	3	100%
1996	40	22	16	13	9	100%
White families						
1949	18	18	21	21	22	100%
1996	16	19	21	22	23	100%
Hispanic families						
1949	n.a.	n.a.	n.a.	n.a.	n.a.	
1996	37	25	18	12	9	100%
Families residing in central cities						
1949	14	15	22	24	25	100%
1996	28	21	17	17	18	100%
Families residing in Southeast and East-South-Central regions						
1949	32	23	17	17	11	100%
1996	23	21	20	18	19	100%
Children						
1949	15	22	22	22	19	100%
1996	28	19	19	18	16	100%

Sources: U.S. Department of Commerce, Bureau of the Census (1975b), tabulations of
the 1950 Decennial Census Public Use Microdata Sample files and the March 1997
Current Population Survey
Note: Rows may not add to 100 percent due to rounding.
n.a. = not available

As we move up the 1949 distribution, these characteristics reverse.
Families were less likely to be elderly or headed by a single woman
and more likely to be headed by a middle-aged man. Workers were
less likely to be in agriculture or service occupations and more likely
to be in blue-collar or white-collar work. In the fifth (top) quintile,

where family incomes were $32,300 or more, 99 percent of the families had at least one worker. Almost half of these family heads had white-collar jobs while one-third had blue-collar jobs. Among residents of the Southeast and East-South-Central regions, only 4 percent of black families and 13 percent of white families were in the top quintile, but the quintile contained 25 percent of the families who lived in U.S. central cities.

By 1996, many of these patterns had changed, beginning with the elderly's improved position. The bottom quintile in 1996 contained families with incomes below $20,100 and received, by census estimates, 4.2 percent of all income going to families. The proportion of the bottom quintile who were elderly declined slightly: Elderly families were more numerous in the population but their improved economic status had raised them into higher quintiles. Now the bottom quintile was increasingly populated by the growing proportion of female-headed families: 42 percent of the quintile in 1996 versus 15 percent in 1949. In a similar way, 28 percent of all children were now in the bottom quintile, an increase from 15 percent in 1949.

Geographic patterns within the distribution changed as well. Between 1949 and 1996, southern families became more evenly spread through the distribution as regional economic distinctions faded. At the same time, central city families were increasingly concentrated in the distribution's bottom quintile as differences grew between city and suburban income.

Finally, occupations changed throughout the distribution. Over almost fifty years, farm work became much less frequent while professional and managerial work rose substantially. Patterns of work effort changed as well. In the first quintile, the proportion of families with a working head declined from 62 percent to 52 percent. In the top quintile (income over $76,800), the proportion of families with working wives rose from 32 percent to 81 percent, a trend that was repeated to various degrees in every quintile.

In chapter 1, we noted that family income inequality was larger in 1996 than it had been following World War II. These patterns add another dimension to the comparison. Today, we think of inequality in terms of people who occupy overlapping worlds: the bond trader and the mail room clerk in the same financial house; the female family head and the suburban commuter who live in the same metropolitan area and see the same television commercials.

Inequality at the end of World War II had a different feel. An important part of 1940s inequality was tied to age. For many families, to be old was to have a low income and so this part of inequality was broadly shared.[30] Much of the rest of income inequality was tied to very low southern and rural incomes. In those years, the South and other rural areas were largely unconnected to the rest of the country by mass media or easy travel. To someone living in New York, Detroit, or San Francisco, this regional aspect of inequality might as well have been describing differences among nations.

The conditions that shaped the bottom quintile in 1949 changed dramatically over the next fifty years.[31] The South now competes on a largely equal footing with the rest of the nation. Farm families are now a much smaller fraction of the population. Since 1970, elderly incomes have risen at a rate much faster than the national average. Taken alone, each of these trends would have caused a substantial decline in family income inequality. Family income inequality did decline through the late 1960s. Since the mid-1970s, however, it has risen again and is now larger than it was in 1949. In the chapters that follow, we explain why.

CHAPTER 3

Economic Change, Government Policy, and the Evolution of Living Standards

B Y THE end of World War II, the nation had lived through seventeen years of putting material aspirations on the shelf.[1] During
the Great Depression, there was no income. During the war, income returned, but there were no consumer goods. The experience
left us ambivalent.

We had high hopes for the postwar economy, but we also had a
sense of foreboding. If a Great Depression could happen once, it
could happen again, especially since war production was ending. Depression was not the only danger. When the government relaxed wartime wage and price controls, producers quickly pushed up prices
and labor staged a wave of strikes to recoup forgone wartime pay
increases. In a 1946 Gallup poll, economic worries topped the list of
the most important problems facing the country, a position that such
concerns would not hold again until the mid-1970s.[2]

Making up for Lost Time: 1947 to 1959

Yet the fears were not borne out: the economy did very well, even if
life was not perfect. Between 1947 and 1959, there would be another
war, three bouts of inflation, and three recessions, the last of which
would be quite serious. Over this same period, however, median family income would grow from $19,500 to $26,800 (1997 dollars). Had
poverty statistics been kept, they would have shown the proportion

of the population in poverty declining from 32 percent to 22 percent (see table 3.1).*

Why did incomes grow so fast? The answer is instructive because it illustrates something of what government macroeconomic policy can and cannot accomplish. The growth from 1947 to 1959 was a case where policy was quite passive.

Gross domestic product (GDP), the dollar value of the economy's total annual output, is a popular topic of discussion, but economists also talk about *potential* GDP, the value of output that would be produced if the economy were operating at full employment.† Federal government macroeconomic policies—monetary, tax, and expenditure policies—regulate demand for the economy's output. By regulating demand, they attempt to make actual GDP coincide with potential GDP, avoiding unemployment and forgone production (when demand falls below potential GDP) and inflation (when demand exceeds potential GDP).

While macroeconomic policies are important, they can raise living standards only in the short run. If the economy is in recession, increased demand can stimulate GDP to reach its potential and raise average incomes in the process. Additional income increases depend on the growth of potential GDP and, in particular, on the growth of output per worker. In the long run, the level of output per worker sets limits on a worker's income. Economists refer to output per worker as labor productivity, and so the growth of incomes over time depends on the growth of productivity.‡

In the first part of this century, output per worker-hour grew by 2 percent to 2.5 percent per year, a result of a more educated workforce, the mechanization of agriculture, the adoption of electricity, and general technological change.[3] This growth in productivity continued through the Great Depression, but from 1947 to 1966 output per

---

* See Murray (1984) figure 4.5. As we see in chapter 7, the government measures poverty by comparing a family's income to a standard that remains fixed in real terms (that is, inflation-adjusted terms). A falling poverty rate means that real incomes are rising in the bottom part of the distribution.

† This definition evades the problem of assigning a number for the "full employment" unemployment rate. In theory, full employment is the lowest unemployment rate the economy can achieve without causing inflation to accelerate. In practice, government economists used a 4 percent full employment rate in the 1950s and 1960s and about a 6.5 percent rate in the 1970s and early 1980s. The difference in rates was partly due to the growing proportion of teenagers and older women in the labor force, two groups that have historically done more "job-shopping" and so have traditionally exhibited higher unemployment rates.

‡ For brevity, I use the term "productivity" to refer to labor productivity. A second productivity measure is multi-factor productivity—the gain in output controlling for all inputs, not just labor. Multi-factor productivity will not be discussed here.

Table 3.1   Living Standards in the 1950s

	1949	1959	Growth per Decade (Percent)
Median family income (1997 dollars)	$18,800	$26,800	43%
Federal income and payroll taxes as a percent of income for the average four-person family (does not include state or local taxes)	7.35[a]%	9.47%	
Ratio of black-to-white median family income	0.51	0.52	
Percent of all family income received by lowest quintile of families	4.5%	4.9%	
Percent of all persons in poverty	32.0% (est.)	22.4%	
Government expenditures per person (1997 dollars)			
All government expenditures	$2,443	$3,665	50%
National defense	571	1,289	126%
Payments to individuals	480	714	49%
All other expenditures	1,392	1,661	19%

Sources: Median family income, the ratio of black-to-white median income, and income shares come from U.S. Department of Commerce, Bureau of the Census, *Current Population Reports* (various years). Tax burdens come from U.S. Department of the Treasury, Office of Tax Analysis (1998). The 1949 estimate of the poverty rate comes from Charles Murray (1984) figure 4.5. The 1959 estimates of poverty come from U.S. Department of Commerce, U.S. Bureau of the Census (1985a). Statistics on goverment expenditures come from U.S. Department of Commerce, Bureau of Economic Analysis, *National Income and Product Accounts of the United States* (various years).
Notes: The 1949 recession depressed 1949 income below 1947 income by 5 percent, which made decadal growth higher than it otherwise would have been.
[a]Tax burden for 1955; 1949 estimate unavailable.

worker grew at nearly 3.5 percent a year, a remarkably high figure. This 1 percent difference in growth rates may not seem very large, but as the economist Herbert Stein noted in a different context: "The difference between a growth rate of 3 percent and a rate of 4 percent was not one percent as commonly thought at the time but 33.3 percent. This means that in some sense we would have to increase the total of resources devoted to producing growth—the investment, the research, the education and so on—by one-third [to obtain the higher growth]."[4] Stein was speaking metaphorically, for there is no precise relationship between various "inputs" and increased productivity. Nonetheless, the unusually high productivity growth from 1947 to 1966 did have some concrete explanations. One was a stockpiled set of innovations in electronics, transportation, and petrochemicals that had been developed during the Great Depression and World War II. Another was favorable demographics in the form of a very experienced but slow-growing labor force. A third explanation was that the American public wanted to put the Great Depression behind it and would sacrifice personal convenience to make money.

Equally important were the rapidly expanding markets facing producers. The country was starved for basic durable goods. Our trading partners had been devastated by the war, and their needs further increased U.S. demand. These markets created a climate for improved productivity in both obvious and subtle ways. Donald F. Barnett and Louis Schorsch describe the direct links:

> Booming markets foster the construction of new plants, which are generally larger and more advanced technologically; both of these characteristics reduce labor requirements [and so increase output per worker]. . . . Rapid market growth also tends to boost profits and cash flow. The availability of funds for investment then accelerates the modernization of existing facilities. Finally, rapid market growth makes it easier to maintain high operating rates, lowering unit costs and thus improving profitability. All of these characteristics contribute to productivity growth.[5]

In a less obvious way, expanding markets improved productivity by reconciling divergent corporate goals. In 1932 Adolf Berle and Gardner Means addressed the tensions that arise in a modern corporation because the owners (shareholders) and senior management are not the same people. A shareholder wants improved productivity in order to achieve higher profits. Unless senior management's compensation is tied to profits, its goals may be more diffuse. Senior managers may, for example, want to expand the firm beyond what is profitable because a larger firm brings more power and prestige. Today a manager's compensation often includes stock options, and most managers face strong shareholder pressure to achieve high returns. Fifty years ago, managers often had neither incentive, but when the economy was expanding rapidly, a corporation could become larger and more profitable simultaneously and these tensions did not arise.[6]

Even after taking into account innovations, demographics, and expanding markets, productivity growth from 1947 to 1966 simply seemed to benefit from a dose of good luck.*

In the glow of remembrance, rising living standards suggest a tranquil Ozzie and Harriet economy. A more accurate picture comes from Joseph Schumpeter's term "creative destruction," the process by which old products, firms, and areas are displaced even in a healthy economy.[7] Over the 1950s, the number of persons employed on farms dropped from seven million to four million, a decline equal to 5 percent of the nation's labor force. Total manufacturing employment was growing, but within the total, steel employment fell by 25,000 (−4 percent), while aircraft employment increased by 363,000 (+139 percent). Changing industrial patterns led to changing plant locations: over the decade, manufacturing production jobs in the ten largest central cities declined by one-fifth.[8] Dislocations abounded, but the era's technological change was largely skill neutral so that people who lost jobs could often find comparable jobs elsewhere. The combination of skill neutrality, fast growing productivity, and a fast growing average wage meant that more people (including many of the dislocated) won than lost.

How was the new money spent? Largely to make up for the time lost since 1929. The automobile market had been brought to a halt by the depression and the war, but at the war's end it exploded. The number of private automobiles on the road had grown by only three million in all of the 1930s, but it grew by twelve million between 1946 and 1950, and twenty-one million more between 1950 and 1960. By 1960 there were sixty-two million cars on the road, one for every 1.8 adults.

Over the same period, the number of owner-occupied homes almost doubled, from seventeen million to thirty-three million. As with cars, the demographics for home ownership had been present throughout the depression. The problem was insufficient income, but after the war, incomes were growing. At the same time, housing was more affordable. The availability of automobiles opened up whole new areas to construction because building sites were no longer tied to public transportation. The new land combined with improved mass construction techniques to keep housing prices low. In the mid-1950s, the average home in Levittown, New Jersey, had monthly carrying charges of $745, while the average family had monthly income of

---

* For example, in the work of Edward Denison (1985), quantifiable factors can account for about two-thirds of productivity growth during the period; he refers to the unexplained remainder as the "residual"—that proportion of the rapid growth that cannot be explained by observable factors.

$2,500 (in 1997 dollars). On a national basis, the average thirty-year-old man could carry the mortgage on an average home for 14 percent of his gross pay.[9] With cars and housing now so affordable, the middle-class dream was becoming available on an increasingly wide basis.

More important than the consumption of housing and cars was our "consumption" of children. Children, like consumer goods, cost money, and hard times, ceteris paribus, are marked by falling birth rates.* From 1929 to 1944, the number of children under age fourteen *declined* by 1.5 million, but between the end of the war and 1960, the number of children under fourteen increased by 20.3 million in what we call the baby boom. Some of these children represented births that had been postponed during the depression and the war, but most were the children of younger men and women who had been raised in the depression. They had lived first on low incomes and then on rationed consumption. When they formed their own families in the 1950s, they found that they truly could have it all—they could live better than they had seen their parents live, and they could have large families, too.†

The fast-growing number of children led to a statistical paradox. The income of the average *family* was growing rapidly, but consumption expenditure per capita—that is, per man, woman, and child—was growing far more slowly, a reflection of growing family size. Usually slow growth is a sign of trouble, but here it reflected an optimism that workers could support large families.

Living standards improved by other measures as well. The proportion of households with radios grew from 85 percent to 95 percent. The proportion of households with televisions grew from essentially nothing to 85 percent. Families acquired vacuum cleaners, washing machines, and other time-saving devices that would ultimately help women enter the labor force.‡

Diets changed: per capita consumption of beef and veal increased by one-quarter; per capita consumption of potatoes declined by one-fifth; lard consumption declined; butter and margarine consumption increased; the introduction of frozen foods increased the availability of vegetables and juices throughout the year.[10] In today's world of

---

* The qualifying ceteris paribus is important. In the mid-1960s, the birth rate began to fall from its baby-boom high levels even though times were very good. At least part of the reason was an expanded set of opportunities for women, together with a growing interest among women in working outside the home. Chapter 7 discusses this change in greater detail.

† This argument has been developed most elegantly by Easterlin (1980).

‡ I am thankful to Maureen Steinbruner for this point.

wraps, radicchio, and the continuing Cajun revolution, these improvements seem tame, but they brought about gains in nutrition (and fat).[11] Because agricultural productivity grew so fast (the opposite side of farm worker dislocation), improved diets did not require increased food expenditures.

We have focused on the increased consumption of goods. Consumption of services rose just as rapidly. Expenditures on medical care, recreation, telephones, personal care, and other consumer services all increased such that services accounted for one-fifth of all consumer expenditures in both 1947 and 1959. Twenty years later, increasing service consumption and growing service employment would be used as evidence of a second-rate economy, but during the 1950s it was just another part of the larger theme of making up for lost time.

The Drive for Full Employment: 1960 to 1969

Some of us have few memories of the 1950s, but clearer memories of the 1960s. It was a decade when government assumed a much larger role in taxing, spending, and managing the economy.

The new economic intervention was a natural development of the 1950s growth. From 1947 through 1959, the economy had experienced rapid growth in productivity and potential GDP, but it had also seen three recessions. Each time a Keynesian-activist president might have tried to reduce unemployment through tax cuts and/or increased government spending, but neither President Truman nor President Eisenhower was predisposed to such activism. Both men were concerned about the corrosive effects of inflation. Eisenhower, in particular, felt that periodic economic slumps kept inflation in check and attempts to shorten recessions would ratchet inflation upward. His view was politically acceptable because both the 1949 recession (under Truman) and the 1954 recession had been mild. The 1958 recession, however, was both deep and long, with unemployment averaging a then high 5.4 percent from 1958 to 1960. Nonetheless, Eisenhower held firm against activist policies.*

---

* The description as it applies to Truman is a little unfair. In 1948 the Republicans had forced Truman to accept a cut in taxes from their wartime high levels. When the economy entered the recession of 1949, Truman felt that since a tax cut had recently been passed and presumably was just starting to work, a second tax cut designed specifically to fight the recession was unnecessarily risky.

Eisenhower's reluctance to stimulate the economy has been detailed by Richard Nixon (1962). Nixon and his adviser Arthur Burns feared that a continued recession would cost Nixon the 1960 presidential election. He appealed to Eisenhower to take some action to stimulate the economy, but Eisenhower refused.

Compared with the Great Depression, the 1958 recession was not serious, but a decade of postwar recovery had made the depression a fading memory. People were less ready to accept any economic downturn at all and more willing to see the government experiment with antirecession policies. John Kennedy's 1960 campaign promise to "get the country moving again" was an attempt to tap this feeling.[12]

In contrast to the Truman-Eisenhower years, the Kennedy-Johnson years were a high point of Keynesian activism, and the initial success was enormous. A number of authors have described the role of good decisions in this success.[13] Less obvious were the roles of luck and circumstance, which made the 1960s an ideal Keynesian test case.

Consider the context. Productivity growth remained above 3 percent per year, permitting average wages to increase by 3 percent per year without creating inflationary pressures. In addition, Kennedy (and then Johnson) inherited low inflationary expectations. Getting the country moving through Keynesian stimulation could lower unemployment, but it ran the risk of increasing inflation. Had we entered the 1960s with high inflation, Keynesian policies would have been ruled out. Eisenhower's policies had kept the economy slack, however, and inflation averaged only 1 percent per year from 1958 to 1960. In this way, Eisenhower had removed a potential obstacle to the Keynesian experiment.

A second Eisenhower legacy was a federal budget with, in economists' terms, a large "full employment surplus." Keynesian policies mandated deficits only in recessions. If taxes are already low vis-à-vis expenditures, a further stimulating tax cut can leave a permanent (or "structural") budget deficit that continues even when the economy reaches full employment and stimulation is no longer needed. During the late 1950s, Eisenhower ran a stringent fiscal policy, so that had the economy been at full employment, the budget would have shown a large surplus. This full-employment budget surplus provided Kennedy and Johnson with the margin for Keynesian tax cuts: they could cut taxes knowing that the budget would come into balance as the economy reached full employment.*

To list these happy circumstances is to belittle neither economic policy nor the role of policy-makers. Many presidents have squandered opportunities, whereas the Kennedy-Johnson application of Keynes began brilliantly. But the opportunity was there. If we miss this point and think that rising incomes in the 1960s reflected smart

---

* This, in fact, happened. In 1965 the federal budget ran a small surplus, and in 1966 it ran a small deficit.

policies alone, we will conclude that post-1973 stagnation came only from government ineptitude, and that is simply wrong.

The early results of the Kennedy-Johnson policies were all that could be hoped for. After 1963 unemployment declined steadily. In 1965 it stood at 4.4 percent, and median family income stood at $31,800 (in 1997 dollars), a $5,000 increase in six years. The increased income reflected both sustained productivity growth and the Keynesian stimulation that was getting more people into jobs. Despite the brisk recovery, inflation was running at under 2 percent per year.

From many perspectives, 1965 was a pivotal year. It was the first year of Lyndon Johnson's second term, a year he began with an enormous legislative agenda. The nation was gripped by the civil rights revolution and the march in Alabama from Selma to Montgomery, which culminated in the Voting Rights Act of 1965. But 1965 was also the year in which the country became increasingly involved in the Vietnam War. Increased military commitments required increased expenditures. Since the war was too unpopular to permit new taxes, Johnson financed its opening phase with new deficit spending.[14] In the process, he turned economic folk wisdom on its head. A war was supposed to be good for the economy. It was, after all, the only time when government could increase spending and run deficits—that is, practice Keynesian economics—with a straight face. Attitudes had changed in the early 1960s, however, and by 1965 the government, without the benefit of a war, had stimulated the economy to nearly full employment.

This made the Vietnam deficits a very mixed blessing. In the short run, the deficits further stimulated the economy and produced much faster growth and lower unemployment than any president would have dared to choose—a boom of enormous proportions. At the same time, this boom sowed the seeds for stubborn inflation that would prove very difficult to break.

The boom accelerated income growth for the rest of the decade. As the economy approached full employment, worker productivity began to grow more slowly, averaging 2.5 percent per year (versus nearly 3.5 percent per year from 1947 through 1966). Slower productivity, however, was offset by falling unemployment, and over the decade median family income grew from $26,800 to $37,800 (table 3.2), a growth rate comparable to that of the 1950s. Moreover, low unemployment enabled income gains to be distributed more equally than would otherwise have been the case.

For example, throughout the postwar period, the unemployment rates for black men were about twice those of white men, but the 1960s expansion made this two-for-one relationship something posi-

Table 3.2   Living Standards in the 1960s

	1959	1969	Growth per Decade (Percent)
Median family income (1997 dollars)	$26,800	$37,800	41%
Federal income and payroll taxes as a percent of income for the average four-person family (does not include state or local taxes)	9.47%	13.54%	
Ratio of black-to-white median family income	0.52	0.61	
Percent of all family income received by lowest quintile of families	4.9%	5.6%	
Percent of all persons in poverty	22.4%	12.1%	
Government expenditures per person (1997 dollars)			
All government expenditures	$3,665	$5,608	53%
National defense	1,289	1,558	21%
Payments to individuals	714	1,333	87%
All other expenditures	1,661	2,717	64%

Sources: Median family income, the ratio of black-to-white median income, and income shares come from U.S. Department of Commerce, Bureau of the Census, *Current Population Reports* (various years). Tax burdens come from U.S. Department of the Treasury, Office of Tax Analysis (1998). Poverty estimates come from U.S. Department of Commerce, Bureau of the Census, *Current Population Reports,* series P-60 (various years). Statistics on government expenditures come from U.S. Department of Commerce, Bureau of Economic Analysis, *National Income and Product Accounts of the United States* (various years).

tive. For every one-point drop in the white unemployment rate, the black rate dropped two points. In both 1968 and 1969 the black male adult unemployment rate stood at 3.8 percent, six percentage points below its 1955 to 1965 average, and about 4.5 points below its 1997 level.

Low black unemployment was strong medicine for black incomes. The proportion of black families headed by women had risen from 15 percent in 1950 to 22 percent in 1960, and 31 percent in 1969 (see chapter 7). By itself, this trend should have caused the black-white income gap to grow, but the improved economy was so powerful that the ratio of black-to-white median family incomes increased from .52 to .61. More generally, the income share of the lowest quintile increased, and the combination of rising and more equal incomes caused the proportion of the population in poverty to fall from 22 percent to 12 percent (table 3.2).

By the end of the decade, Congress had raised taxes to pay for Vietnam, but after-tax income had still risen sharply over the decade. Expenditures on cars and houses grew, but at slower rates than in the 1950s; the most urgent postwar needs had been filled. At the margin, consumption was shifting toward services. Per capita expenditures on recreation and meals had grown slowly in the 1950s, but over the 1960s they grew by 40 percent. Per capita expenditure on medical care grew even faster in the 1960s than it had in the 1950s.

The shift toward services was also evident in the apparently rapid growth of government spending. We say "apparently" because government spending in the 1960s was characterized not so much by an accelerated growth in dollars spent as by a growth in new initiatives. While the 1950s are commonly viewed as conservative, government expenditures (federal, state, and local) actually grew faster than private consumption spending in that era (table 3.1). That fact did not make news because the lion's share of the money went into traditional programs: public education (the baby boom), national defense, and Social Security. Only a few initiatives—the new network of federal highways, for instance—stood out.

Over the 1960s, government expenditure per person grew only slightly faster than it had grown in the 1950s (table 3.2). At the federal level, traditional programs took a smaller portion of the increment, and new money went into new programs: health insurance for the elderly and poor families (Medicare and Medicaid), community action antipoverty programs, aid to elementary and secondary education, and so on.

Behind the new programs was a fortuitous alignment of economics and politics. Between World War II and the mid-1960s, family incomes had increased by 56 percent. The government apparently could avoid recessions as well as depressions, and economic growth was beginning to look automatic. Cars and single-family homes were widely available, and an increasing proportion of the population saw itself as middle-class. We were ready to consider increased public spending to "make the society a better place."*

During the 1950s, the congressional Democrats had built an agenda of domestic programs, but Eisenhower generally was not interested.[15]

---

* In 1964, 44 percent of respondents saw themselves as middle-class or higher, up from 37 percent in 1952. On the complementary relationship between private consumption and public expenditure, see Hirschman (1982) and Levy (1985).

In a curious sense, his attitude may have further stimulated public receptivity to the Democrats' ideas. Had Eisenhower tried, say, a war on illiteracy that subsequently failed, the public might have become skeptical about what government could accomplish. With no initiatives, however, there also could be no failures, and so the public was willing to listen to ideas about what government could do.

By the mid-1960s, Eisenhower's caution had been swept away. The civil rights movement was gaining strength. Kennedy had been assassinated, and Lyndon Johnson assumed office. Johnson skillfully presented the Democratic agenda as a way to heal the nation.[16] Congressional Republicans might have blocked the agenda on fiscal grounds, but many of them were dragged from office by Senator Barry Goldwater's disastrous presidential candidacy in 1964. Their Democratic replacements found a delightful prospect: the economic expansion was raising tax revenues so fast that the government had to initiate new spending, cut taxes, or do both. To do nothing would create large budget surpluses that would slow down the economy. Under Johnson's prodding, with the civil rights revolution as backdrop, the 1965–1966 Congress passed Medicare and Medicaid, compensatory aid for disadvantaged students, the original War on Poverty legislation, and a substantial increase in grants to state and local governments as well as the Voting Rights Act of 1965 and a major liberalization of the country's immigration laws.

Even more ambitious than the actual legislation were the promises they embodied. Some were performance promises, like the promise that government dollars could teach all poor children how to read. Others were promises of entitlement: the government, for example, would provide certain levels of medical care for the elderly, or absorb significant numbers of immigrants, no matter how expensive these actions became. The assumption behind these promises of entitlement was that long-run economic growth would continue. If it did not, things would get very expensive.

The Troubles Begin: 1970 to 1972

When the economy goes badly, politicians get the blame, and so it is not surprising that they should want the credit when things go well. Johnson took full credit for the sustained boom of the 1960s, and Keynesian economists confidently talked of "fine-tuning" the economy to achieve maximum performance. This view obscured the underlying factors that lay beyond any politician's immediate control. Three of these factors we have already noted: rapid productivity growth, skill neutrality, and the absence of inflationary expectations. A fourth factor was stability in raw materials prices. By the early 1970s, these factors began to reverse. Incomes (and politicians) suffered correspondingly.

Inflationary expectations began to form in the late 1960s. The economic boom had left the country with very low unemployment but a high (for that time) inflation rate of 5.5 percent. When Richard Nixon took office in 1969, he planned to induce a short recession, break the inflation, and stimulate a new expansion in time for the 1970 midterm elections.[17] History was on his side. In each of the earlier postwar recessions (1948, 1954, and 1958 to 1960), one year of recession was sufficient to bring inflation below 1 percent, but in 1970 the plan did not work. By August 1971, after eighteen months of recession, inflation was still running at 4.7 percent while unemployment was at almost 6 percent.

This was the first evidence of inflationary expectations, or "stagflation": employers and workers anticipating inflation and pushing for higher wages and prices even though the economy is slack.* The result is a self-fulfilling prophecy. In retrospect, it can be seen that this early stagflation was a problem created by Keynesian policy itself. The late Arthur Okun, a key architect of the 1960s economic success, summarized the relationship well:

> In subtle ways, I believe the depression mentality [and the drive to combat recession] fostered inflation vulnerability. There was an imbalance in policy: it is inconceivable that a four-year recession would have been tolerated in the way that a four-year boom was tolerated in the late 1960's. And when the economy is made depression-proof and deflation-proof, private expectations and conventions become asymmetrical, introducing inflationary bias into the system.[18]

Nixon, feeling the pressure of the upcoming election, responded with a mixed policy. He instituted wage and price controls to break inflation and accepted a monetary expansion by the Federal Reserve to lower unemployment. He also freed the international value of the dollar from the gold standard, a point we return to later.

The combination of policies represented a distinct gamble. Wage and price controls can reduce inflation when the economy is slack—when there is no underlying scarcity—but because monetary policy was stimulating the economy, scarcities were sure to arise. Controls could suppress inflation only until they were removed, or until they

---

* Here, as in many other things, an excellent source is the work of the late Arthur Okun. See *Prices and Quantities* (1981), his work on stagnation and the "invisible handshake": the tacit agreement by which employers and employees came to expect cost-of-living salary adjustments even in slack markets.

simply broke down. Nixon, by pursuing both policies, was gambling that the controls would at least hold through the 1972 election.

The gamble worked. Inflation cooled, unemployment fell, and 1972 median family income reached $39,300, $1,500 more than it had been in 1969. As the controls were lifted, however, inflation began to reappear.

The Quiet Depression

In the late 1960s, the unemployment rate was below 4 percent and the economy was clearly in a boom. If we think in terms of income growth rather than unemployment, the entire period from 1947 to 1973 was a twenty-seven-year boom. The point is not that unemployment is unimportant—clearly it is very important—but over the long run rising wages and incomes are a better index of the nation's progress. During Dwight Eisenhower's two terms in office (1953 through 1960), the economy experienced one mild and one quite serious recession, but the average family's real income still rose by 24 percent. The full employment of the Kennedy-Johnson years drew more people into the labor force and so distributed growing incomes more equally, and the average family's real income grew by 30 percent. During these years, the American middle class grew, not so much because inequality declined (though it did), but because the *whole income distribution* kept moving to higher levels as most people improved their situation (figure 3.1).

Today such income growth seems remarkable. In the eight years following Richard Nixon's first term (1973 through 1980), the average family's real income did not grow at all. From Ronald Reagan's first year in office through most of Bill Clinton's first term (1981 to 1996), it grew by a total of 9 percent. In my 1987 book *Dollars and Dreams*, I referred to the years after 1972 as "the Quiet Depression."[19] The phrase may have been excessive, but it helped focus attention on the years after 1972 as a period of consistently slow productivity and average wage growth, a time when the average family suddenly found economic gains much harder to come by (figure 3.2). Along other dimensions, the economy's performance varied sharply during these years, and it is to these variations that we now turn.

Economic Stasis: 1973 to 1979

In 1973 few people saw the long-run productivity problems that lay ahead.[20] What people could see was plenty of short-run trouble in the form of shortages in the supply of two key raw materials.

The first was the 1972 to 1973 food shortage, which led to a rapid inflation in food prices. The shortage was driven by a worldwide crop failure and a bad Peruvian harvest of anchovies, a critical ingredient in animal feeds.[21] In the United States, the situation was made worse by a large and disadvantageous wheat sale to the Soviet Union. Between 1972 and 1974, food prices in the United States rose by 34 percent.

The rise of food prices was quickly followed by the 1973 to 1974 oil shortage. Unlike the food shortage, the oil shortage was contrived, a policy imposed by the Organization of Petroleum Exporting Countries (OPEC) in the wake of the 1973 Arab-Israeli War. It resulted in a tripling of oil prices. While the price rise was buried in the rhetoric of the exhaustion of natural resources, it is best understood as OPEC's attempt to run oil production as a monopoly cartel.* The Arab-Israeli War served as the catalyst for cartel cooperation.

These "supply shock" inflations were quite different from inflation in the late 1960s. The earlier inflation came from an overstimulation of demand for output and was at least accompanied by low unemployment. Shortages in food and oil could cause rapid inflation (and strengthen inflationary expectations) even when the economy was stagnant and unemployment was high.

The OPEC increase in particular could not have come at a worse time. The country remained divided over the Vietnam War. Vice President Spiro Agnew had been forced to resign, under threat of trial for corruption, and Nixon himself was besieged by the Watergate hearings.† The administration was left with little authority to face a very difficult problem because the OPEC price increase did more than exacerbate inflation; it also caused large amounts of income to be sent overseas to foreign oil producers. These oil payments were equivalent to a giant tax and so helped to increase unemployment even as inflation was accelerating. By the time President Nixon was forced to resign and Gerald Ford took office, inflation had reached 12 percent per year and unemployment was 5.6 percent and rising fast. Not until 1976 would the economy begin to recover.

The food and oil inflations caused a substantial erosion in average family income. Median family income continued to rise in 1973 to a postwar high of $40,400, but between 1973 and 1975 it fell by $1,800 to slightly above its 1969 level. Under normal circumstances, this income loss would have been erased by little more than two years of

---

* An alternative explanation is that demand in the 1960s had expanded rapidly while petroleum producers had allowed their prices to remain low. In this view, the 1973 to 1974 price increase was merely a "catch-up" to free market levels.

† I am indebted to Robert Reisner of Washington, D.C., a former member of President Nixon's administration, for reminding me of these connections. On one particular evening, the newscaster Walter Cronkite had to expand the *CBS Evening News* from its normal half-hour to one hour to cover the events of the day, which included the Agnew resignation and the continuing Arab-Israeli Yom Kippur War.

Figure 3.1 The Family Income Distribution, 1949 to 1973

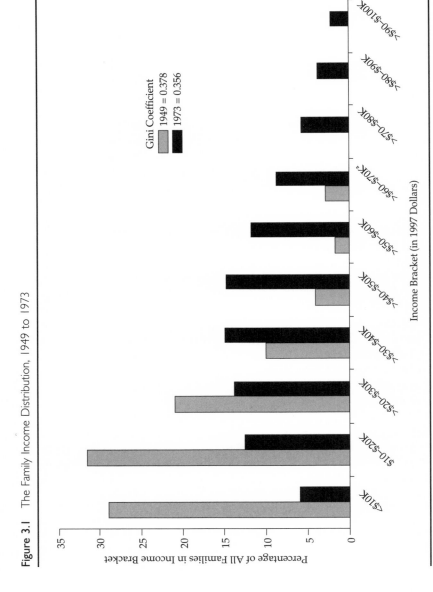

Sources: Author's tabulations of the 1950 Decennial Census Public Use Microdata Sample files and the March 1974 Current Population Survey.

[a]For 1949, the income bracket >$60,000–$70,000 contains all families with incomes above $60,000.

Figure 3.2 The Family Income Distribution, 1973 to 1996

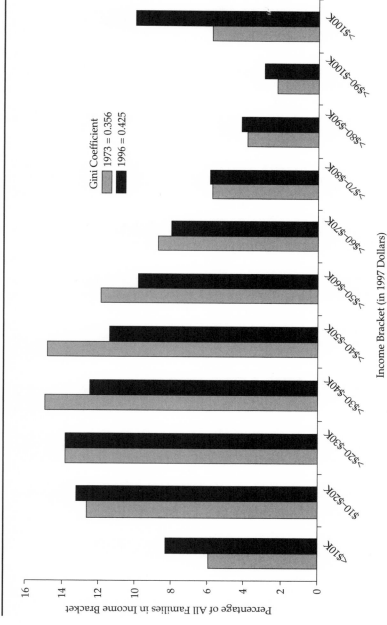

Sources: Author's tabulations of the March 1974 and March 1997 Current Population Survey.

economic growth. In the final bit of 1970s bad luck, however, productivity growth collapsed.

In the 1950s and early 1960s, rapid productivity growth (3.3 percent per year) had created rapid income gains. After 1966 productivity growth slowed to something like its historical trend of 2.3 percent per year, a change that caused some worry. Beginning in 1973, productivity growth slowed to about 1 percent per year, a growth rate that continued through at least 1995.*

The sudden productivity slowdown† is one of the central events of this book. It has no definitive explanation,‡ but the most careful studies point to factors like these:

- The rapid increase in energy prices suddenly changed the techniques required to achieve efficient production, making certain kinds of capital equipment obsolete and so lowering the amount of capital per worker.

- During the 1970s, maturing baby boomers and older women entered the labor force in great numbers, lowering average labor-force experience. They also caused the labor force to grow rapidly enough to further dilute capital equipment per worker.

- Increased government regulation of business diverted research efforts away from more efficient production (as measured in productivity statistics) and toward the reduction of pollution and increased worker safety.§

---

* As this book was being finished, the most recent data showed productivity growth averaged 1.6 percent for 1996–1997. Economists disagree sharply on whether this higher growth rate will continue. If it were to continue, it would make a big difference in the life of the nation. We return to this point in chapter 8.

† As Robert Samuelson notes, the very sharp slowdown after 1973 may have been an artifact of Nixon's wage and price controls. Recall that productivity measures the growth in output per hour. The wage and price controls forced all of the early 1970s economic recovery into output, allowing none of it to go into inflation. Without the controls, the recovery might have generated somewhat greater inflation and a somewhat smaller growth in output, and the slowdown in productivity might have been spread over several years.

‡ As careful scholars of the subject have shown, it is far easier to reject causes of the productivity slowdown than to accept them. For example, the fact that the slowdown occurred so suddenly rules out an explanation like the shift of employment to the service sector, which had proceeded gradually over many years. Similarly, other industrialized countries also experienced productivity slowdowns after 1973, a fact that throws doubt on uniquely U.S. explanations like the glut of baby-boom workers. See Denison (1985) and Baily and Blair (1988) for fuller discussions.

§ For a case study of how antipollution regulations may have diverted research efforts from ways to increase output, see Baily and Chabrabarti (1985). Because we measure a firm's output by its sales, we have no way of correcting for the fact that the output is accompanied by clean, rather than dirty, air. To the extent that the 1970s were characterized by less output but cleaner air, standard productivity statistics will understate the gains in well-being.

Even when these factors are all considered, they predict only a part of the observed slowdown, thus opening the door to a more speculative explanation. The speculation begins with the fact that increased productivity requires technological change, which, as David Landes writes, is often painful to implement:

> Technological change is never automatic. It means the displacement of established methods, damage of vested interests, often serious human dislocations. Under the circumstances, there usually must be a combination of considerations to call forth such a departure and make it possible: (1) a need or opportunity for improvement due to inadequacy, present or potential, of prevailing techniques; and (2) a degree of superiority such that the new methods pay sufficiently to warrant the cost of change.[22]

To take a contemporary example, management's decision to purchase a set of personal computers and to put them on employees' desks is straightforward enough. It is more difficult to think through a reorganization of work so that the computers can share information in real time. It is more difficult still to implement the reorganization: to train employees to use the new software, to give employees the incentive to share the information they develop, to lay employees off if part of their work becomes so automated that they are no longer needed. In an uncertain world, these changes involve big risks, and they give the status quo a strong appeal.*

When markets are growing rapidly, as they did in the 1940s, 1950s, and 1960s, a business can confine innovation to its new capacity and so change can be less disruptive (recall Barnett and Schorsch's comments on the link between growing markets and productivity). By contrast, changes made to existing capacity can be very painful. Often, a firm changes only under intense market pressure that has put the firm's future in doubt. Managers and line personnel may prefer the status quo to any reorganization, but when the status quo is untenable, work reorganization becomes more acceptable.†

In the early 1970s, the collapse of productivity growth was a sign that U.S. firms had to organize work in new ways. From 1973 to 1979, however, four factors undercut what should have been competitive pressure to restructure.

---

* Less painful investment alternatives include "working around" existing employees by hiring additional people to run the new technology and adding new technology by acquiring other companies that use it.

† For example, during the 1980s, the credible threat of plant closings caused the United Auto Workers to agree to substantially modify work rules and job classifications in a number of automobile plants.

The first was regulation. Since the late 1940s, better transportation and communication had laid the groundwork for a more competitive economy. The interstate highway system, begun under Eisenhower, had reduced the costs of moving goods among regions. Major cities were now linked by jet airliners. Long distance calls could now be dialed directly (rather than requiring operator assistance) and at significantly reduced costs. In many industries, however—telephones, interstate airlines, interstate trucking, railroads, banking, electric power—competitive forces were held in check by government regulation. Regulation limited a new firm's ability to enter the industry and an existing firm's ability to change prices, both of which reduced possibilities for competition.

The second, as we have seen, was inflation. Between 1973 and 1979, prices at both the wholesale and retail levels rose by more than 100 percent. Rapid inflation increased uncertainty and so discouraged long-term investments as it also undercut managers' ability to make intelligent decisions.* While inflation created demands for higher money wages, employers could hold real wage costs in check by giving "cost-of-living" raises that lagged behind inflation. In several ways, then, inflation helped to obscure many firms' weakening positions.

A third factor undercutting competitive pressure in the early 1970s was the declining foreign value of the dollar. Recall that when President Nixon adopted wage and price controls in 1971, he also abandoned the dollar's link to the gold standard and allowed the international value of the dollar to be set in foreign exchange markets.† By 1975 President Ford was fighting the post-OPEC recession by encouraging low interest rates, a policy continued by President Carter. While low interest rates stimulated domestic spending, they also lowered

---

* When inflation is high, a firm runs the risk of underestimating its cost of capital because it is simpler to value equipment at historical cost—the price the firm actually paid for it—rather than the price the firm would have to pay for it today. When managers make this mistake, a project can appear to be profitable even though it is actually lowering the firm's asset value. I am indebted to my cousin, Dan Levy, for this insight. Consistent with this idea is Mueller and Reardon's finding (1993) for a sample of seven hundred U.S. corporations that the rate of return on equity, properly calculated, was negative during this period.

† Under the gold standard, a foreign nation holding dollars could require the United States to redeem the dollars with gold at a fixed exchange rate. Beginning with the Vietnam War buildup, the United States began to run substantial trade deficits, which resulted in growing dollar holdings abroad. Nixon's action reflected the reality that soon there would not be enough U.S. gold reserves to redeem the growing foreign holdings.

the dollar's international value.* Between 1973 and 1979, the dollar fell by 31 percent against the deutsche mark, 20 percent against the yen, and 15 percent against a trade-weighted average of currencies.[23] The declining dollar tilted the playing field toward U.S. manufacturers. In Europe and Asia, the prices of U.S. exports (in francs, deutsche marks, or yen) declined steadily. In the United States, the price of imported goods rose steadily. Both trends protected U.S. manufacturers from foreign competition.

Finally, labor-force demographics provided a buffer of a different kind. Its numbers amplified by the baby-boom cohorts and older married women, the labor force was growing at a very rapid 30 percent per decade. The fast-growing number of persons with paychecks led to higher aggregate spending. In the 1960s, total consumption expenditure, adjusted for inflation, grew by 53 percent. Between 1973 and 1979, aggregate consumption still grew at 33 percent per decade, despite now-stagnant wages, because the number of workers was increasing so fast. From the perspective of a state tax collector, an automobile manufacturer, or a bank with checking accounts to sell, more paychecks were substituting for richer paychecks in supporting revenue growth, thus further undercutting pressure for change.

Taken together, regulation, inflation, the falling dollar, and demography created a period of economic stasis in which firms were protected from the pressure to restructure.† In a roundabout way, these same developments also helped to limit earnings inequality. As the well-educated baby boomers entered the labor force in large numbers, they sharply increased the supply of college graduates and so narrowed inequality between the earnings of college and high school graduates. A wave of restructuring might have offset this effect by reducing demand for blue-collar workers, but as we have seen, this did not happen. The falling value of the dollar protected U.S. manufacturing and so supported demand for production workers. The worldwide crop failures and the OPEC price shock also stimulated blue-collar jobs in agriculture and energy production. Between the

---

* Foreigners acquire dollars to purchase U.S. government securities, among other reasons. When U.S. interest rates are low, demand for U.S. securities declines, and the demand for dollars declines correspondingly.

† As noted earlier, the productivity slowdown was not unique to the United States. Productivity growth also fell sharply in most European countries and Japan after 1973. European productivity subsequently revived only because countries there were willing to tolerate historically high rates of unemployment. The fact that so many countries faced productivity problems immediately after 1973 suggests the central role of the inflation and uncertainty of the post-OPEC economy. See Denison (1985) p. 7, and the references cited therein. Note that we do *not* list the shift of employment to the service sector as a cause of the productivity slowdown. We explain why in chapter 4.

mid-1960s and the late 1970s, the earnings gap between a thirty-year-old man with a bachelor's degree and a thirty-year-old man with a high school diploma had closed from about 30 percent to 15 percent—for better or worse, a force for greater earnings equality.

The earnings of young college graduates and high school graduates were converging toward a common average, but because of slow productivity growth, the average wage itself was growing only slowly. The easy money policies of Ford and Carter succeeded in lowering unemployment, but by 1979 median family income was $41,800, only $1,400 higher than it had been in 1973. This growth was equivalent to 6 percent per decade, far less than the 40 percent per decade of the 1950s and 1960s.

The situation continued to deteriorate. Because productivity was growing so slowly, workers' push for higher wages and firms' push for higher profits resulted in higher inflation. In the first half of 1979, prices were increasing at 12 percent per year, a dangerously high figure, and people were beginning to worry that inflation was of control. On other fronts, President Carter was moving to reform the economy through the deregulation of interstate airlines, trucking, and railroads, while the courts were deregulating long distance telephone service. Inflation, however, overshadowed Carter's efforts and economic problems once again reached the top of the Gallup poll's problem list.[24] On July 25, 1979, Jimmy Carter responded by appointing Paul Volcker chairman of the Federal Reserve Board. It was not an appointment Carter wanted to make. He knew Volcker was an inflation hawk, a man who would quickly raise interest rates to break inflation, even at the cost of a recession. No president up for reelection wants a recession, but given the national fear of inflation, Carter had little choice.

As Volcker settled into the job, new problems arose. In late 1979, a coalition of secular and fundamentalist Iranians overthrew the shah of Iran. With Iranian oil production disrupted, OPEC announced a fourfold increase in the price of oil. The cycle began again. By the fall of 1980, inflation still exceeded 11 percent and mortgage rates exceeded 12 percent even though unemployment was 7.5 percent and rising. These conditions helped set the stage for Jimmy Carter's election defeat by Ronald Reagan.

The Rise of Competitive Pressures in Manufacturing

In the 1980 presidential campaign, Ronald Reagan had argued that the economy's problems stemmed from government intervention. Limit the role of government; give people and business strong incentives to produce more; let free markets operate; and the economy would thrive. While no Keynesian Democrat would have called for limited government, Reagan and the Democrats did agree on two points. Both believed in the continuing deregulation of markets, a process President Carter had initiated. Both also believed that incomes would grow rapidly if government simply did the right thing (though, of course, they disagreed on what the right thing was). Implicitly, the second point meant that government policy could raise the rate of productivity growth, an idea of enormous hubris under either laissez faire or Keynes. A new wave of technology—computers, for example—might take a long time to bear fruit no matter what government policies were followed.

When Reagan took office, his economic program promised a painless end to inflation and an immediate return to rapid economic growth.* It was an impossible boast. The 1979 OPEC price increase had given inflation a big boost, leaving Reagan with a painful choice: reduce inflation or reduce unemployment, but not both at once.

Confronted with the choice, Reagan moved first to fight inflation. In the process, he ushered in an era of rising competition and restructuring, the effects of which were first felt in manufacturing.

As Volcker pursued his tight monetary policy, the president offered strong support. By the end of 1981, the oil price shock and tight money policies had together pushed the economy into deep recession—the adult male unemployment rate was more than 9 percent—but Reagan, consistent with his sense of limited government, made it clear that he would not intervene. A second signal of Reagan's outlook was his firing of the air traffic controllers (a group whose union had supported him) when they went on strike in 1981.

At the same time, Reagan laid out his strategy for future growth by proposing a series of supply-side tax cuts.† Today the combination of Reagan tax cuts and no corresponding budget cuts is properly blamed for the large budget deficits that extended into the 1990s. We should remember, however, how popular the policies were at the time. After seven years of stagnant earnings, tax cuts had enormous

---

* For example, the Reagan administration predicted that if its program were adopted, 1984 inflation would stand at 5.5 percent, unemployment at 6.4 percent, and real gross domestic product at $1,718 billion in 1972 dollars (then the standard benchmark for real GDP). In 1984 inflation more than met the target, standing at 4.3 percent, but unemployment was 7.1 percent and GDP was $1,639 billion, about the level the administration had forecast for 1983. See U.S. Office of Management and Budget (1981).

† In theory, Keynesian tax cuts are aimed at stimulating demand in an economy that is working at less than full capacity. Supply-side tax cuts are aimed at increasing the economy's capacity by raising incentives to invest more and work harder. Very roughly speaking, one would associate Keynesian GDP growth with falling unemployment rates and supply-side GDP growth with faster productivity growth.

political appeal since they would put money into people's pockets. By the same logic, budget cuts would have been counterproductive since any cut—in defense, in Social Security, in farm subsidies—would have taken money *out* of someone's pocket. The combination of big tax cuts and much smaller expenditure cuts was what most people wanted. The resulting deficits, however, would have important consequences in the years that followed.

By 1981 Volcker's policies, with Reagan's support, had slowed inflation much more quickly than observers had expected. December-to-December consumer price inflation fell from 13.3 percent in 1979 and 12.5 percent in 1980 to 8.9 percent in 1981 and 3.8 percent in 1982, a major achievement. Other things being equal, the end of inflation should have spelled the end of high interest rates. The end of inflation coincided, however, with the beginning of the Reagan fiscal policy and big budget deficits. The Treasury's need to borrow large amounts of money and the markets' fear that deficits would spur future inflation kept interest rates high. By 1982 the *real* interest on the three-year government securities rate—the interest rate adjusted for inflation—exceeded 6 percent, three times its normal postwar level.

High real interest rates made U.S. securities very attractive to both U.S. and foreign borrowers. When foreign investors purchased these securities, they first had to convert their own currencies into U.S. dollars. The resulting demand for dollars quickly reversed the dollar's falling value, which, during the 1970s, had kept foreign competition at bay. By 1984 the average value of the dollar against foreign currencies was 55 percent higher than it had been five years earlier.[25]

U.S. manufacturing firms had already been weakened by the deep recession. The rising dollar weakened them further by making U.S. exports very expensive overseas and foreign imports cheap. Simultaneously, the high interest rates raised investors' standards for an acceptable rate of return, standards that many manufacturers now could not meet.* The result was a wave of manufacturing downsizing and reorganization that included the introduction of new technology and the outsourcing of production to foreign countries. By the end of the 1980s, U.S. manufacturers would face another source of pressure: the collapse of the Soviet Union resulted in reduced U.S. defense procurement.

---

* See Blair and Schary (1993). As they note, high real interest rates help explain the start of the leveraged buyout boom, but deals continued, pushed by a process of imitation and encouragement by investment bankers, long after interest rates subsided.

These wrenching changes helped to revive manufacturing productivity growth, but the restructuring was heavily skill biased and the demand for blue-collar labor collapsed. During the 1980s, total durable goods employment declined by a net 1 million workers: employment in skilled positions increased, but 1.4 million semiskilled blue-collar jobs—machine operators, assemblers, inspectors, and the like—disappeared. By the mid-1980s, the oil and agricultural markets had also moved into surplus, further decreasing blue-collar demand. Between 1979 and 1985, the college–high school earnings gap reopened dramatically, though, as we shall see, this development was not all due to changes in manufacturing employment. We return to skill bias and the gap between college and high school earnings later in this chapter and again in chapter 4.

For the decade of the 1980s, manufacturing productivity grew at about 2.6 percent a year,* a growth rate close to that of the booming 1950s. Service-sector productivity remained weak, however, and since services employed three-quarters of the labor force (chapter 4), economywide productivity growth and wage growth remained weak as well. The recession hit bottom in 1982. From 1982 to 1989, unemployment fell steadily, but by 1989 median family income stood at $43,600, only $1,400 (4 percent) higher than its level a decade earlier (table 3.3).

Stagnant Wages and Rising Consumption

It is natural to assume that if wages and family incomes grew slowly after 1973, living standards grew slowly as well. Surprisingly, the assumption is wrong, at least by standard measures. Between 1973 and 1989, real consumer expenditure per capita grew at a rate of 34 percent per decade. Much of the new money went to such necessities as housing, utilities, and medical care. Still, the growth in spending per capita was faster than in the Eisenhower 1950s, suggesting that growth after 1973 was actually quite dynamic.

The contradiction is easily reconciled. The post-1973 growth in consumption per capita did not reflect a booming economy in the 1950s sense, but rather two national trends: the growing proportion of the

---

* I recognize that my story of broad manufacturing gains runs counter to the official data of the Bureau of Labor Statistics. Those data hold that manufacturing productivity gains were heavily concentrated in one industry—nonelectrical machinery (principally computers)—but census data show that semiskilled labor was eliminated throughout manufacturing; anecdotal evidence suggests that these changes led to productivity gains in automobiles, steel, and a variety of other industries.

Table 3.3   U.S. Living Standards, 1973 to 1996

	1973	1989	1996	Growth over Twenty-Three Years (Percent)
Median family income (1996 dollars)	$40,400	$43,600	$43,200	7%
Federal income and payroll taxes as a percent of income for the average four-person family (does not include state or local taxes)	14.96%	16.87%	16.88%	
Ratio of black-to-white median family income	0.58	0.56	0.59	
Percent of all family income received by lowest quintile of families	5.5%	4.6%	4.2%	
Percent of all persons in poverty	11.1%	12.8%	13.7%	
Government expenditures per person (1997 dollars) All government				
expenditures	$6,118	$8,517	$9,291	52%
National defense	$1,213	$1,557	$1,021	−16%
Payments to individuals	$2,003	$3,161	$4,067	103%
All other expenditures	$2,901	$3,798	$4,203	45%

Sources: Median family income, the ratio of black-to-white median income, and income shares come from U.S. Department of Commerce, Bureau of the Census, *Current Population Reports* (various years). Tax burdens come from U.S. Depatment of the Treasury, Office of Tax Analysis (1998). Poverty estimates come from U.S. Department of Commerce, Bureau of the Census, *Current Population Reports,* series P-60 (various years). Statistics on government expenditures come from U.S. Department of Commerce, Bureau of Economic Analysis, *National Income and Product Accounts of the United States* (various years).

population who worked and our increased willingness to take on debt.

We have seen how a rapidly growing labor force in the 1970s—thanks to the entry of older women and baby boomers of both sexes—was one force that postponed restructuring. The fact that most of these people found jobs was the major success of the post-1973 economy.* These work patterns also influenced statistics on income per person. Middle-aged families increasingly relied on two paychecks rather than one. Younger men and women postponed both marriage and children as they entered the labor market (see chapter 7). More workers and fewer children meant that the proportion of the entire population in the labor force rose from 41 percent in 1970 to 49 percent in 1989, despite the fact that older men were retiring at earlier ages.

Not even an economist would argue that these trends were all induced by the stagnant economy,† but they helped offset the effects of stagnant wages on consumption. Because an increasing proportion of the population was at work, income and consumption per *capita* (that is, per man, woman, and child) could grow fairly rapidly even though income per *worker* grew slowly. In this way, the decade was a reversal of the 1950s. Then, income per worker was growing by over 30 percent per decade, but consumption spending per capita grew at half that rate because of the baby boom and the large number of little "capitas" it included.

There is also a plausible argument that the growth in income per capita after 1973 overstates gains in living standards. The missing issue is time. GDP accounts and census income statistics measure work done in the market for pay. Unpaid housework by women or men is not counted. When a wife takes a paid job outside the home, the family suffers some loss of her work at home or of her leisure time. GDP accounts and per capita consumption numbers do not count either loss, and so the wife's pay is treated as a pure gain. If the family compensates by hiring an outside person to clean or cook or mind the children—services the wife used to perform—the payments to the outside person are counted as an additional income gain.

Beyond demographics, the growth of consumption was reinforced by both government and private decisions to take on new debt. Debt comes in many varieties: consumer debt, the government's debt, the debt in our international trade balance. In the GDP accounts, these different pieces can be combined into a single equation:[26]

Personal +	Savings by +	Government +	Foreign	=	Domestic
Savings	Business	Savings	Capital		Investment
			Inflow		

---

* In this, it was quite unlike the European economies, which developed historically high rates of unemployment that persist today.

† In particular, the birth rate began falling sharply and women's labor force participation began growing sharply in the 1960s when the economy was strong. These trends are discussed in chapters 5 and 7.

This accounting equation describes the way in which each dollar of investment must be financed by a dollar saved from one of four sources: individuals, businesses (through their retained earnings), the government sector (through budget surpluses), or capital borrowed from foreign countries. By comparing the elements of this equation in the early 1970s and the mid-1980s, we can see how the country's financial position changed:

- The individual savings rate declined from 5.4 percent to 3.8 percent of GDP, but the business savings rate increased by an offsetting amount, from 11 percent to 14 percent of GDP.

- The government sector (federal, state, and local) moved from running a small surplus in the early 1970s to running a deficit equal to 3.4 percent of GDP per year, a reflection of the large annual deficit in the federal budget. Government thus changed from being a small generator of savings to a significant user of savings. The total domestic savings rate (individual plus business plus government) fell from 16.8 percent to 14.7 percent of GDP.

- The rate of investment remained constant at 16.5 percent of GDP, despite reduced domestic savings, because we were borrowing heavily from abroad. In the early 1970s, we were a net supplier of capital for other countries. By 1985 our net borrowing from other countries equaled 3.5 percent of GDP per year.

As we have seen, the emergence of the federal budget deficit in the early 1980s was in part a response to slow-growing earnings. It reflected our willingness to cut taxes, coupled with our reluctance to cut expenditures. The effect of these policies was to put more money in our pockets to keep consumption growing, but the choice was possible only because foreign countries were lending us money.

Foreign borrowing was not automatically bad. If foreign funds had increased the level of U.S. investment, both the United States and foreigners would have benefited. The U.S. rate of investment was no higher in the late 1980s, however, than it was in 1973, despite the foreign capital.* Foreign funds had been used to offset government deficits and thus to finance extra U.S. consumption.† This was a strat-

---

* One could reasonably argue that the rate of investment should have been greater than it had been in 1973 to keep up with rapid labor-force growth, and so our relatively constant rate of investment was insufficient.

† That is, the deficit reflected the fact that government wanted to cut taxes without making corresponding cuts in government expenditure. Tax cuts without expenditure cuts was a way to increase consumption spending.

egy for postponing stagnation's effects, but it involved borrowing from the future.

The Rise of Competitive Pressure in the Service Sector

Through the early 1980s, restructuring was concentrated in manufacturing and the impacts were focused on blue-collar labor.* By the mid-1980s, competitive pressure had grown in the service sector as well. In services, restructuring eventually would affect workers of all educational levels, though here, too, the lion's share of the change was skill biased, with less-educated workers bearing the largest costs.

Recall that in the 1970s many service-sector industries had been protected by government regulation, inflation, and a rapidly growing labor force that produced automatic increases in customers. By the late 1980s, each of these forces had collapsed. Deregulation in airlines, railroads, and trucking had begun under President Carter in the late 1970s and would extend to other industries in the 1980s. Paul Volcker and President Reagan, working together, had effectively broken inflation by 1982.

The slowdown in labor-force growth toward the end of the 1980s was the result of predictable trends. The last of the baby-boom cohorts had now entered the labor force. At about the same time, the surge of women into the labor force had leveled off at 58 percent.† These developments together reduced the growth of the labor force from 30 percent per decade to about 12 percent per decade, ending the automatic flow of new customers.

A final competitive pressure (in manufacturing as well as in services) was the growing computerization of work—first through mainframe computers and ultimately through networked personal computers. Initially, computers replaced semiskilled workers who had performed routine clerical tasks. As we have seen, implementing new technology like computers carries risks, but through the 1980s increased competitive pressure often made the risks worth taking. Over time, computers also expanded the kinds of information that could be transferred instantaneously and at low cost. With fast and cheap information, a well-managed firm could target customers more carefully, while the rapid transmission of information sped up competi-

---

* Recall that by the early 1980s the demand for blue-collar labor had also been reduced as energy and agriculture markets moved from shortage to surplus.

† That is, 58 percent of all adult women were either employed or looking for work. The corresponding figure for men was about 75 percent—down by about twelve points since the 1950s.

tion: a firm had less time to profit from a new product before competitors arose.*

In both manufacturing and services, then, competition was increasing and jobs were becoming less certain. All of these trends were well under way by the end of President Reagan's second term, and they would be particularly troublesome for Reagan's successor, George Bush.

The White-Collar Recession: 1989 to 1992

By the late 1980s, most people knew that wages were growing slowly, but growing job instability, particularly among white-collar workers, was something new. In the 1950s, a highly recruited worker could tell the manager of a small Connecticut manufacturing firm that he was happy to join the firm, but he would stay only until there was an opening at the telephone company because a job at the telephone company was "a job for life."[27] Between 1985 and 1989, AT&T, one of the deregulated successors to the "telephone company," reduced employment by 76,000, about one-fifth.

The pace of layoffs accelerated in 1989 as the economy entered recession. In contrast to the blue-collar recession of 1980 to 1982, this was a white-collar recession in which middle managers and other better-educated workers were laid off as well. According to data compiled by the outplacement firm Challenger, Gray, and Christmas, layoff announcements by major corporations totaled 111,285 in 1989, 316,047 in 1990, and 555,292 in 1991.[28]

The layoffs that began in the late 1980s generated a simple sound bite: college-educated men in their forties and fifties were losing their jobs and now no one was safe.[29] What was less clear from the headlines was a sense of context. Most media stories were written around specific corporate layoffs involving several thousand persons, but few stories tried to place these layoffs in the context of the whole labor force. Some economists countered that media reports were alarmist, since economywide data showed no decline in the length of the average job. The media reports were more important than economic data in shaping public opinion, and this opinion began to run against George Bush.

In 1989 Bush had enjoyed enormous popularity as the result of his

---

* One might ask why, if computers have had such impact, productivity has not grown faster. For two quite different reviews of the explanations, see two papers presented at the 1998 Allied Social Science Association Meetings in Chicago: Jack Triplett, "The Solow Paradox: What Do Computers Do to Productivity?" and Robert J. Gordon, "The Great Productivity Speed-up and Slowdown: How Much Is Mismeasurement?"

leadership in forcing Iraq to withdraw from its invasion of Kuwait. By 1992, with the economy in white-collar recession, Bush's popularity fell sharply. In November 1992, he lost a three-way presidential election to Bill Clinton.

A New Style of Recovery: The Economy Since 1992

Like most economic stories, this chapter should be written in a loose-leaf notebook, since the story continues to evolve. In late 1992 the economy began to recover, but it soon became clear that economic recovery looks different when competitive pressure is high. Firms, unsure of their position, paid overtime and stretched salaried personnel to avoid hiring new workers. Even though GDP was now growing, layoffs continued, unemployment remained high, and in the media the talk was about a "jobless recovery."

Nevertheless, the recovery continued, and by 1994 unemployment began to fall steadily. As more data came in, the downsizing issue became clearer. The rate of job loss was indeed up, albeit moderately, and the pattern of job loss was shifting. Older college graduates were still less likely to be laid off than younger high school graduates, but layoff rates between the two groups were getting closer. Workers responded to downsizing by holding on to their jobs when they could. This explained the economists' finding that the average length of time on a job was not declining: more persons were being laid off, but fewer persons were quitting.[30]

While the downsizing was not as dramatic as portrayed by the media, perceptions of job security had changed.* This change, in turn, gave President Clinton an ironic benefit. Layoffs and threats of layoffs had made people cautious about pushing for wage increases. As the labor market improved and the unemployment rate fell, there were few signs of the inflationary pressure that usually terminates an economic upswing.

These events provided the basis for the first of the three stories in chapter 1: the good news on inflation and unemployment. In June 1998, the unemployment rate stood at 4.3 percent, its lowest level since the late 1960s, yet inflation was not a problem. Because the economy (and tax revenues) had been growing, Clinton and the Republican Congress had been able to agree on a five-year plan to balance the budget. All this was very good news.

---

* For example, in the *NBC News/Wall Street Journal* poll of January 13–16, 1996 (question 12a, form b), 30 percent of respondents said that downsizing had "affected them personally."

The second of the three stories—slow wage growth—remained true as well. Despite more than a decade of restructuring, the officially measured growth of labor productivity remained fairly weak. In 1996 and 1997 productivity growth averaged 1.6 percent per year (up from about 1 percent in the previous decade), but economists remained skeptical that the revival was permanent. Permanent or not, the revival was so recent that it had had very little effect on income growth. In 1996 (the latest statistic available) median family income stood at $43,200 (in 1997 dollars), about equal to its value in 1986, and $400 below its value in 1989.

Chapter 1 introduced a third story—the large and rising inequality of incomes. Understanding this third story requires looking at a wider set of factors: industries that rise and fall, an occupational distribution that responds to changing consumption patterns as well as to technology and trade; people who move in search of opportunity and who change the rates at which they marry and have children. We explore all of these factors in the chapters that follow.

CHAPTER 4

Industrial Change: Is There Life After the Service Sector?

OR TWO decades, the most durable economic sound bite has been the nation's shift to a service economy. Of the three economic stories that opened chapter 1, two were problems—the slow growth of wages and the high level of inequality. The shift of employment to the service sector has been blamed for both.[1] Sound bites leave out too much information. Recall that as early as 1947 more than half of all hours of employment were already in service sector industries (chapter 2). Despite the service sector's already large size, the 1950s and 1960s were a kind of golden age in which incomes grew rapidly and equally. It was not until the early 1980s that service sector growth became something sinister. This peculiar timing implies a case of mistaken identity in which the service sector is blamed for problems caused by other forces. If the implication is correct, it does not make slow wage growth or high inequality any less serious, but it allows us to see those problems more clearly. To tell this story, we first answer two central questions:

Did the growth of the service sector cause the slowdown in wage growth?

Did the growth of the service sector cause increased earnings inequality?

In examining each question, we will find some smoke but not much fire. We will then reexamine the service sector in light of macroeconomic history (chapter 3), and the causes of the mistaken identity will come clear.

The Service Sector and Stagnant Wages

Over the long run, the growth of the economy's wage level is driven by the growth of labor productivity. We saw how the post-1973 productivity slowdown was prolonged by a combination of factors—rapid inflation, regulated markets, a falling dollar, a fast-growing labor force—that allowed firms to postpone painful changes (chapter 3). These factors, however, do not explain why the productivity slowdown began in the first place. We know that productivity in some services grows very slowly. Musicians today require the same time to play the Brandenburg Concertos as when Bach wrote them. A barber takes the same time to cut a head of hair as a barber took in 1947.* Could not the shift of employment to services have contributed to the initial productivity slowdown?

If a contribution existed, it was modest. Begin with the fact that barbering and concert performances are very labor-intensive. They provide little scope for capital and new technology to raise output per worker. In this respect, they differ from most other service industries with greater technological possibilities. Since World War II, airlines—a service industry—have moved from propeller planes to jets. Travel agents—another service industry—have moved from telephones, pencils, and mail to computerized reservation systems. Telephones themselves have moved through a dizzying sequence. In the late 1940s, literally every call involved speaking to an operator; then rotary dialing allowed local calls to be made without operator assistance; area codes enabled customers to direct dial many long distance calls; touchtone phones allowed calls to be dialed much faster; today voice recognition software further reduces the need for operator assistance.† Imagine airlines without jets, travel agents without computerized bookings, or a telephone system in which operators make all connections by hand, and the productivity gains become obvious.

Official statistics confirm this trend. From 1947 to 1973 labor productivity in the service sector rose by an average 1.9 percent per year (table 4.1).‡ This growth rate was slower than productivity growth in agriculture (about 4 percent per year) or in manufacturing (2.6 percent per year), but it was sufficient to help justify growing wages.

Because productivity grows more slowly in the service sector than in other sectors, a gradual shift of labor toward services could have forced a gradual decline in the rate of productivity growth. After 1973 labor productivity growth slowed abruptly, however, and the decline

---

* Beauticians' productivity has improved. See Fuchs (1968) chap. 6.

† A majority of white-collar service employees now have personal computers on their desks, holding out the possibility of future productivity gains. As early as 1985, some analysts argued that mainframe computers had put capital per worker in services on a par with capital per worker in manufacturing. See the work of financial economist Stephen Roach, as quoted in Kirkland, Jr. (1985).

‡ This calculation was made by the author based on National Income and Product Account data.

Table 4.1   Labor Productivity Growth Since World War II
(Annual Growth Rates of Non-Farm Labor Productivity)

	Economy-Wide	Manufacturing Only	Service Sector Only
1947 to 1973	2.8%	2.6%	1.9%
1973 to 1979	1.1	1.2	.5
1979 to 1990	1.0	2.6	.4
1990 to 1996	1.2	3.5	.2

Sources: Economy-wide and manufacturing only productivity statistics calculated from productivity data on the web site of U.S. Department of Labor, Bureau of Labor Statistics (http://stats.bls.gov). Service sector only productivity data is author's estimate using *National Income and Product Accounts* data and includes government output.

took place *within* manufacturing and *within* services (table 4.1). The contrast is sharp. Between 1947 and 1973, labor productivity in services grew at 1.9 percent per year. Between 1973 and 1979, combined productivity for services, goods production, and agriculture grew at only 1.1 percent per year. The slowdown, moreover, occurred in both the United States and most other industrialized countries at about the same time.[2] The broad collapse, across both industries and countries, points to macroeconomic shocks rather than the U.S. service sector as the initial source of the problem.*

When we turn from the initial slowdown to why the slowdown continued, the service sector looks more culpable. After 1973, productivity in manufacturing recovered fairly quickly while service sector productivity remained weak until very recently (table 4.1). Part of this weak growth actually may reflect the problems of measuring improvements in service output and so may be too pessimistic.[3] Nonetheless, it appears that problems within the service sector—problems that did not exist before 1973—help to explain why economy-wide productivity growth has been slow to recover. One explanation for these problems is the way in which the service sector remained insulated from competitive pressure long after manufacturing had been forced to restructure by recession and foreign competition (chapter 3).

---

* The effect of slower productivity growth on wages was amplified in the 1970s and 1980s because prices of consumer goods—for example, medical care—were rising faster than prices in the economy as a whole. This "terms-of-trade" effect enters the data because productivity is based on real GDP (adjusted for inflation using changes in the GDP price level) while wages are adjusted for inflation using changes in the prices of consumer goods only. In the 1950s and 1960s, the effect had worked in the opposite direction with the prices of consumer goods rising more slowly than prices in the economy as a whole.

If barbers and cellists are unusual cases, they still raise an important question about wage growth: Since barbers' and cellists' productivity cannot rise, how can their incomes rise? To answer the question, imagine what would happen if barbers' wages had not increased. In 1949 the typical barber was earning about $12,000 (in 1997 dollars). Barbering is an occupation that requires both skill and training. If that same salary held today, skilled people would have better opportunities and, to paraphrase Groucho Marx, "I would not want my hair cut by anyone who wanted to cut it." In reality, the typical full-time barber now earns about $22,000. Embedded in this salary is the fact that the real cost of haircuts has risen relative to the cost of oranges, calculators, or televisions, each of which are products of industries with higher rates of technological progress.* Over fifty years, however, our real incomes have also grown, and we can afford the higher haircut costs. In this way the benefits of high productivity industries are spread throughout the economy.†

The Service Sector and Inequality

Since at least the early 1980s, the shift of employment to the service sector has been blamed for growing earnings inequality. Bruce Steinberg, then a writer for *Fortune* magazine,[4] gave one early summary:

> [T]he decline of the middle [of the income distribution] really began during the long expansion of the late Seventies, when families began to find the economic ground under them shifting. The key to what's going on lies in the explosive growth of the service economy, which has brought on massive upheaval in employment patterns.[5]

Steinberg argued that the service sector's earnings distribution was inherently less equal than the earnings distribution in goods-producing industries: mining, construction, and manufacturing.‡ These good-producing industries paid middle-class wages, while service sector earnings ranged from the minimum wage of fast food outlets to surgeons' high fees. Like many other authors, Steinberg believed

---

* For example, in 1950 the cheapest portable radios (which were very heavy) cost substantially more than a typical man's haircut. Today, the cheapest portable radio and a man's haircut cost similar amounts. Today's radio, moreover, is substantially lighter and has better reception than its 1950 counterpart.

† The reader may recognize this as the argument of economist William Baumol explaining why certain labor-intensive services—the arts, domestic help—seem to become so expensive over time. See Baumol (1967).

‡ Technically, agriculture is also in the good-producing sector. Agricultural earnings are relatively low and highly unequal, and no one argues that the declining share of the labor force in agriculture has increased earnings inequality. For this reason, we will treat agriculture as a separate sector rather than treating it as part of the goods-producing sector.

that the shift from manufacturing to services was creating a two-tier job market—the very high paid and the very low paid, with a shrinking number of jobs in the middle.*

Applied to the entire labor force, Steinberg's story went too far. Three million elementary and high school teachers were in the service sector and they were neither very poor nor very rich. The same is true of chefs, accountants, medical technicians, airline stewards and stewardesses, advertising copywriters, and the average lawyer. Restricted to men who have not gone beyond high school, the story makes more sense.† In politically incorrect language, the service sector contained two kinds of work: jobs for people with a good education, and women's jobs.

Consider an automobile production worker who had not gone beyond high school but earned enough at Ford in the late 1960s to own a summer home in northern Michigan. From an economic perspective, his good wage reflected a combination of factors. Automobile production required large amounts of machinery, and so wages were not the only source of cost reduction. In those years before a well-developed import market, automobile production was dominated by three large firms who restricted competition so that pressure to reduce costs was limited. Because production was concentrated in a few large plants, unions were better able to organize the industry's work force and bargain for higher wages. Much of the work was physically hard, and so by custom, most women would not compete for jobs.[6]

These circumstances were most common in durable manufacturing industries. They were less present in nondurable manufacturing industries like food processing or textiles, in which wages were lower.‡ Nonetheless, as recently as the late 1970s, the combination of durable and nondurable manufacturing provided jobs to almost one-third of male high school graduates and dropouts, aged twenty-five to fifty-four, and the annual earnings of these men averaged $34,500 per year.

With some exceptions,§ these circumstances were less likely to occur in service-sector industries. Service firms were often labor intensive and so wage costs were important. Production was often spread over many locations and so unionization and wage bargaining were

---

* See, for example, Cyert (1984), Bluestone and Harrison (1982), and Kuttner (1983). Among the authors who disagreed are Rosenthal (1985), Samuelson (1983), and Lawrence (1984).
† The issue was less relevant for women because, as I explain later, most women have always worked in the service sector.
‡ Earlier in this century, textile industries left New England for the South to escape high wages and unionization.
§ For example, airlines, a capital intensive industry, in which airline mechanics were heavily unionized and received high wages.

harder. Where many manufacturing jobs required physical strength, sales and clerical jobs required "soft skills" that women were supposed to have and less educated men were supposed to lack, putting the men at a disadvantage. Among men of the same age and education who worked in services, earnings in the late 1970s averaged about $31,800 per year, or about 8 percent less than in manufacturing.

Based on this picture, a shift of employment to services should have lead to more male high school graduates and dropouts in low wage jobs and greater earnings inequality. In reality, this picture is correct but incomplete. To see this, return to 1979, on the eve of the 1980 to 1982 blue collar recession and the beginning of restructuring. Figure 4.2 compares the earnings distributions for twenty-five- to fifty-four-year-old men—"prime age" men—in the service sector in 1979 and 1996. Figure 4.1 makes the same comparison for prime age men in the goods producing sector—manufacturing, mining, and construction. Consistent with Steinberg's story, 1979 earnings in services were less equal than 1979 earnings in goods production. Between 1979 and 1996, however, earnings inequality increased *within* each sector: more jobs below $20,000 and above $70,000; fewer jobs between the two limits. In economic terms, there was a surge in skill bias in both sectors that widened the earnings gap between men who had not gone beyond high school and men who had at least some college.

The surge occurred, moreover, when labor productivity and the economy's average wage were growing slowly. Slow growth is a hidden message in the two figures. In each figure, two earnings distributions, one for 1979, the other for 1996, sit roughly on top of each other because average earnings changed very little in the intervening seventeen years, a period that extended over four presidents. Because the economy's average wage level had not grown, the earnings of male high school graduates and dropouts declined relative to college graduates and in absolute terms: these are the men making less than $20,000. In the service sector, the median earnings of prime age male high school graduates (excluding dropouts) fell from $34,000 to $26,500. Within manufacturing, the median earnings of prime age male high school graduates fell from $37,500 to $29,600.

In one sense, these results should not surprise us. Within any part of the nation, goods production firms and service firms draw from the same labor market. If demand for a particular kind of worker falls in one sector, lower wages eventually will ripple through to the other sector. The more basic question is why the demand for less educated men fell in the first place. We return to that question in a moment.

Among women the earnings gap between college graduates and high school graduates widened as well, but in a more benign fashion:

Figure 4.1   Goods Production Total Earnings, Men Twenty-Five to Fifty-Four, 1979 and 1996

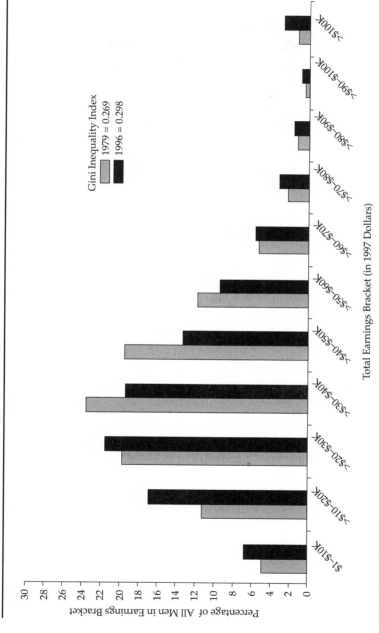

Sources: Author's tabulations of the March 1980 and March 1997 Current Population Survey.

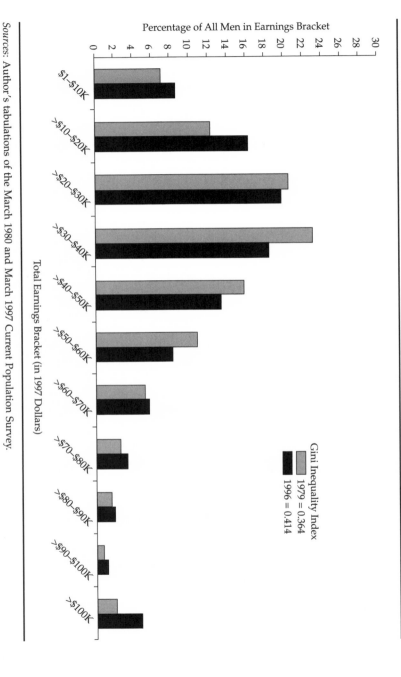

Figure 4.2   Services: Total Earnings, Men Twenty-Five to Fifty-Four, 1979 and 1996

Sources: Author's tabulations of the March 1980 and March 1997 Current Population Survey.

the earnings of female high school graduates fell slightly while college graduates' earnings rose significantly (figures 4.3 and 4.4). In chapter 5, we discuss why earnings patterns for men and women differed in this way.

Why the Service Sector Grew

To this point, we have put three facts on the table. The growth of average wages slowed dramatically after 1973. A surge in skill bias widened the college-high school wage gap after 1979. The service sector played only a modest role in these developments. To complete the picture, we will trace the sevice sector's growth, this time in the context of recent macroeconomic history (chapter 3).

Nearly sixty years ago, the distinguished economist, Colin Clark, described a growing service sector as a positive sign: "the most important concomitant of economic progress, namely, the movement of the working population from agriculture to manufacture and from manufacture to commerce and services."[7] Clark's quote may sound strange today, but he had two specific factors in mind. One is the tendency for business and consumers to demand more services as they grow richer. The other is the way in which service industries use relatively large amounts of labor.

In chapter 3 we noted that services became an increasingly important part of personal consumption spending as family incomes rose. It is easy to see why. When a family's income doubles, they do not double the amount of food they eat at home. They often more than double their expenditures on services like restaurants, vacation travel, medical care, life insurance, or college education for the children. Added to this is the family's increased demand for publicly provided services—better schools, better libraries, more parks.

Business demand for services grew in a similar way. At the end of World War II, a manufacturer of kitchen stoves needed telephones, transportation, utilities, retail outlets, and other service providers as normal parts of production. As the economy matured, business expanded its service demand to include more lawyering, accounting, data processing, and management consulting. Because of these demands, businesses consumed about one-third of growing service sector output throughout the postwar period.

As the nation's GDP doubled over time, then, demand for services more than doubled. This is part of what Clark meant, but there was a second factor. If the service sector experienced very rapid productivity growth, the sector could produce this increased output with a constant or declining share of the labor force. Because service sector productivity is relatively low (table 4.1), an increase in service de-

Figure 4.3 Goods Production Total Earnings, Women Twenty-Five to Fifty-Four, 1979 and 1996

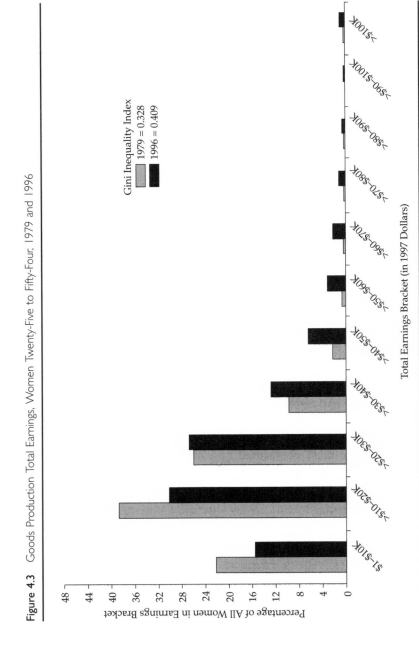

Sources: Author's tabulations of the March 1980 and March 1997 Current Population Survey.

Figure 4.4 Services Total Earnings, Women Twenty-Five to Fifty-Four, 1979 and 1996

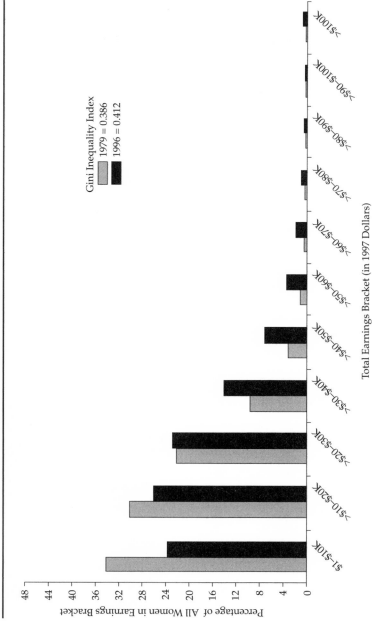

Gini Inequality Index
1979 = 0.386
1996 = 0.412

Sources: Author's tabulations of the March 1980 and March 1997 Current Population Survey.

Table 4.2   Distribution of Full-Time Equivalent Employment by Sector and Industry, 1947 to 1996

	1947	1959	1969	1979	1989	1996
Persons engaged in production (in thousands)	57,320	63,770	78,478	94,332	113,450	123,666
Share by sector and industry (percent)						
Agriculture	11.3%	7.4%	4.0%	3.3%	2.7%	2.7%
Goods-producing sector						
Mining	1.7	1.2	0.8	0.9	0.6	0.5
Construction	5.6	5.5	5.4	5.8	5.7	5.6
Manufacturing	26.5	25.6	25.5	22.1	17.1	15.0
Durable goods	(14.4)	(14.6)	(15.2)	(13.5)	(10.2)	(8.8)
Nondurable goods	(12.1)	(11.0)	(10.3)	(8.5)	(7.0)	(6.2)
Service-producing sector						
Transportation, communication, and public utilities	7.4	6.4	5.7	5.5	5.0	5.1
Wholesale trade	4.6	5.2	5.1	5.6	5.6	5.3
Retail trade	14.6	13.9	13.3	14.6	15.8	16.1
Finance, insurance, and real estate	3.3	4.2	4.6	5.5	6.3	5.9
Services industry	13.0	14.6	16.8	19.5	25.2	29.5
Government and government enterprises	11.8	16.2	18.7	17.1	16.0	14.7
Total	100%	100%	100%	100%	100%	100%

Sources: U.S. Department of Commerce, Bureau of Economic Analysis (1981) table 6.11B; Survey of Current Business (July 1983) table 6.11B, (July 1990) table 6.10B, and (June 1998) table B.8.
Notes: Persons engaged in production equals the number of full-time equivalent employees plus the number of self-employed persons working in an industry. Numbers may not add to 100 percent due to rounding.

mand means a relatively large increase in service sector employment. When adjusted for inflation, service sector *output* as a fraction of real GDP has grown at a moderate rate. Service sector *employment* as a proportion of the labor force has grown more rapidly.

As the date of the Clark quote implies, none of this is new. In the United States, service sector industries account for 53 percent of all hours of employment in 1947 and they account for about 77 percent today (table 4.2). In this shift employment in the "old line" service industries—transportation, communication and utilities, wholesale trade, retail trade—has grown in line with total U.S. employment. Finance, insurance, and real estate grew faster but from a small base. The bulk of new service sector employment has come in government and the "service industry," a group of small industries within the service sector.

The growth of government employment followed the growth of government expenditures (chapter 3). Between 1947 and 1969, total U.S. employment increased by twenty-one million persons (on a full-time equivalent basis), and almost eight million of these jobs were in government. The new jobs ranged from teachers of the baby boom children to air force colonels to federal administrators who designed the Great Society. After 1970, the growth of government employment slowed, but governments at all levels still employ almost one worker in seven.

The census-defined service industry is a grouping of services that are too small to merit individual classification: personal services such as hotels, barber shops, and private hospitals; entertainment services such as movie theaters, theme parks, and restaurants; business services like law firms, data processing firms, and consulting firms. Within this group, restaurant employment has been growing quickly, but the largest employment gains have been in health care and business services. The growth of business service employment underlines the ambiguous meaning of some of these shifts. If the kitchen stove company had an accountant on its payroll, she would have been tabulated as a manufacturing employee. If the accountant had left to join an accounting firm, taking the stove company's business with her, she would be retabulated as a service sector employee even though she did the same job. Similarly, some manufacturing firms now employ production workers supplied by temporary firms. In government statistics, the production workers work for the temporary firms and therefore appear as service sector employees.[8]

Through the early 1970s, then, the service sector's history was benign—even boring—with little to inspire alarmist articles in business magazines. One reason is that total goods production employment continued to grow in the 1950s and 1960s. The employment shift to services simply meant that service sector employment was growing faster.

During the 1950s and 1960s goods producing firms added six million new jobs. Because of this increase, the proportion of working men employed in mining, construction, and manufacturing stood at 39 percent in 1949, 41 percent in 1959, and 41 percent in 1969. In the same years, service sector employment grew by twenty-two million persons (full-time plus part-time). Almost three-quarters of the increase represented women who were then entering the work-

Figure 4.5   Number of Men and Women Workers by Sector of Employment

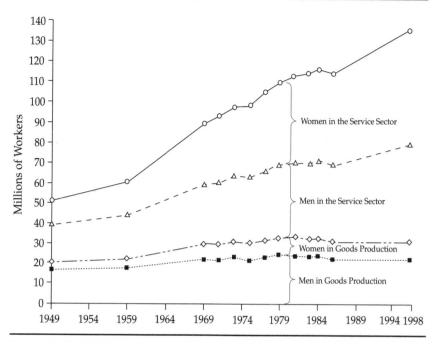

Sources: Author's tabulations of the 1950, 1960, and 1970 Decennial Census Public Use Microdata Sample files and the Current Population Survey (various years).

force (figure 4.5). Among traditional women's occupations, clerical work is distributed across all industries, but all other traditional occupations—teachers, nurses, sales personnel, and so on—are in the service sector. Victor Fuchs notes that this growth contained an element of feedback: More working women induced a need for more restaurants (supermarkets had deli counters but not prepared foods), daycare teachers, dry cleaners, and other service jobs.[9] In these years, then, service sector growth did not mean goods production decline.

The alarm bells also were silent because the economy's wage level was growing rapidly.

Wage Growth as a Safety Net

To this point, we have discussed the rate of wage growth in abstract terms. In fact, wage growth influences day-to-day life in a number of ways, including the shape of an individual's career and the nation's ability to cope with economic restructuring. Start with the fact that even in the strongest economies, some fraction of jobs are always being lost. Beginning in the 1890s, New England steadily lost textile mills, first to the Southeast and then to overseas manufacturers. During the 1950s, the number of workers on farms dropped by 2.9 million, or about 5 percent of the U.S. labor force. From the end of World War II through 1963 Chicago lost one-third of its blue collar manufacturing jobs. This churning is all part of what Joseph Schumpeter meant by "creative destruction":

> The opening up of new markets, foreign or domestic, and the organizational development from the craft shop and factory to such concerns as U.S. Steel illustrate the same process of industrial mutation—if I may use that biological term—that incessantly revolutionizes the economic structure *from within*, incessantly destroying the old one, incessantly creating a new one. This process of Creative Destruction is the essential fact about capitalism. It is what capitalism consists in and what every capitalist concern has got to live in.[10]

As the name implies, creative destruction involves substantial dislocation and pain. When productivity and the economy's average wage are growing, this pain is substantially reduced. From the end of World War II through 1973, that is exactly what happened.

To appreciate the meaning of average wage growth, it is useful to distinguish between two questions:

1. At this moment, how much more do forty-year-olds earn than thirty-year-olds?

2. At this moment, how much more do forty-year-olds earn than forty-year-olds earned ten years ago?

The first question involves what economists call age-earnings profiles, the point-in-time relationship in which people's earnings rise with the promotions and the more responsible jobs that come from increased experience. We can see the relationship for men by running our finger down any of the columns in table 4.3. For example, in 1949 the average thirty-year-old earned $16,833 while the average forty-year-old earned $18,670.[11] If a thirty-year-old in 1949 had wondered what he might be making in ten years, $18,000 to $19,000 would have been a reasonable guess.

Average wage growth refers to the second question, the way in which rising productivity can lift the economy's entire wage structure. During the 1950s, our thirty-year-old man saw himself elbowing up a crowded flight of stars as he competed for promotions. Unknown to him, productivity growth was turning the flight of stairs into an up escalator, raising both his wages and the wages of those with whom he was competing. His income grew due to this economy-wide wage

Table 4.3   Men's Income Growth Before and After 1979 (in 1996 Dollars)

Age	1949	1959	1969
Twenty-five to thirty-four years	$16,833	$24,222	$32,193
Thirty-five to forty-four years	$18,670	$25,923	$36,193
Forty-five to fifty-four years	$18,058	$24,936	$33,793

High School Graduates			Four Year College Graduates (no Advanced Degree)		
Age	1986	1996	Age	1986	1996
Twenty-five to thirty-four years	$26,076	$23,873	Twenty-five to thirty-four years	$36,217	$35,707
Thirty-five to forty-four years	$33,320	$30,606	Thirty-five to forty-four years	$43,573	$46,929
Forty-five to fifty-four years	$36,217	$30,963	Forty-five to fifty-four years	$49,255	$46,474

Sources: Author's tabulations of the 1950, 1960, and 1970 Decennial Census Public Use Micro-data Sample files and the March 1987 and March 1997 Current Population Survey.
Notes: Figures represent men's median income for the cohort and year in question.

growth as well as his promotions and so he moved from a thirty-year-old's income in 1949 to a forty-year-old's income in 1959 ($25,923) a much larger gain than he might have predicted.

In this way, the economy's rate of wage growth reshaped the typical career. For example, by the time most men are forty, their biggest promotions are behind them. Based on promotions alone, they cannot expect to see big income gains as they pass from forty to fifty.* Because the economy's average wage was growing during the 1950s, men who passed from age forty to age fifty saw incomes rise substantially: $18,760 at age forty and $24,936 ten years later. During the 1960s a similar passage from age forty to fifty increased earnings by nearly one-third. Wage growth was extending the years of a man's career in which his earning power increased.

Wage growth also helped to cushion the shocks of creative destruction. Throughout the postwar period, workers in the service sector

---

* We can see this in the upper part of table 4.3 where the income of forty-year-old men and fifty-year-old men are similar. This is equivalent to saying that the age-earnings profile levels off in the early-to-mid 40s.

earned 5 to 10 percent less than manufacturing workers for reasons we discussed earlier. Wages in both sectors were rising so fast, however, that these differences were muted. In 1959 a thirty-year-old man in durable manufacturing earned about $26,000. Had he been laid off and taken a service sector job, he would have earned about $1,200 less. Over the next ten years, however, thirty-year-old men in both sectors would see their earnings increase by about $12,000. The loss of the manufacturing job did not mean permanent downward mobility. In this way, the fast rate of average wage growth was a safety net for change. By the time of the 1981 blue-collar recession, this safety net had disappeared.

Manufacturing, Services, and Macroeconomics

In the sound bite story, the growth of the service sector is undermining the economy. The more accurate argument runs the other way. Economy wide forces—good and bad—shape all the economy's industries. From World War II through the early 1970s, productivity growth was strong and services and goods production both did well. At that point, both sectors began to face problems.

Employment in goods production—particularly manufacturing—is sensitive to economic downturns. When unemployment rises, demand for cars, houses, and investment equipment all slow even as the demand for services continues. The years after 1969 were a series of recessions: Richard Nixon's planned recession to break inflation in 1970 and 1971; the deep recession that followed the 1973 to 1974 OPEC price increase; the deep blue-collar recession that followed the 1979 to 1980 OPEC price increase (chapter 3). Each recession extracted a cost in goods production employment. Over the 1950s and 1960s, mining, construction, and manufacturing had created six million new jobs. From 1969 through 1979 these industries created only 2.1 million additional jobs and the proportion of male workers in goods production fell modestly. As Robert Lawrence writes: "There is no puzzle in explaining [the slow growth of] aggregate manufacturing production: it is almost exactly what one should have expected given the performance of the total economy."[12]

In reality, manufacturing in the 1970s was weaker than Lawrence suggests. In the 1950s and 1960s U.S. corporations relied on the rapid growth of markets to reconcile improved productivity (and profits) and the managerial desire for expansion. By the early 1970s, demand for U.S. manufactured goods was growing more slowly. The most pressing postwar domestic needs had been filled and producers in West Germany and Japan were providing formidable competition in products like automobiles, machine tools, and consumer electronics. Frequent recessions and rising energy prices made the situation worse. Much of U.S. manufacturing was ripe for restructuring, and it was only the combination of inflation, demographics, and the falling dollar that held restructuring at bay (chapter 3).

Within the context of slow-growing goods production, job loss became more frequent as older firms stumbled and younger firms grew, often in other regions.[13] Job loss would have been hard in any circumstances, but after 1973 incomes rose slowly even for workers who held their jobs. Workers who lost a high-wage job faced a long-term cut in their standard of living. Moving to a higher paying job seemed the only way to get ahead, and the slow growth of high-wage manufacturing jobs became a source of real worry.

The worst was yet to come. The blue-collar recession of 1980 to 1982 struck a tremendous blow to manufacturing. In the subsequent recovery, the large budget deficits led to an overvalued dollar which overpriced U.S. exports abroad and made foreign imports cheap (chapter 3). The results were clearest in the high wage durable manufacturing belt that ran from Baltimore and Pennsylvania west through the Great Lakes states. What had been a fairly prosperous region in the 1970s was now transformed into the Rust Belt (chapter 6).

This was the beginning of the surge in skill bias in which high school graduates and dropouts—particularly men—saw their economic prospects suddenly collapse. An early assessment of the damage came from the Bureau of Labor Statistics' surveys of displaced workers. The bureau defined a displaced worker as a person over twenty years old, who had worked at his or her job for at least three years, and who had lost his or her job due to plant closings or employment cutbacks between January 1979 and January 1984.[14] By this definition, the bureau counted 5.1 million displaced workers, or about 5 percent of the entire U.S. work force. One-half of these displaced workers were in manufacturing, which then accounted for only one-quarter of total U.S. employment (men and women). Many of the displaced were blue collar workers with limited education, and there was no general wage growth to cushion the blow. As of January 1986, two years into economic recovery:

- 30 percent of the displaced workers were reemployed at wages equal to or better than those in the job they lost;

- 30 percent were reemployed at wages lower than those in the job they lost;

- 40 percent were unemployed or had dropped out of the labor force.[15]

Falling demand for semiskilled manufacturing workers was reinforced by a sharp decline in union power. Some of the biggest employment losses were in durable manufacturing firms where unions had been strongest. In reality, an excess of union power had made some of these firms vulnerable.* On balance, however, unions protected semiskilled workers from the sharpest effects of the market. By the early 1980s, unions were facing both a loss of unionized jobs and an unsympathetic president. President Reagan made his position clear by firing striking air traffic controllers and by refusing to intercede in the economy as unemployment rose sharply (chapter 3). Both were signals that power was shifting away from workers, and employers could drive increasingly hard bargains without fear of government intervention.† We return to the power shift in chapter 5.

Dramatic pictures of huge, shuttered steel mills were the symbols of the time, but the impact of restructuring was not confined to the Rust Belt. By the middle 1980s, deregulation, new technology, and the slowdown in labor force growth were forcing restructuring on service industries. In services, too, restructuring involved a significant degree of skill bias.[16]

An example is economist David Marcotte's study of Maryland commercial banks.[17] Through the 1970s commercial banking was heavily regulated, even to the rates banks could pay on deposits. Between regulation and a rapidly growing customer base, many banks could succeed without heavy marketing or cost-cutting. By the end of the 1980s, the banking industry was far less regulated and the customer base was growing more slowly. Banks were under great competitive pressure to both cut costs and build market share. To reduce costs, they increasingly used computers, rather than people, to perform routine tasks—automatic teller machines (ATMs) are a prime example. To expand market share, they focused their remaining labor force on marketing—in particular marketing multiple services to

---

* For example, by the early 1970s major steel producers felt they had been seriously hurt by strikes. In exchange for no-strike pledges, workers were given a substantial wage increase and an automatic cost-of-living adjustment to protect against future inflation. In the early 1970s, an inflation rate of 5.5 percent was considered politically unacceptable (chapter 3). In 1974, however, oil price increases pushed inflation to 12 percent, and only once in the next eight years did inflation fall below 6 percent. During these years, most wages in the economy lagged behind inflation while wages in big steel kept pace. By 1979 production workers in the steel industry had weekly earnings 50 percent higher than average weekly earnings in durable manufacturing and 80 percent higher than average weekly earnings in nondurable manufacturing. The high wages translated into high costs, which made the major producers particularly vulnerable to import competition. Unionized auto workers also received automatic cost-of-living provisions in the early 1970s creating similar problems for the automobile industry.
† McKinley L. Blackburn, David E. Bloom and Richard B. Freeman estimate that the decline of unionization was responsible for perhaps 15 percent of the growth in the earnings differential for college versus high school educated men. See Blackburn, Bloom, and Freeman in Burtless, ed. (1990) table 12.

high-income customers.* As a result, banks and many other kinds of service firms were looking for two kinds of people: computer analysts who could improve the bank's systems, and persons with the interpersonal skills to attract high-income consumers. Some of those laid off were well-educated—middle managers who had grown up in stable, regulated environments and did not know how to sell. More severely, the sharply reduced demand for less-educated workers added to the economy's growing skill bias.

A Summing Up

By the mid-1990s, the hemorrhage of manufacturing employment had ended. Manufacturing employment was not growing much, however, and it was clear that large majorities of both men and women would be employed in services. This was not the benign process Colin Clark had celebrated, but we can now see why Clark and Bruce Steinberg viewed the process so differently.

To begin with, the pace of restructuring in the 1980s was far more than the normal employment shift to services. The blue-collar recession, the overvalued dollar, deregulation, and the slowdown in labor force growth combined to compress something like two decades of gradual change into seven or eight years. Beyond this, Steinberg and other contemporary writers were reacting against trends that went well beyond the service sector: an economy in which wages were growing slowly, in which less-educated men and women would have a harder time earning a middle-class income, in which there was a distinct shift of power away from employees and toward employers.

In particular, the falling demand for high school graduates and dropouts raised serious questions about how U.S. society was evolving. To the layman, a person's years of education refers to time spent in the classroom. To the social scientist, a person's years of education might be a surrogate for the person's family background or genetic intelligence. By the 1990s, it was not unusual to hear arguments that the economy was now favoring a cognitive elite—an elite based on genes—and greater equality was now beyond the reach of any policy. In the next chapter, we evaluate this argument in greater detail.

---

* As marketing expert Garth Hallberg writes, "The way consumers truly differ is in the inherent profit opportunity they present to the marketer—their profit differential." (Hallberg [1995] p. 7). In the interest of full disclosure, Garth Hallberg is my cousin's husband.

CHAPTER 5

Occupational Change:
Can the Economy Still Produce
Good Jobs and, If So,
Who Gets Them?

I N CHAPTER 4, we began our analysis of the job market by examining the economy's industrial structure. It was a safe choice. While we do not often say it, we believe that in fifty years the U.S. economy still will have industries. Whether these industries will provide good jobs, even for educated workers, is a separate question and a source of some anxiety.

In this chapter, we examine trends in American jobs since World War II—the nature of the work, how much a job pays, the job's security. We will look at the progress of different groups—for example, black women or white men—within this occupational structure. Finally, we will examine the evidence for two overlapping pictures of today's job market that have received substantial attention. One is that earnings are now tightly tied to genetic intelligence and so earnings inequality cannot be moderated by policy. The second is that we have entered a winner-take-all market in which the very highest incomes grow enormously while all other incomes stagnate.

What Is a Good Job?

To tell this story, we need to define a good job. A starting point is a joke told forty-five years ago by the comedian Sam Levinson. Two young women, casual friends, meet by chance for the first time in several years. One of the women is pushing a stroller with two young children. The other woman asks the children's ages. The first woman replies: "The doctor is one and a half. The lawyer is six months old."

In the 1950s, Levinson could tell this joke knowing that his audience would equate doctors and lawyers with success. The question is, why? At that time, people saw both doctoring and lawyering as noble professions—saving lives, upholding the law. People respected schoolteachers too, yet Levinson (a former schoolteacher) never would have said, "The schoolteacher is six months old." In addition to their nobility, the doctor and the lawyer were perceived as successful because each performed well-paid, clean, steady work in pleasant surroundings where they largely could be their own bosses.* Each job also required significant education.

These characteristics—good pay, clean work, job security, autonomy—are what make a job good. They do not necessarily come together in any one job. One artist may be autonomous and eat well, while another is autonomous and starves. A bond trader with an extravagant income may be fired at a moment's notice. A good job in 1950 might not be a good job forever. In March 1995, the *Wall Street Journal* profiled the problems of Patrick Kwan, a new medical school graduate in anesthesiology. After years of training, Kwan was piecing together several part-time assignments because tighter health insurance reimbursements were eliminating anesthesiologist positions.[1] Kwan was not the only doctor to feel such pressure. Two years later, the American Medical Association (AMA) issued a joint statement with other medical groups calling on the United States to train fewer doctors. As the organization said, "The current rate of physician supply—the number of physicians entering the work force each year—is clearly excessive." The solution proposed by the AMA was to limit the number of foreign medical school graduates accepted into U.S. internships.†

To an economist, Kwan's situation is part of normal economic life. Even in a very strong economy, the supply of people entering a particular occupation can catch up with demand.‡ When this happens, openings are harder to come by, wages start to fall, and the occupation has fewer good jobs. Or the opposite can happen: demand leaps ahead of supply, creating new opportunities. If Levinson had said,

---

* As distinct from, say, factory workers, who at that time did nothing but respond to other people's orders.

† See Pear (1997) p. 9. In fairness, doctors have always said there are too many of them. In June 1986, the AMA issued a report in which it argued that physicians were in oversupply. Dr. Arnold Relman, an author of the report and editor of the *New England Journal of Medicine*, said at that time: "There is more pressure on the doctor to maintain his income than is good for the public or the profession." A half-century earlier, in 1934, the president of the AMA had said: "A fine piece of education work could well be done if we were to use only half of the 70-odd medical schools in the U.S." See Freudenheim (1986) and Freeman (1976) p. 118. In the mid-1990s, the average salary for all doctors was $154,000 (1995 dollars, before taxes, after expenses). See Doyle (1996).

‡ In the case of anesthesiologists, stricter insurance reimbursement is shrinking demand for surgeries as well.

"The software engineer is six months old," his 1950s audience would have been mystified, but in January 1998 good software engineers were as much in demand as good football quarterbacks.*

At the same time, occupational markets are part of the broader economy and are also shaped by broad economic trends. In earlier chapters, we identified four such trends:

- The post-1973 slowdown in wage growth.

- The post-1979 surge in skill bias that lowered demand for high school graduates and high school dropouts.

- The long-term employment shift away from agriculture and goods production and toward the service sector.

- An increasingly competitive environment and a shift in power away from employees and toward a firm's shareholders.

Because these trends work in various directions—more "clean" work in the service sector, lower wages for semiskilled work—their net impact on the number of good jobs is not clear. We will see some evidence, however, that the public believes that "good" jobs are harder to come by, even for college graduates. This anxiety helps to explain several social trends and provides one justification for the growth of big salaries at the top of the earnings distribution. We discuss both the anxiety and winner-take-all salaries as the chapter progresses.

We begin our story by describing the occupational progress of white men, a group who comprised two-thirds of the 1940 labor force and make up about 41 percent of the labor force today. "White men" covers a wide ground—the West Virginia coal miner, the San Francisco stockbroker, the Wyoming chef—but one generalization that can be made about them is that throughout the postwar era, white men have faced fewer constraints of custom and legal segregation than most other groups in the labor force. For this reason, we will also use white men's experience to illustrate general labor market trends and as a baseline by which to measure other groups' experience.

Occupations and Earnings: White Men

In chapter, 2 we defined an occupational structure using five classifications:

---

* Unlike the doctors who would compete with immigrants, high-tech executives have been lobbying for *increased* immigration of software engineers. See Rogers (1998).

1. Professional and managerial workers

2. Other white-collar workers

3. Blue-collar workers

4. Service workers

5. Farmers and farm-related occupations

Many occupations require at least some training, and even in an era of downsizing, most people do not change careers often.* It follows that the occupational structure evolves slowly as each new cohort of workers chooses a different set of careers.

Within the slow evolution of the occupational structure, the major occupational trend among white men has been the shift into white-collar work. In the 1950 census, 32 percent of white men were in white-collar occupations (table 5.1). By 1980 the proportion had climbed to 43 percent.[2] The shift was a broad-based trend and included well-paid lawyers and engineers, midlevel technicians, and lower-paid workers in retail sales and administrative support.

To a large extent, more white-collar jobs were the occupational equivalent of employment growth in the service sector. The government expansion of the 1950s and 1960s was concentrated in white-collar employment, as was the growth in health care and business services (chapter 4), but even in manufacturing, employment was becoming more white-collar as more managers, engineers, and accountants were hired. Bureau of Labor Statistics data show that within durable goods manufacturing nonproduction (white-collar) workers constituted 17 percent of employment in 1948, rising to 31 percent by 1980.[3]

In the years since 1980, the growth of white-collar employment for all workers—not just for white men—has centered on two occupational catagories: managers and administrators, and sales occupations. Both have grown at astounding speed. In 1979 managerial and administrative positions accounted for about 10 percent of all jobs in the economy, but they accounted for 18 percent of the net jobs added

---

* In the early 1980s, research suggested that most men, after an initial period of job-shopping, spent the bulk of their career in two or three long-term jobs. See Hall (1982). As we saw in chapter 3, the rate of layoffs has recently increased, but the rate of voluntary quits has decreased, so that overall time on a job has not changed appreciably. There are, of course, exceptions to these long job tenures, including the period during which mechanization forced large numbers of agricultural workers off farms and into urban areas.

Table 5.1 Occupational Distribution of White Male Workers, 1949 and 1979, and Non-Hispanic White Male Workers, 1996

Occupational Group	Percentage of All White Men in Group	Percentage of All White Men in Group	Percentage of All Non-Hispanic White Men in Group
	1949	1979	1996
Professional and managerial workers			
Executives, administrators, and managers	10.5%	9.8%	12.8%
Management-related occupations	1.4	2.8	2.8
Engineers and natural scientists	1.9	3.5	5.5
Doctors, dentists, and other health diagnostic occupations	0.7	0.9	0.9
Elementary and secondary school teachers	0.9	2.0	2.0
Post-secondary school teachers	0.2	0.7	0.8
Lawyers and judges	0.4	0.8	0.8
Miscellaneous professional specialties (ministers, social workers, and so on)	1.3	2.4	3.0
Other white-collar workers			
Health aides and technicians	0.4	0.7	1.1
Technicians other than health technicians	1.0	2.7	2.5
Sales-related occupations	7.0	8.9	11.4
Administrative support workers	6.8	6.4	5.5
Blue-collar workers			
Craftsmen and precision workers	20.8	21.5	19.7
Machine operators	13.4	9.5	6.6
Transport equipment operators	6.7	7.3	6.9
Handlers, laborers, and so on	6.7	6.1	5.3
Service workers			
Household workers	0.1	0.0	0.0
Protective service workers (police, fire, and so on)	1.5	2.2	2.6
Food services, building services (except household), childcare, restaurant, and personal services workers	3.4	5.5	5.5
Farmers and farm-related occupations	12.7	4.1	2.9
Armed forces	2.4	2.3	1.2
Total	100%	100%	100%

Sources: Author's tabulations using the 1950 and 1980 Decennial Census Public Use Microdata Sample files and 1997 March Current Population Survey.
Note: Data restricted to males aged eighteen to sixty-five with positive earnings.

from 1979 to 1989.* Sales occupations accounted for 10 percent of all jobs in 1979, and one-quarter of net jobs added over the next ten years.† Some new sales positions were in the expanding financial sector—stockbrokers and bond traders are classified as sales occupations—but sales positions grew in most industries, reflecting the economic changes of the 1980s: deregulation, more foreign competition, a slow-growing customer base, and slow-growing average wages, all of which increased competitive pressure on firms to expand market share (chapters 3 and 4).

By 1996, 49 percent of white male workers were in white-collar jobs, up from 32 percent in 1950. In a related trend, white men increasingly acquired college educations. That second trend, however, was far from smooth.

Since many white-collar jobs require education beyond high school, the post–World War II economy put college graduates in demand. Claudia Goldin and Robert Margo show that in 1940, on the eve of World War II, young male college graduates had weekly earnings about 70 percent higher than those of young male high school graduates.[4] By 1950 World War II veterans were entering the labor force, their college educations financed by the GI Bill. Nonetheless, demand for college graduates remained well ahead of supply, and thirty-year-old white men with four or more years of college earned on average 27 percent per year more than thirty-year-old white men with high school diplomas.

This pattern continued through the 1950s. Among whites in their late twenties, the proportion with four or more years of college rose from 6 percent in 1947 to 12 percent in 1959. Demand grew as well, however, and the gap between college and high school earnings in 1960 was 30 percent, slightly higher than in 1950.

As illustrated by the story of Patrick Kwan, the young anesthesiologist, supply-and-demand gaps do eventually close. Among young college graduates, closure occurred in the 1970s. The principal reason was the continued increase in supply. In the early 1970s, large numbers of young men went to college, both to raise their earnings and to avoid being drafted into the Vietnam War. By 1979, 28 percent

---

* A note of caution: these numbers come from census tabulations, in which people self-report their occupations. Reports by *employers* to the Bureau of Labor Statistics show a somewhat slower growth of managerial positions. Even these data, however, show that the number of managerial positions for all workers grew by 33 percent from 1984 to 1995, while total employment grew by 22 percent.

† I calculate net jobs added by subtracting the number of persons in an occupational category in April 1980 from the corresponding number of persons in April 1990. Over this period, managers and administrators grew from 11.3 million to 15.6 million, sales positions grew from 10.4 million to 16.6 million, and total employment grew from 109.2 million to 132.6 million.

of twenty-five- to twenty-nine-year-old white males had four years of college (or more).[5] Richard Freeman calculates that in 1952 there were 2.2 managerial, administrative, and professional jobs for every college graduate (regardless of race and sex). By the early 1970s, the ratio had declined to 1.6 to 1.[6] The surge in supply increased job competition among college graduates and exerted downward pressure on their wages.

By itself, the downward pressure on college graduates' wages would have closed the educational earnings gap, but the gap was also closing from below: the 1970s was the decade when macroeconomic events were driving up the wages of high school graduates. The falling international value of the dollar was stimulating U.S. manufacturing, while crop failures abroad and the oil price shock were stimulating food and energy production (chapter 3). In each of these industries, higher production spelled higher demand for blue-collar workers.

By 1979, thirty-year-old white men earned about $36,200 with a bachelor's degree, and $33,300 with a high school diploma. In percentage terms, the gap was 9 percent, less than half of what it had been in 1960. As strange as it sounds today, Freeman and others could reasonably speculate that college might no longer be a good investment in purely economic terms.*

In chapter 4, we noted that rapid productivity growth and wage growth can serve as a safety net for economic change. The 1970s surge in college graduates is a case in point. If productivity and wages had continued to grow rapidly during the 1970s, college graduates would have gotten richer and high school graduates would have gotten richer faster (beginning from a lower starting point). Because the surge in college graduates occurred after 1973, wage growth had slowed in all occupations (table 5.2) and a relative wage decline could also become an absolute wage decline.

This was the beginning of the anxious perception that there were no longer enough good jobs to go around. In one sense, the perception was crazy. After all, a thirty-year-old white male with a bachelor's degree had average 1979 earnings of $36,200. Nevertheless, the bad economic news—the surge of graduates, the oil and food price shocks, slow productivity growth—had taken its toll: these earnings were about $4,000 less than what thirty-year-old white men with a bachelors degree had made in 1969 (in 1997 dollars).

The anxiety was compounded by young workers' high expectations. In the 1970s, young men and women had grown up exclusively

---

* See Freeman (1976). Assessing college as an investment requires balancing tuition costs and forgone earnings while attending college against the gain in earnings that accrues to college graduates throughout their careers.

Table 5.2   White Men's and Non-Hispanic White Men's Median Earnings by
Occupation and by Year (in 1997 Dollars)

	1949	1979	1996
All white males	$16,833	$30,928	$30,606
Professional and managerial workers			
Executives, administrators, and managers	22,955	47,069	48,970
Management-related occupations	23,567	40,522	40,808
Engineers and natural scientists	26,627	49,051	52,030
Doctors, dentists, and other health diagnostic occupations	37,033	89,767	102,019
Elementary and secondary school teachers	20,506	35,618	35,707
Post-secondary school teachers	24,791	42,655	45,909
Lawyers and judges	32,748	61,848	76,515
Miscellaneous professional specialties (ministers, social workers, and so on)	18,670	27,729	30,606
Other white-collar workers			
Health aides and technicians	20,812	31,993	34,687
Technicians other than health technicians	19,894	34,664	36,727
Sales-related occupations	18,670	31,993	30,606
Administrative support workers	18,670	29,947	26,525
Blue-collar workers			
Craftsmen and precision workers	18,670	31,993	28,566
Machine operators	16,833	27,729	25,505
Transport equipment operators	17,445	29,861	25,709
Handlers, laborers, and so on	12,548	17,068	14,283
Service workers			
Household workers[a]	—	—	—
Protective service workers (police, fire, and so on)	18,670	31,993	32,646
Food services, building services (except household), childcare, restaurant, and personal services workers	12,548	14,904	12,753
Farmers and farm-related occupations	8,264	17,041	15,303
Armed forces	10,100	17,964	26,525

Sources: Author's tabulations of 1950 and 1980 Decennial Census Public Use Microdata
Sample files and March 1997 Current Population Survey. Data inflation-adjusted using
the personal consumption expenditure deflator.
Notes: Data restricted to white males ages eighteen to sixty-five with positive earnings
in the previous year. The 1996 sample excludes Hispanic whites.
[a]Denotes too few observations for a meaningful estimate.

in the post–World War II economic boom. Unlike their parents, who had known the war and something of the Great Depression, these young people had very high expectations, and even a temporary pause in wage growth was a big comedown.

An early sign was the shift in attitudes among college freshmen, whose views had been surveyed since the late 1960s by the American Council on Education. In these surveys, students were asked to rank the importance of each of a series of values in their lives. Between 1968 and 1972, about 40 percent of all freshmen felt that "being very well off financially" was "essential" or "very important," the highest and second-highest ratings. In the fall of 1973, as oil prices were rising and wages stopped growing, this proportion jumped to 62 percent, and it continued to climb: by the late 1980s, it had reached 75 percent, about where it stands today.[7] We can say (with a smirk) that freshmen suddenly abandoned flower power for Datsun 240-Zs. It is more likely, however, that freshmen saw the face of a different economy. In the late 1960s, when wages were growing and the unemployment rate was below 4 percent, a white male college student could major in anything and know he would graduate with a well-paying job (by the standards of the time) provided he could avoid the draft. By the mid-1970s, the sense of effortless upward mobility had disappeared.

Anxiety surfaced in other ways. Since the early 1950s, the proportion of young persons who described themselves as middle-class had increased steadily, but after 1970 it began to decline modestly.[8] In the mid-1960s, when all careers paid well (by historical standards), only 10 to 12 percent of freshmen majored in business administration. As the economy stalled, business administration majors increased, reaching 25 percent of all freshmen in 1987 before the proportion fell back modestly.[9] Pre-med and pre-law (Levinson's occupations), and later, computer science, enjoyed similar popularity.

Until 1980 financial anxiety did not automatically translate into college attendance. The gap between college and high school earnings had become too small for that, and by the end of the 1970s the proportion of male high school graduates enrolling in college had actually leveled off. But everything changed in the blue-collar recession of 1980 to 1982, when the educational earnings gap reopened dramatically. Between 1979 and 1985, the educational earnings gap among younger white men expanded from 9 percent to about 32 percent— about $36,200 for the college graduate and $27,500 for the high school graduate. The corresponding earnings gap for women expanded at a more moderate pace.

Young people saw these changes, and the fraction of high school graduates who went on to college began to rise. The response among some of the least-educated older male workers, however, was to drop

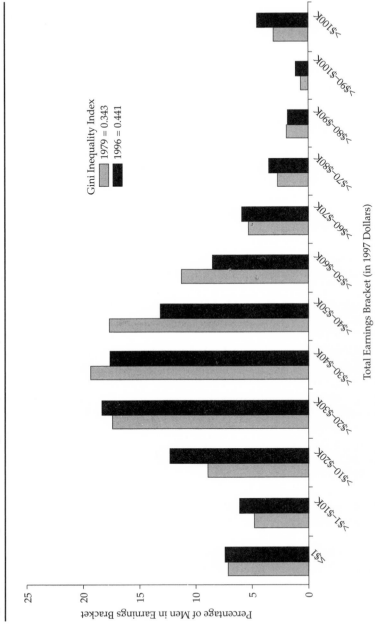

Figure 5.1 Earnings of White Men Age Twenty-Five to Fifty-Four, 1979 and 1996

Gini Inequality Index
1979 = 0.343
1996 = 0.441

Percentage of Men in Earnings Bracket

Total Earnings Bracket (in 1997 Dollars)

Sources: Author's tabulations of the March 1980 and March 1997 Current Population Survey.

out of the labor force entirely. Between 1970 and 1996, the labor-force participation rate of prime-age white men fell from 97 percent to 93 percent, and among high school dropouts in this group, the rate declined from 94 percent to 80 percent.[10] The growing educational-earnings gap redefined good jobs and bad jobs within the occupational distribution. In 1979 white male managers and administrators (of any age) averaged $47,100 annually, while white male machine operators and assemblers averaged $27,700, a difference of $19,400. By 1989 managers and administrators averaged $49,000, while machine operators (now a declining occupation) averaged $25,500, a difference of $23,500. These numbers did not receive the attention given to the extraordinary gaps that emerged between production workers and CEOs—a subject to which we will return—but they did serve to stretch the middle of the earnings distribution and so contributed to earnings inequality.

Beyond the educational earnings gap, a second, less discussed source of earnings inequality was the growing difference in earnings among men (and among women) with the same age, race, education, and other observable characteristics. We can see examples of both types of inequality in figures 5.1 and 5.2.

Figure 5.1 compares the earnings distributions for prime-age white men in 1979 (the last year before demand for high school graduates fell) and 1996. The two distributions have similar medians, reflecting the lack of growth in the average wage during the period. The 1996 distribution has greater fractions of men with earnings below $30,000 (including those not working) and above $60,000. Much of the widening difference occurred along educational lines.

Figure 5.2 compares the 1979 and 1996 earnings distributions of twenty-five- to thirty-four-year-old white males with exactly four years of college. Even within this apparently homogenous group, the distribution spreads out over time.

This "within group" earnings inequality—earnings inequality among apparently similar people—was not new. It had been growing since at least the late 1960s, and even today its causes are not well understood. We might suppose that these earnings differences reflect the fact that people of the same age and education have different levels of skill (as measured on standardized tests) or work in different occupations or industries. Such explanations have been tested, and none can explain why within-group earnings differences have grown.* Because of this aspect of earnings inequality, total male earnings in-

---

* The term "within-group inequality" comes from the statistical technique of analysis of variance: a population is divided into homogeneous groups—in this case, groups based on age, education, gender, race, and so on—and inequality is divided into within-group and between-group differences. For a discussion of sources of within-group earnings inequality, see Levy and Murnane (1992).

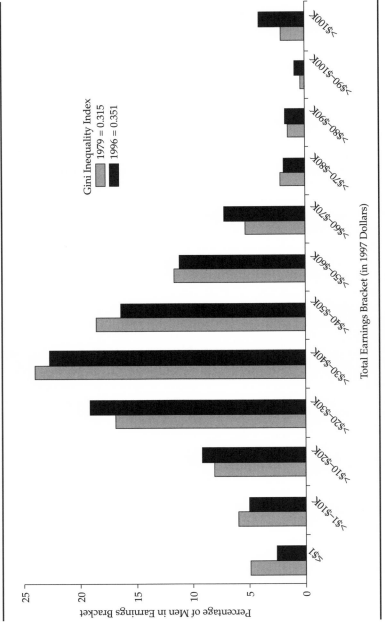

Figure 5.2 Earnings of White Male College Graduates Age Twenty-Five to Thirty-Four, 1979 and 1996

Sources: Author's tabulations of the March 1980 and March 1997 Current Population Survey.

equality through most of the 1970s was a kind of stand-off: earnings differences within groups of apparently similar men were increasing, but earnings differences between more- and less-educated men were falling. After 1979 both kinds of inequality were growing, and so overall earnings inequality increased sharply.*

By the late 1980s, the concept of within-group earnings inequality (if not the term) had entered the media in stories about the growing "lower tail" of new college graduates who were forced to take "high school" jobs.[11] The stories resonated because many people knew a recent college graduate who was living at home while working as a waiter in a restaurant or (in Seattle) a latte bar. The market for college graduates, it was said, had collapsed.

The latte bar stories were exaggerated, but they held kernels of truth. The first thing to know about young college graduates is that in both the 1970s and the 1980s many started slowly. In 1989 the average twenty-three-year-old white male with a bachelor's degree earned $14,300 (in 1997 dollars). In that same year, the average twenty-nine-year-old white male with a bachelor's degree—someone who had found his niche—earned about $34,700, about the same as 1979. These slow starts reflect a softness in demand that enabled employers to enforce apprenticeship terms in journalism and other overcrowded occupations. More important, $34,700 was a median figure: higher within-group inequality meant that the fractions of graduates doing significantly better or worse than this median had both increased since the 1970s (figure 5.2). Finally, a college graduate in the late 1980s carried more tuition debt than graduates in the 1970s. For most individuals, college was still the best game in town—but college per se could not guarantee protection against all economic change.† This realization further increased anxiety and helped fuel the crush of students applying to Ivy League and other elite four-year colleges. It was as if good jobs were scarce prizes, like winning lottery tickets; perhaps "the right college" could provide a winning edge.[12]

In addition to the latte bars, a second change in the demand for white-collar labor was the the slow reduction in job security. Earlier, we described how the combination of deregulation, trade, and technology reduced the demand for semi-skilled workers (chapters 3 and 4). Economists call this a demand shift: on a supply-demand diagram,

---

* Kevin Murphy (personal communication) was the first to point out to me this way of thinking about earnings inequality.
† Moreover, many "high school jobs" now have higher skill requirements—for example, production workers in a modern automobile plant must monitor the quality of their work using statistical process control. See Tyler, Murnane, and Levy (1995) for a discussion of these points.

Figure 5.3 Alternative Changes in the Demand for Labor Demand

A: A Declining Demand for Semi-Skilled Workers

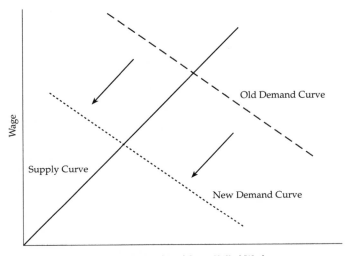

Number of Employed Semi-Skilled Workers

B: A More Elastic Demand for All Labor

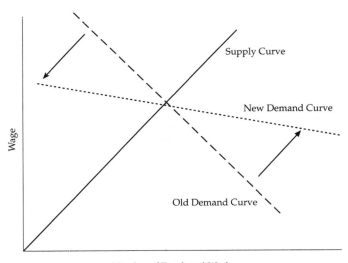

Number of Employed Workers

the whole demand curve moves in (figure 5.3, panel a). A different kind of change occurs when a demand curve becomes more "elastic"—flatter—and the quantity demanded becomes more sensitive to a small change in price (figure 5.3, panel b). The demand for labor or for any other "product" is more elastic when the product has close substitutes. If consumers view all brands of gasoline as interchangeable, Exxon will find that Exxon gasoline sales drop sharply when its price rises as customers switch to Gulf and Mobil.

The economist Dani Rodrik notes that while increased trade shifted down the demand for blue-collar workers, it also increased the elasticity of demand for all workers by giving management a new possibility for substitution: sending complex production work to other countries. What Rodrik writes about globalization is equally true about increased technology: in some organizations, the principal function of middle managers is to collect and distribute information, a task that networked computers now can partially perform.*

Introducing a new technique or moving production overseas is risky business. Because of the risk, the existence of a new technique does not guarantee its adoption.† The 1980s environment favored adoption: increased industrial competition; weakened unions; U.S. presidents—first Ronald Reagan, then George Bush—who firmly embraced free markets and would not intercede if restructuring caused large layoffs. Firms found it easier to restructure and threats of future restructuring had new credibility. The bargaining power of the average worker was reduced, which is the same thing as the demand curve for labor becoming more elastic.

In practical terms, a more elastic demand for skilled workers meant somewhat more tenuous white-collar employment—the downsizing and layoffs described in chapters 3 and 4. In the recovery years between 1993 to 1995, about 2.7 percent of managers and administrators lost their jobs each year. This rate was lower than the 5 percent rate for blue-collar workers, but both rates were at levels normally found in a deep recession—not an economic recovery.[13] Tenuous employment also appeared in the growth of temporary and contract employment—job arrangements in which employees (including some blue-collar employees) work on short-term jobs, often without health insurance or other fringe benefits. The economist Susan Houseman

---

* See Rodrik (1997). I have benefited from numerous conversations with Rodrik, who is my neighbor. Note that technology reinforces globalization by making it easier to exchange information with firms in other countries, thereby expanding the range of products that can be produced offshore.
† Recall David Landes's comments, quoted in chapter 3, regarding the adoption of technical change.

estimates that on a typical day in 1995 about 1.5 percent of all employed workers (of any race or sex) were assigned from temporary help agencies, while another 2.3 percent of all workers were short-term hires. Some workers preferred this arrangement. Others used the temporary job to find a permanent job, or they saw the temporary job as their best opportunity.[14]

Like the stories about college graduate waiters, the modest increase in white-collar job insecurity was news, and it received intense media attention. By focusing on layoffs (rather than on the people who kept their jobs), the stories often exaggerated the changes under way. In reality, white-collar workers reacted to the changes by becoming more cautious and less willing to quit jobs voluntarily. Thus, layoffs were up, quits were down, and the average worker's length of time on a job did not change much. Increased caution was itself, however, a sign of a large psychological impact. As we saw in chapter 3, this same caution helped explain why wage inflation was so low in the late 1990s despite low unemployment.

In chapter 1, we introduced the idea that we can make sense of the economy only by looking simultaneously at several different stories— there is no single punch line. White men's occupations show the same complexity. The shift into white-collar work—clean "brain" work— continues to improve job quality over time, but earnings for most occupations have not improved in recent years; indeed, earnings in occupations with low skill requirements have declined. In 1996 a typical white male in his fifties with a bachelor's degree had earnings of about $51,000, and he was almost certain to have health insurance. In the previous ten years, however, his earnings had grown by only 7 percent, and if he read the papers, he knew that there was a possibility, small but real, that he would soon be let go. He could be excused for thinking that comparable men two decades ago had it better. A white-male high school graduate of similar age had no doubts on this point. He was making about $31,300, about $2,000 to $3,000 less (in 1997 dollars) than he had made when he was forty, and there was an almost 10 percent chance that he did not have health insurance. As far as he could tell, his children would have to go to college to have a chance at the middle class.

Occupations and Earnings: Black Men

On the eve of World War II, half of all black men worked in the rural South, the poorest part of the country (chapter 2). Another quarter lived in southern cities. Only one-third had gone beyond the seventh grade (compared with three-quarters of whites). Black men were restricted to agriculture, service work, and low-level blue-collar jobs. In

1939, their nationwide earnings averaged $5,000 (in 1997 dollars), about two-fifths of the earnings of white men.

Beyond this was the pressure of legal and informal discrimination, not only in the South but in the North as well. Philly Joe Jones was a world-renowned jazz drummer who came to prominence in the Miles Davis Quintet of the late 1950s.* In August 1944, Jones, then a World War II veteran, and seven other men were hired as the first black conductor-trainees for the Philadelphia Transportation Company (PTC). Six thousand white PTC conductors and motormen called a wildcat strike in protest. State liquor stores and bars were ordered closed to prevent racial violence. The strike was settled only after the secretary of war ordered military personnel to take over the system.[15]

In the years since then, black men as a group have passed through two distinct phases: substantial gains through the mid-1970s, and fragmented gains and declines since then. Through the mid-1970s, the civil rights movement and legal pressures to end discrimination were both important in the economic progress made by black men, but equally important was traditional upward mobility. As with white men, sons acquired more education than their fathers had, achieving some of the things the fathers could not. Through this difficult process of slowly and painfully changing its membership, a group thus improves its position in society. Occasionally, however, some larger event advances or retards the progress of most group members—not just the new ones. Over the postwar period, three such events affected black men: the movement out of agriculture, the 1960s boom, and industrial restructuring, which reached cities earlier than it reached the rest of the nation.

The movement out of southern agriculture reached its peak in the 1940s and 1950s. It was during that time that black men faced both the pull of manufacturing jobs in the North and the push of declining farm employment (chapter 6). Over these two decades, one-third of the southern black population migrated to cities in the North and, to a lesser extent, the Far West.

Migration did not lead to enormous occupational mobility. Once in cities, the migrants still faced extensive discrimination, and well under half had finished high school. They moved into blue-collar jobs and personal service jobs; white-collar jobs of any kind were out of reach. In 1960, only 12 percent of black men held white-collar jobs. This was one-third of the rate for white men, and the underlying disparity was greater because few of the black jobs were in the pri-

---

* This was the first Miles Davis Quintet to record on a major label (Columbia) and to reach large white audiences.

Figure 5.4 Median Individual Income of Black and White Men, 1948 to 1996 (in 1997 Dollars)

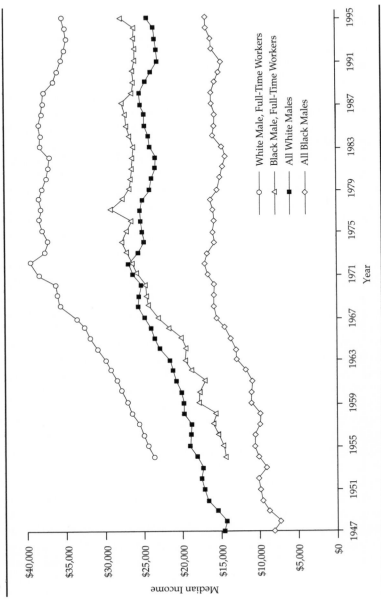

Sources: U.S. Department of Commerce, Bureau of the Census (1985d) table 40 and author's tabulations of the Current Population Survey.
Note: Medians restricted to men with positive incomes.

vate sector. Most were in teaching, administrative support personnel, and other government positions, including large numbers of jobs in the postal service.[16]

Nevertheless, migration substantially increased black male incomes because southern agriculture had paid so little. In 1950 a black man in rural Georgia earned less than $3,000 (in 1997 dollars). When a man moved from agriculture to almost any blue-collar or service job, it was a big step up—an income jump comparable to the move from being a convenience store clerk to a computer technician.

Black men who could make the move and obtain full-time work were closing the gap with whites. By 1960 black men who worked full-time earned about 58 percent as much as their white counterparts. Many black men, however, were not finding full-time work. In the late 1950s, black men's unemployment rate averaged 10 percent, compared to 4 percent for white men. In terms of income, *all* black men (including men who worked less than full-time) had earned income equivalent to 47 percent as much as their white counterparts, a ratio lower than it had been in 1948 (figure 5.4).[17]

The migration out of agriculture could boost black incomes, but the process had obvious limits. By 1960 the proportion of black men in agriculture had fallen to 11 percent, and there were few men left to migrate. At that point, a second event boosted black progress—the very low unemployment rates of the late 1960s.

The 1960s boom came at a good time. During the 1950s and 1960s, manufacturing jobs were rapidly leaving central cities, and in some cities the weakening economy left many black men stranded (chapter 6). By 1963 the national economy had recovered from the recession of 1958 to 1960, but the unemployment rate for black adult men still stood at 8 percent, more than twice the rate for white men. Then Keynesian tax cuts and Vietnam War deficit spending began to stimulate the economy (chapter 3). As high demand exhausted the white labor pool, increased demand focused on blacks.

Relative to earlier years, black men did well. In the last half of the 1960s, black men averaged 4.5 percent unemployment, their best rate since unemployment statistics had been collected by race. Low unemployment translated into big relative income gains. By 1969 the black-white income ratio for full-time male workers stood at .67 (up from .58 in 1959), while the income ratio for all men stood at .57 (up from .47 in 1959).

Tight labor markets also led to modest occupational mobility. By 1969, 17 percent of black men were in white-collar jobs, up from 12 percent in 1960. Movement was still confined to the lower tier of white-collar jobs (administrative support positions, public school teachers); black men's white-collar employment still relied disproportionately on the public sector; and the proportion of black men in these jobs was still half that of white men. Nonetheless, it was progress.

In chapter 3, we saw that it was also in the 1960s that the number of black families headed by women increased rapidly. How does this picture fit with the progress just described for black men? There is no single answer, but a part of the answer begins with the remark by W. E. B. Du Bois quoted in chapter 2: "The conditions of life for men are much harder than for women." Du Bois was writing about Philadelphia in 1896; black men faced better conditions in cities in the 1960s. Nevertheless, a significant fraction of black men were simply dropping by the wayside.* In 1969, a banner year for low unemployment, 6 percent of twenty-five- to fifty-four-year-old black men reported no earned income, while 32 percent reported total income below the federal poverty standard for a family of four.[18]

These statistics understate the true situation because they fail to adjust for the number of black men whom the census simply did not count. For example, in 1969 census statistics show 1.39 million black women but only 1.18 million black men aged twenty-five to thirty-four, a difference of 15 percent.[19] As the economist Robert Lerman notes, the Census Bureau had developed independent population estimates from birth and death certificates suggesting that only one-third of this gap was real, reflecting high rates of homicide and incarceration among black males.† If we assume that most of these uncounted men had low earnings, the suggestion is that something over one-third of prime-age black men had very low earnings in a very tight labor market.‡ There is more to the story of black female-headed families than black male joblessness, but the poor circumstances of many black males surely played a part. We return to the subject of female-headed families in chapter 7.

The many black men who did progress in the 1960s and early 1970s benefited from more than tight labor markets. Discrimination was slowly eroding, and affirmative action also played an important role, particularly in the South and in firms with government con-

---

* Figure 5.4 is based on men who report positive incomes. The growing number of black men who reported no income would not be included in calculating the median. To the contrary, if men moved over time from reporting low incomes to reporting no incomes, their dropping out could raise the median of persons who continued to report income.

† Personal communication (1986).

‡ Using the census estimates, we can say that approximately 10 percent of all prime-age black men were uncounted, and we can assume that most of them had low incomes. We also know that about 25 percent of black men who *are* counted reported very low incomes. Taken together, these numbers indicate that something like one-third of all blacks prime-age men had very low incomes.

tracts.[20] Young blacks were closing the educational gap with whites in terms of years of schooling, though differences in reading and mathematics test scores were closing more slowly.[21] Low unemployment enhanced the impact of these changes, however, and when labor markets went slack after the 1973 OPEC price rise, most progress for black male workers stopped as well. The post-OPEC combination of sharp inflation and recession hurt many central city economies by accelerating the closing of older manufacturing plants and forcing cutbacks in municipal employment (chapter 6). Both kinds of job loss hurt less-educated black men. In the late 1970s, the incomes of black men who worked full-time were 71 percent of those of their white counterparts—up modestly from the late 1960s (69 percent). At the bottom of the distribution, the number of poorly educated black men who dropped out of the labor market continued to grow. In 1978, a fairly good year, 10 percent of prime-age black men reported no earned income from any source, a figure twice what it had been in the late 1960s. While some of these men may have actually had earnings from the underground economy, others were living on disability assistance or, more often, from the income of other family members.

Among all men (including those reporting no earnings), the early 1970s was the point of greatest black-white equality. Since that time, black-white male earnings differences have grown, but not for any single reason. John Bound and Richard B. Freeman have described the different mechanisms at work.[22]

- *Restructuring in manufacturing (black male high school graduates)* Bound and Freeman report that in the 1970s, before the development of the Rust Belt, more than 40 percent of young black male high school graduates in the Midwest (the Great Lakes and the Great Plains states) were employed in durable manufacturing. In 1989 the fraction had fallen to 12 percent. This represented a significant loss of unionized high-wage jobs. More generally, the continued closing of older, central-city manufacturing plants during this period undermined the position of young black men in many large cities.

- *More college graduates and the end of affirmative action (black male college graduates)* In the early 1970s, young black and white male college graduates were roughly on a par—equal earnings, equal proportions working as managers and administrators, and so on. After 1976 this parity eroded sharply; today thirty-year-old black male college graduates earn about 17 percent less than their white counterparts. Bound and Freeman show that part of this decline reflects a rapid increase in the number of black male college graduates; it also likely reflects the end of affirmative action pressures to increase the occupational status of blacks.

• *Crime (black male high school dropouts)*   Crime affects reported income statistics both by creating possibilities for illegal (unreported) income and by giving people criminal records, which lower their chances of being hired for legitimate work. Among black men, the crime problem is most acute among younger high school dropouts, men ages eighteen to twenty-nine. Bound and Freeman estimate that in 1988, 20.1 percent of such men were incarcerated, while another 25 to 30 percent had been incarcerated earlier in their lives.

Figure 5.4 looks at income equality between all black and white men with positive incomes. In terms of the labor market, we can argue that this measure of equality is too broad: we should expect income equality only among men of a similar age and education.* Bound and Freeman show that since the mid-1970s earnings have become less equal under this narrower definition as well as under the broader one.

It is useful to take the comparison one additional step. Earlier, we noted that the gap in years of schooling between black and white young adults had narrowed substantially, but the gap in reading and math skills, as measured on standardized tests, was closing more slowly.† Since a person's test scores directly measure what he or she knows, test scores may be better surrogates for job skills than years of education. Correspondingly, we should look at wage differences among black and white men with similar test scores. In exploring this difference, we assume that a test score at age seventeen or eighteen reflects a mix of the quality of an individual's education, the individual's innate ability, the individual's family background, and so on.

The economists Derek A. Neal and William R. Johnson have made such a comparison for younger workers (ages twenty to twenty-nine) in the early 1990s. Their analysis is based on the Department of Labor's National Longitudinal Survey of Youth in which all participants had been given the Armed Forces Qualification Test (AFQT) in 1980—a year in which the participants ranged in age from fifteen to age twenty-three.‡ Neal and Johnson first estimate that the average earnings gap between black and white young men of the same age and education

---

* Perhaps we should ask why blacks and whites have different amounts of education in the first place.

† One example is the National Assessment of Educational Progress (NAEP)—the "Nation's Report Card." In 1992 a national sample of seventeen-year-olds averaged 307 on the NAEP mathematics test. Within this average, whites averaged 312 and blacks averaged 286. The national average reading score was 290, with whites averaging 297 and blacks averaging 261 (U.S. Department of Education 1994).

‡ Young persons took the AFQT as part of the sample design, regardless of whether they had plans to join the military.

(regardless of AFQT score) was about 20 percent. Among black and white workers of the same age and same AFQT score (regardless of education), the earnings gap closes to 7 percent. Other studies suggest that similar test measures can explain some of the significant fraction of young black men who report no earnings from any source.

In sum, as education and skills have become more important in the economy, the poor quality of black education and disadvantaged family background can explain some, but not all, of the reemerging earnings differences between black and white men. Crime and arrest records also play a part in this gap, as does a mix of discrimination and the changing nature of work. In particular, we have seen that industrial restructuring has increased the demand for both hard skills—reading, math—and "soft" skills, such as the ability to market products to customers. In assessing soft skills, an individual's personal attributes—his accent, his understanding of a customer's frame of reference—can become confounded with employer prejudice or fears of customer prejudice. In the last decade, both employer interviews and experiments involving equally qualified black and white job applicants indicate that residual prejudice continues to hurt black men's employment chances.[23] Prejudicial attitudes have been declining over time—witness the growing number of black elected officials—but it is hard to imagine that they will disappear in day-to-day life very soon.

In 1997 several widely discussed books argued that blacks have made substantial progress over the last half century.[24] As we shall see, the description more accurately fits black women than black men, but it is undeniable that black men have made significant progress. In 1949 less than 2 percent of employed black men were managers or administrators; nearly 6 percent are today (table 5.3). In 1949 more than one-fifth of black men worked in agriculture, mostly as farm laborers; less than 3 percent have such jobs today.

If we shift the frame of reference from the last fifty years to the last twenty years, the picture is cloudier. Since the mid-1970s, slow wage growth, the falling demand for less-skilled men, crime, and the end of affirmative action have combined to slow substantially the progress of black males. The year 1996 was a reasonably good one, with national unemployment averaging 5.6 percent. Yet in that year Current Population Survey data show that 22 percent of prime-age black males reported no earned income (figure 5.5). Two-thirds of these men were high school dropouts. Assuming these statistics are exaggerated by unreported income, they remain startling.

It follows that the debate surrounding these recent books is not about their description of the past but about their uses of the past to project the future. Will future black male progress look like the last

Table 5.3   Occupational Distribution of Black Male Workers, 1949, 1979, and 1996

Occupational Group	Percentage of All Black Men in Group			Percentage of All Non-Hispanic White Men
	1949	1979	1996	1996
Professional and managerial workers				
Executives, administrators, and managers	2.0%	3.7%	5.7%	12.8%
Management-related occupations	0.1	1.5	2.0	2.8
Engineers and natural scientists	0.1	1.1	1.4	5.5
Doctors, dentists, and other health diagnostic occupations	0.1	0.2	0.3	0.9
Elementary and secondary-school teachers	0.7	1.6	1.6	2.0
Post-secondary-school teachers	0.1	0.4	0.3	0.8
Lawyers and judges	0.0	0.2	0.3	0.8
Miscellaneous professional specialties (ministers, social workers, and so on)	0.7	1.8	2.8	3.0
Other white-collar workers				
Health aides and technicians	0.1	0.8	1.0	1.1
Technicians other than health technicians	0.1	1.5	1.9	2.5
Sales-related occupations	1.2	3.5	6.5	11.4
Administrative support workers	3.3	8.6	8.2	5.5
Blue-collar workers				
Craftsmen and precision workers	9.3	15.1	15.8	19.7
Machine operators	14.4	14.6	9.8	6.6
Transport equipment operators	7.3	10.6	10.4	6.9
Handlers, laborers, and so on	24.3	11.7	11.4	5.3
Service workers				
Household workers	0.7	0.1	0.0	0.0
Protective service workers (police, fire, and so on)	0.4	2.8	4.2	2.6
Food services, building services (except household), childcare, restaurant, and personal services workers	12.9	12.3	12.6	5.5
Farmers and farm-related occupations	20.2	3.2	2.2	2.9
Armed forces	2.0	4.6	1.6	1.2
Total	100%	100%	100%	100%

Sources: Author's tabulations of the 1950 and 1980 Decennial Census Public Use Microdata Sample files and 1997 March Current Population Survey.
Note: Data restricted to workers ages eighteen to sixty-five with positive earnings.

Figure 5.5 Earnings of Black Men Age Twenty-Five to Fifty-Four, 1973 and 1996

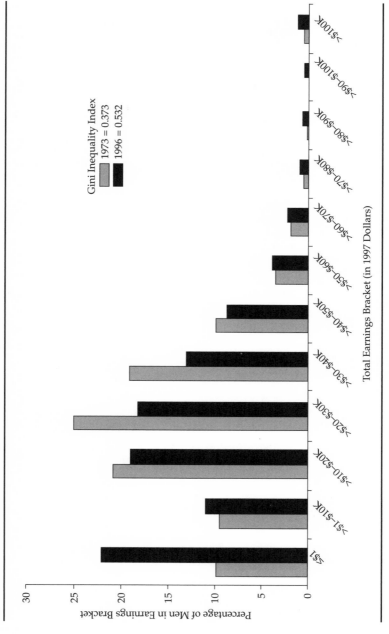

Sources: Author's tabulations of the March 1974 and March 1997 Current Population Survey.

Figure 5.6 Median Individual Income of Black and White Women and White Men Who Worked Year Round and Full Time, 1955 to 1996 (in 1997 Dollars)

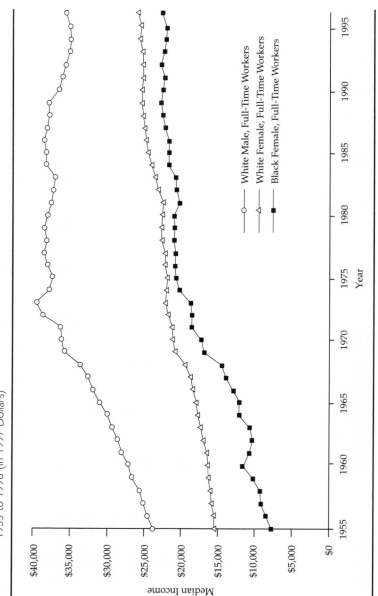

Sources: U.S. Department of Commerce, Bureau of the Census (1985d) table 40 and author's tabulations of the Current Population Survey.

Note: Medians restricted to persons with positive incomes.

fifty years or the last twenty? Whatever else the answer depends on, it depends critically on the quality of education, a subject to which we return in chapter 8.

Occupations and Earnings: White Women

For white women, as for black men, the story of the last fifty years divides into two distinct subperiods. From World War II through the end of the 1970s, white women's occupational mobility was limited. Since 1980 white women have made significant gains. Progress was not spread evenly—as with other groups, progress among white women divided along educational lines. Nonetheless, white women's gains after 1979 stood out in a period when many other groups were at best staying even.

In the late 1970s, on the eve of this progress, the economic data for white women seemed to raise a paradox. Anyone could see that the number of women lawyers, doctors, and managers was growing, yet in 1979 white women who worked full-time had average income of $22,700, 40 percent less than the earnings of white men who worked full-time (figure 5.6). The percentage gap was almost as large as in 1955, the first year it was published.[25]

The paradox was reconciled by three facts:

- Over the postwar period, the number of white women in the labor force increased far more rapidly than the number of white men.

- The rapid increase in working women raised the number of women lawyers and managers, but also the number of women teachers, sales clerks, and secretaries. Thus, the overall occupational distribution of white women did not change very much.

- Within most occupations, women still earned less than men, even when age, education, and hours worked were held constant.

Even during World War II working women were an exception. In 1944, at the peak of the war, about 35 percent of all women over the age of fourteen were employed. It was a high rate for the time, but far less than today's rate of 58 percent of white women over the age of sixteen.

The low postwar labor-force participation rate for women reflected a straightforward career pattern: work for pay (if you work at all) before marriage and children, then stop. Among younger white women age eighteen to twenty-four, about one-half worked. Among prime-age white women (twenty-five to fifty-four), one-third worked. Women showed little tendency to return to work after their children were grown, but this would soon change. By the late 1950s, almost half of all white women age forty-five to fifty-four were working, and women in their late thirties were returning to work as well. The women most likely to have young children—those age twenty-five to thirty-four—still remained out of the labor market in large numbers.[26]

During the 1960s, labor-force participation grew moderately among women of all ages, but during the 1970s it exploded, particularly among women in their twenties and early thirties, the traditional child-raising years. Among women age twenty-five to thirty-four, labor-force participation rose from 46 percent in 1970 to 66 percent in 1979.

The huge influx of white women workers helped reshape the labor force. Between 1955 and 1980, the number of adult white male workers grew by twelve and a half million, while the number of adult white female workers increased by twenty million.[27] Since most of these women held white-collar jobs in the service sector, their large numbers accelerated the economy's transition to a service society (chapter 4). These numbers also created the paradox of women's economic position. Consider two questions:

- Among all employed white women in 1979, what proportion were managers and administrators?
- Among all managers and administrators in 1979, what proportion were white women?

In 1979 only 5 percent of employed white women worked as managers and administrators. This figure was not much larger than in 1949 (4 percent). To the contrary, in 1979 nearly half of all working white women were in three traditional occupations: administrative support and clerical (32 percent); sales (12 percent); and education (7 percent). Since the end of the war, white women's occupational distribution had advanced no more rapidly than the distribution for white men.

The proportion of managers and administrators who were white women was a different issue. Because the number of white women in the job market had grown so rapidly, women became more numerous and visible in every occupational category even without significant occupational mobility. Thus, the proportion of all managers and administrators who were white women rose from about 13 percent in 1950 to more than 27 percent in 1979. In this way, white women appeared to be making giant strides even as their occupational distribution improved only gradually.

Beyond occupational segregation, female-male earnings differences continued to exist *within* occupations. In the 1980 census, white women who worked full-time earned 20 to 30 percent less than white men of the same age, education, and occupational category.[28] Some of the difference was easily explained. At that time, women classified as year-round, full-time workers actually worked 10 percent fewer hours than men in the same category.[29] With the rapid growth in women's labor-force participation, many women (especially those above age thirty) were relatively new to the job, and their wages reflected their relative lack of experience.[30] Nevertheless, part of the earnings gap reflected simple discrimination. For example, the idea continued to prevail that married women could rely on their husbands' paycheck and did not need money as much as did men.

During the 1980s, these traditional patterns began to change. In a decade when many dimensions of inequality increased, the gap between women's and men's earnings closed, for both good and bad reasons. On the positive side was the continued erosion of occupational discrimination, a particular benefit for white women who had graduated from college. The fraction of white women who held managerial or administrative positions rose from 5 percent in 1979 to 10 percent in 1996 (table 5.4), while the proportion in administrative support (clerical) work fell. More generally, college-educated women (most of them white) were the only group to show consistent wage gains during the 1980s and 1990s. Between 1979 and 1995, the median earnings of twenty-five- to thirty-four-year-old white women with sixteen years of education rose from $23,400 to $26,500.

Earnings converged among less-educated women and men for a more negative reason: white women's earnings fell by less than white men's did. In chapter 4, we saw that the earnings of male high school graduates and dropouts declined by 15 to 20 percent during the 1980s. While these earnings fell across all industries, the largest declines took place in high-wage durable goods manufacturing—industries that employed few women. When women worked in manufacturing at all, it was in textiles, apparel, or food processing, industries with lower pay scales. Coming into the 1980s, then, blue-collar women had less to lose than did blue-collar men. Over the decade, wages of high school-educated white women fell by only 3 to 5 percent, bringing men's and women's earnings closer.

A different dimension of convergence in men's and women's earnings was traceable through changing patterns in labor-force participation. As discussed earlier, during the 1970s and 1980s the least-educated prime-age men (with the weakest earnings prospects) began to drop out of the labor force. Among white women, labor-force participation rose among all education groups, but it rose highest among the well-educated. Among prime-age white women, college graduates' labor-force participation rose from 55 percent in 1970 to 83 percent in 1995. Among high school dropouts, labor-force participation rose from 44 percent in 1970 to 53 percent in 1995.

Table 5.4   Occupational Distribution of White Female Workers, 1949, 1979, and 1996

Occupational Group	Percentage of All White Women in Group 1949	Percentage of All White Women in Group 1979	Percentage of Non-Hispanic White Women 1996	Percentage of All Non-Hispanic White Men 1996
Professional and managerial workers				
Executives, administrators, and managers	4.1%	5.1%	9.8%	12.8%
Management-related occupations	0.6	2.3	4.7	2.8
Engineers and natural scientists	0.3	0.5	1.6	5.5
Doctors, dentists, and other health diagnostic occupations	0.1	0.2	0.4	0.9
Elementary and secondary-school teachers	6.4	6.5	7.4	2.0
Post-secondary-school teachers	0.2	0.6	0.8	0.8
Lawyers and judges	0.0	0.2	0.4	0.8
Miscellaneous professional specialties (ministers, social workers, and so on)	1.8	2.8	4.1	3.0
Other white-collar workers				
Health aides and technicians	4.4	5.3	6.9	1.1
Technicians other than health technicians	0.4	1.2	1.4	2.5
Sales-related occupations	10.1	11.9	13.5	11.4
Administrative support workers	32.0	31.7	24.1	5.5
Blue-collar workers				
Craftsmen and precision workers	2.3	2.4	1.9	19.7
Machine operators	20.8	8.9	4.1	6.6
Transport equipment operators	0.2	0.9	0.9	6.9
Handlers, laborers, and so on	0.6	2.2	1.5	5.3
Service workers				
Household workers	3.3	0.8	0.8	0.0
Protective service workers (police, fire, and so on)	0.1	0.4	0.6	2.6
Food services, building services (except household), childcare, restaurant, and personal services workers	10.7	15.1	14.4	5.5
Farmers and farm-related occupations	1.4	1.0	0.8	2.9
Armed forces	0.1	0.3	0.1	1.2
Total	100%	100%	100%	100%

Sources: Author's tabulations of the 1950 and 1980 Decennial Census Public Use Microdata Sample files and 1997 March Current Population Survey.
Note: Data restricted to workers ages eighteen to sixty-five with positive earnings.

Converging earnings and converging labor-force participation were strong forces for income equality. Among year-round full-time workers, the ratio of median white women's earnings to median white men's earnings rose from .59 in 1979 to .73 in 1996. Among younger men and women with at least some college, the ratio stood at .82.* More generally, the hourly wage distribution for men and women, viewed as one group, showed little increase in inequality after the early 1980s. Taken separately, men's wage inequality and women's wage inequality continued to grow. When men's and women's wages were combined, however, the trend toward wage equality between the sexes offset growing inequality within each group.[31]

At the same time, the convergence of men's and women's earnings raised a second paradox. As Francine Blau and Lawrence Kahn point out, U.S. men and women are closer in education, labor market experience, and occupational status than men and women in many other industrialized countries.[32] Yet compared to other countries, the U.S. female-male earnings ratio is relatively low. Why?

As Blau and Kahn show, part of the answer involves the increasingly unequal wage structure among U.S. men. To see this, suppose that the education and work experience of the average working woman make her "equivalent" to men at the fortieth percentile of the male earnings distribution. If the male earnings distribution were very equal, earnings at the fortieth and fiftieth percentiles would be close in dollar terms, and so the female-male ratio of median earnings would be near 1.0. On the other hand, if the male earnings distribution were very unequal, earnings at the fortieth and fiftieth percentiles would be far apart in dollar terms, and the female-male ratio of median earnings would be lower.[33]

We know that the U.S. male earnings distribution became substantially less equal during the 1980s (chapter 4). Working women were gaining on working men in both education and experience. The dollar penalty for being below average was growing, however, and so women were, in essence, swimming upstream. Blau and Kahn estimate that if male earnings inequality had not increased during the 1980s, the female-male earnings ratio for full-time workers would have risen to between .75 and .8.

---

* See Blau (1998). A number of commentators have paraphrased the work of June O'Neill and Simon Polacheck (1993) to argue that there is no longer an earnings gap after controlling for all individual characteristics. O'Neill and Polacheck's work, however, looks only at young workers (where some gap remains) and says nothing about the future of this gap if men and women face differential promotion possibilities and other forms of discrimination.

A cynic would point to a second problem of timing: white women moved into higher-wage white-collar occupations just as those jobs became unstable. There is some truth to this. In the blue-collar recession of 1981 to 1983, a woman college graduate (regardless of age or occupation) had a job loss probability of about 2 percent per year, and the figure for a male college graduate was almost 3 percent per year. The difference reflected the concentration of women college graduates in teaching and other secure positions. By the mid-1990s, women's and men's occupations were more similar, and so women were more exposed to the risks of the wider economy. Between 1993 and 1995, a woman college graduate had a job loss probability of slightly over 3 percent per year, compared to 4 percent per year for male college graduates.

Despite these setbacks, the 1980s were a decade of substantial progress for white women. For better and worse—mostly for better—the market was treating women and men more as equals.

Occupations and Earnings: Black Women

Unlike white women, black women have always worked in large numbers. In the late 1940s, nearly half of all black women worked (compared to about one-third of white women). In those years, black working women shared many of the disadvantages faced by black men: geographic concentration in the low-wage South, limited education, and official and informal discrimination. These barriers could be seen in the jobs they held. In the 1950 census, two out of every five employed black women worked as a household domestic. Another one-fifth worked in cafeterias, on cleaning crews, and in other low-rung service jobs (table 5.5). Low-rung occupations translated into low earnings. Even in the mid-1950s, a black woman who worked full-time had an income of $7,900 (in 1997 dollars), a figure about half as large as the income of her white counterpart (figure 5.6).

With this starting point, it would be no surprise if black women's economic status paralleled that of black men: broad-based progress only through the mid-1970s. In fact, black women's progress was more sustained and their occupational status changed fairly rapidly.

In most ways, the forces behind black women's progress were similar to the forces affecting black men: migration out of the South, attitudes changed by the civil rights movement, the late 1960s Vietnam War–fueled boom. As important as any of these factors were rapid gains in education. In 1950 the average young white woman earned a high school diploma, while the average young black woman did not complete ninth grade. By the early 1970s, a majority of both black

Table 5.5 Occupational Distribution of Black Female Workers, 1949, 1979, and 1996

Occupational Group	Percentage of All Black Women in Group			Percentage of All Non-Hispanic White Men
	1949	1979	1996	1996
Professional and managerial workers				
Executives, administrators, and managers	1.3%	2.9%	4.8%	12.8%
Management-related occupations	0.1	1.8	3.7	2.8
Engineers and natural scientists	0.0	0.3	0.9	5.5
Doctors, dentists, and other health diagnostic occupations	0.0	0.1	0.0	0.9
Elementary and secondary-school teachers	3.9	5.9	5.2	2.0
Post-secondary-school teachers	0.1	0.3	0.4	0.8
Lawyers and judges	—	0.1	—	0.8
Miscellaneous professional specialties (ministers, social workers, and so on)	0.4	2.2	3.0	3.0
Other white-collar workers				
Health aides and technicians	1.8	4.6	5.0	1.1
Technicians other than health technicians	0.1	0.9	0.8	2.5
Sales-related occupations	1.5	6.7	11.3	11.4
Administrative support workers	3.8	25.1	24.1	5.5
Blue-collar workers				
Craftsmen and precision workers	1.1	2.3	2.0	19.7
Machine operators	15.8	13.0	8.9	6.6
Transport equipment operators	0.2	0.9	1.4	6.9
Handlers, laborers, and so on	1.9	3.3	2.3	5.3
Service workers				
Household workers	41.2	4.3	1.2	0.0
Protective service workers (police, fire, and so on)	0.1	0.7	1.8	2.6
Food services, building services (except household), childcare, restaurant, and personal services workers	18.6	23.4	22.6	5.5
Farmers and farm-related occupations	8.1	0.8	0.3	2.9
Armed forces	0.2	0.6	0.4	1.2
Total	100%	100%	100%	100%

Sources: Author's tabulations of 1950 and 1980 Decennial Census Public Use Microdata Sample files and 1997 March Current Population Survey.
Note: Data restricted to workers ages eighteen to sixty-five with positive earnings.

and white young women had graduated from high school though a greater fraction of white women were going on to college.[34]

Improved education allowed many black women to move into the expanding service sector. By the time of the 1980 census, the proportion of black women in domestic work had declined to less than 5 percent, while the proportion in clerical work, health care, and sales had grown from 7 percent to 37 percent. This progress occurred despite the growing number of black families headed by women. During the 1960s, as the number of black female-headed families was growing rapidly, 50 percent of black female family heads were in the labor force, a figure only slightly below the 58 percent participation rate of married black women.*

As black women's occupational status improved, their earnings improved as well. By the mid-1970s, black and white women of similar age and education had approximate earnings parity.[35] As with men, the mid-1970s were a high point of earnings equality between black and white women (see figure 5.6). In the years that followed, however, the experiences of black women and men diverged significantly.

During the mid-1970s, many central cities experienced the restructuring that the whole nation would experience after 1979: an accelerated loss of manufacturing jobs and losses in municipal employment, both of which reduced demand for semiskilled and unskilled workers. Where city employment was growing, it was in services that largely favored the better educated (chapter 6).

Black women and men were both vulnerable to the increased demand for better-educated workers, but black men were hurt by the loss of manufacturing jobs in a way that black women were not. Even in the booming 1960s a significant fraction of black men had low earnings or no earnings at all. The changing nature of central-city economies only compounded the situation.† By contrast, the growing service sector created clerical, sales, and hospital jobs that favored women's soft skills over the skills of less-educated men. For women, this expansion of demand helped to cushion the falling demand for less-educated workers.

---

* More recently, Katheryn Edin and Laura Lein (1997) report that one-half of welfare recipients work (though most of their income is not officially reported). On the labor-force participation and poverty rates of black female household heads in the 1960s, see U.S. Bureau of the Census, *Current Population Reports*, series P-60, no. 76 (1970), table 11. For the labor-force participation of black wives, see *Current Population Reports*, series P-60, no. 80 (1971), table 17. Among black female family heads who were in the labor force in the 1960s, 37 percent were in poverty, about one-half the rate of those who were not in the labor force.

† Here, too, however, other factors were involved: in some cities—for example, New York—black men did not hold manufacturing jobs in any great numbers. See Bailey and Waldinger (1991).

By the 1990s, the economy's shift toward better-educated workers had taken its toll, but black women continued to progress slowly. Black and white women were participating in the labor force at roughly equal rates. As a group, white women had an overall earnings and occupational advantage because of higher rates of college attendance, but racial differences in the labor market were narrowing. Among younger black and white women of the same age and education, the racial gap in wages was 16 percent. Among younger women of the same age and AFQT score (regardless of education), the average racial gap in wages had disappeared.[36]

Occupation and Earnings: The Current Status of Hispanic Men and Women

In chapter 3, we described the wave of legislation passed in Lyndon Johnson's second term: the Voting Rights Act, Medicare and Medicaid, the War on Poverty programs, and, less visible at the time, revisions to U.S. immigration law. Since the 1920s, the country's immigration policy had focused on limiting the number of immigrants and restricting their countries of origin to Britain and northern Europe— the countries from which the original U.S. settlers had migrated. The 1965 revisions allowed for increased numbers of immigrants and substantially expanded the countries from which they could come by emphasizing, for example, immigration that would reunite families.*

By 1970 rapid inflows of immigrants were reshaping parts of the nation's population and labor force. The economists George J. Borjas, Richard B. Freeman, and Lawrence F. Katz have performed a careful analysis of these trends.[37] Table 5.6, reproduced from their work, shows the magnitudes involved.

In 1960, before the new law, foreign-born residents (immigrants) comprised 5 percent of the U.S. population. Four-fifths of these immigrants had been born in Europe or Canada. Between 1960 and the mid-1990s, the number of foreign-born citizens nearly tripled, from 9.7 million to 24.6 million. Immigrants now represented 9.3 percent of the U.S. population. At the same time, the European countries and Canada were no longer the main countries of origin; the immigrant flow from Asia and, in particular, from Latin America and the Caribbean was increasing. While the change was enormous, it was not universally visible because most immigrants settled in one of a half-dozen states: California, New York, New Jersey, Illinois, Florida, and Texas. An issue like bilingual education could become politically charged in California because more than one-quarter of the California population is now foreign-born.

---

* For a brief history of this legislation, see Borjas (1990) chs. 1 and 2.

Table 5.6 The Foreign-Born Population of the United States and Its National Origins, 1960 to 1996

	Foreign-Born Population				
Item	1960	1970	1980	1990	1996
In millions	9.7	9.7	14.1	19.8	24.6
As percentage of entire population	5.4%	4.8%	6.2%	7.9%	9.3%
Distribution by origin (percent)					
Canada and Europe	84%	68%	43%	26%	21%
Caribbean and Latin America	9	19	31	43	50
Asia	5	9	18	25	25
Other	2	4	8	6	4

Sources: From Borjas, Freeman, and Katz (1997), reprinted with permission from the Brookings Institution. Authors' calculations. Data for 1960 are from U.S. Bureau of the Census, *Historical Statistics*, vol. 1 (1975). Data for 1970 to 1990 are from *Statistical Abstract of the United States* (various years). Data for 1996 are from the Census Bureau and are available on the bureau's worldwide web page.

This history is important in discussing the occupational status of Hispanic Americans. Historical data for blacks and whites are, to an extent, pictures of successive generations of the same families interacting with the economy. Data for Hispanics are different. Between 1970 and 1996, the Hispanic American population grew from 14.7 million to 26.5 million, of whom 10.3 million were immigrants. When immigration changes a population to this extent, trends in occupational data depend a great deal on the immigrants' characteristics.

Immigrants to the United States tend to have either very low or very high levels of education—a bimodal distribution that differs sharply from the educational status of the native-born population.* Hispanic Americans are themselves a diverse group, comprised of Cubans, Mexicans, Puerto Ricans, and Central and South Americans. Even among Cubans, the most educated of these groups, less than 70 percent have finished high school. Among all Hispanic American[38] adults (native-born and foreign-born), roughly half have finished high school, a rate much lower than the 87 percent among non-Hispanic whites.

These numbers reflect both schooling in the immigrants' home countries and the problems of adapting to a new culture and lan-

---

* In 1990, 22 percent of all immigrants had less than nine years of schooling, compared to 4 percent of the native U.S. population. In the same year, about 20 percent of all immigrants had four or more years of college, a rate equal to that in the native U.S. population. See Borjas, Freeman, and Katz (1997) table 2.

guage. These problems will ease with time, but for the present, limited education and poor educational quality significantly shape Hispanics' occupational status. Two-thirds of employed Hispanic men now work in blue-collar and service occupations (table 5.7), a figure that compares to 47 percent among non-Hispanic white men. For Hispanic women, as with other women, clerical positions offer greater entry into white-collar occupations. Nevertheless, about 45 percent of Hispanic women currently work in blue-collar or service occupations.

The quantity and quality of Hispanic education can explain most of the earnings differences between Hispanics and non-Hispanic whites. Neal and Johnson show that among working young men of the same age and education, the average wage gap between Hispanics and white non-Hispanics is about 5 percent. Among working young men of the same age and AFQT score (regardless of education) the Hispanic-white wage gap disappears. Among young working women of the same age and education, Hispanics and non-Hispanic whites have similar wages. Among young working women of the same age and AFQT scores (regardless of education), Hispanic women have a 15 percent wage *premium*.

These estimates suggest that Hispanic Americans' job market success depends much more on the education they receive than on labor market discrimination once they have left school. As with blacks, the data point to education's central role in improving the economic status of future generations. At the same time, the large numbers of poorly educated immigrants have played a part in U.S. earnings inequality. Immigrants (from all countries) now comprise a significant fraction of U.S. high school dropouts. These workers have contributed to earnings inequality both through their own low wages and potentially by holding down the wages of less-educated, native-born workers. We return to the issue of immigrant competition in chapter 6.

Markets and Meritocracy

We have seen how a surge in skill bias has made education a major axis of economic inequality. We developed this point using U.S. census survey data that showed the growing association between a respondent's annual earnings and years of schooling. What does this association really mean?

It could mean what it appears to mean: changes in the economy have increased the payoff for skills, and the more time spent in the classroom, the more skills learned. If this interpretation is correct, broader access to quality education becomes a central part of equal opportunity.

We can reach a different conclusion by asking what kinds of people

Table 5.7   Occupational Distribution of Hispanic Female and Male Workers, 1996

Occupational Group	Percentage of All Hispanic Women	Percentage of All Hispanic Men	Percentage of All Non-Hispanic White Men
Professional and managerial workers			
Executives, administrators, and managers	5.2%	5.2%	12.8%
Management-related occupations	3.3	1.1	2.8
Engineers and natural scientists	0.3	1.5	5.5
Doctors, dentists, and other health diagnostic occupations	1.5	0.5	0.9
Elementary and secondary-school teachers	4.4	0.9	2.0
Post-secondary school teachers	0.3	0.3	0.8
Lawyers and judges	0.3	0.2	0.8
Miscellaneous professional specialties (ministers, social workers, and so on)	2.5	1.7	3.0
Other white-collar workers			
Health aides and technicians	1.9	0.4	1.1
Technicians other than health technicians	1.2	1.2	2.5
Sales-related occupations	11.8	7.2	11.4
Administrative support workers	22.0	5.6	5.5
Blue-collar workers			
Craftsmen and precision workers	2.6	19.7	19.7
Machine operators	12.3	12.3	6.6
Transport equipment operators	0.5	7.1	6.9
Handlers, laborers, and so on	2.8	9.2	5.3
Service workers			
Household workers	3.7	0.0	0.0
Protective service workers (police, fire, and so on)	0.6	2.4	2.6
Food services, building services (except household), childcare, restaurant, and personal services workers	20.8	13.9	5.5
Farmers and farm-related occupations	2.0	8.8	2.9
Armed forces	0.1	0.9	1.2
Total	100%	100%	100%

Sources: Author's tabulations of 1997 March Current Population Survey.
Note: Data restricted to workers ages eighteen to sixty-five with positive earnings.

today receive the most education. For example, high school seniors who go to college typically have higher standardized test scores than high school seniors who do not. Similarly, high school seniors who go to college typically come from higher-income families who can teach their children about the white-collar job market and the importance of "soft skills." In census data, a person's years of education could be acting as a statistical surrogate for being "smart" or coming from a high-status background. The market could be rewarding the kind of person who goes to college rather than classroom learning per se. If this second interpretation were correct, broader access to quality education would accomplish very little.

These different interpretations were brought into sharp relief by the 1994 publication of *The Bell Curve* by Richard J. Herrnstein and Charles Murray. The authors argue that a young person's IQ is a far more important determinant of future success than either education or, in fact, parents' status. In one sense, their argument is similar to the one we have developed here: that recent economic developments have increased the demand for skilled workers at the expense of the less-skilled. In Herrnstein and Murray's interpretation, however, the central determinant of a person's skill is genetic inheritance.

In essence, *The Bell Curve* argues that increases in income inequality are an outcome of nature, immune to manipulation by public policy. Christopher C. DeMuth, writing in *Commentary* magazine, captures this spirit:

> [T]he critical *source* of social wealth has shifted over the last few hundred years from land (at the end of the 18th century) to physical capital (at the end of the 19th) to, today, human capital—education and cognitive ability. This development is not an unmixed gain from the standpoint of economic equality. The ability to acquire and deploy human capital is a function of intelligence, and intelligence is not only unequally distributed but also, to a significant degree, heritable. As Charles Murray and the late Richard J. Herrnstein argue in *The Bell Curve,* an economy that rewards sheer brainpower replaces one old source of inequality, socioeconomic advantage, with a new one, cognitive advantage.[39]

Herrnstein and Murray's work, as distinct from the popular interpretation of their work, does not support such strong conclusions. Herrnstein and Murray base their conclusions on the National Longitudinal Survey of Youth (NLSY), the same data used in Neal and Johnson's work discussed earlier. Recall that Neal and Johnson conclude that individuals' scores on the AFQT help to explain average wage differences across groups—for example, the average income difference between young white women and young black women.

Herrnstein and Murray use the same data to conclude that IQ is a major determinant of income differences across individuals. Moving from the first conclusion to the second requires two propositions to be true:

- A young person's AFQT score represents genetically determined IQ and is unaffected by educational quality, years of schooling, or family background.

- Young persons' AFQT scores explain not only income differences between groups—the average income of young white men versus the average income of young black men—but differences among individuals.*

There is evidence against both propositions. On the meaning of the AFQT score, a number of authors have argued convincingly that the Armed Forces Qualification Test is a test of general knowledge, rather than an IQ test, and that AFQT scores are affected by the education a person has received.†

The AFQT's ability to predict individual incomes is summarized in a regression by Thomas Kane.‡ Kane's regression, based on the same NLSY data, summarizes the relationship between AFQT score and income for a set of workers who were between twenty-five and thirty-three years old in 1990. The regression line and the data are displayed in figure 5.7.

(5.1)   Annual Income = \$24,737 + \$5,314 × Normalized AFQT Score
              (223.12)   (223.14)
              R^2 = .117

AFQT Score has been normalized and is expressed in standard deviation units so that approximately 95 percent of the population have a normalized score between -2 and $+2$. Coefficient standard errors are listed in parentheses.

---

* The difference between these two ideas can be seen in an analogy based on height and weight. Across a large sample of men, we expect height and weight to be correlated, just as we expect AFQT score and income to be correlated. Neal and Johnson examine average differences between groups, equivalent to saying: "On average, men who are 6' tall weigh more than men who are 5'10". The popular reading of Herrnstein and Murray examines individual differences and is equivalent to saying "Any man who is 6' tall is extremely likely to weigh more than any man who is 5'10". In the Neal-Johnson statement, individual variations—whether a man exercises, whether a man loves beer—are averaged out in computing the group's average weight. In the Herrnstein-Murray statement, individual differences remain in the data to be explained, a much more difficult job.

† See, for example, the discussion in Neal and Johnson (1996) and in Fischer et al. (1996). Also see the discussion in Korenman and Winship (1995).

‡ Kane is a professor at Harvard's Kennedy School of Government. The regression is part of a larger project Kane is doing in this area and was given to me in a personal communication.

Figure 5.7   The Regression Line Relating an Individual's Annual Earnings to His or Her Score on the Armed Forces Qualification Test (Annual Earnings in 1997 Dollars)

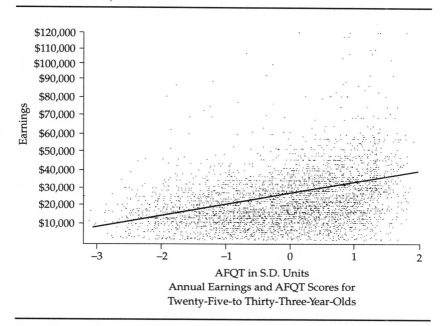

AFQT in S.D. Units
Annual Earnings and AFQT Scores for
Twenty-Five-to Thirty-Three-Year-Olds

Source: Thomas Kane, Harvard University (1998).

DeMuth's quote and many others imply that Herrnstein and Murray show an individual's AFQT score is a very strong predictor of the individual's income. If that were true, most data points in figure 5.7 would lie very close to the estimated regression line. In reality, the figure shows a much cloudier picture in which higher AFQT score leads to higher income on average, but the relationship is very imprecise. The regression estimate confirms this. The value of the squared correlation coefficient (R^2 = .117) means that an AFQT score can explain 11.7 percent of the income variation in the NLSY data used by Herrnstein and Murray.

This weak relationship is not surprising since we know that income depends on many other factors besides IQ. Consider three examples.

Factors that Impact Individual Income

Gender   Based on standardized achievement tests, American women and men have similar IQs. As we have seen, however, American women earn on average 70 to 75 percent as much as American men (figure 5.6). There are a number of explanations for this gap, some of which we have reviewed. Intelligence is not one of them.

College Costs   During the 1980s, the rising gap between the earnings of those with a college education and those with a high school education encouraged a growing fraction of young persons to attend college. College, however, costs money (including forgone earnings while in classes) and the likelihood of a young person attending college is therefore related to family income. Thomas Kane (1995) reports that among children from the top quarter of family incomes, the rate of college attendance rose from .70 in 1977 to .80 in 1993. By contrast, among children from the bottom quarter of family incomes, the rate of college attendance stayed constant at about .28. A young person's intelligence can explain only a part of these enrollment differences. Family income, family background, and the quality of elementary and secondary education all play important roles.

Accounting Rules   Chief Executive Officer (CEO) compensation has grown rapidly since the early 1980s. An important component of this growth is the awarding of large blocks of stock options—options that permit the CEO to purchase shares of the company's stock at a fixed price in some future period. Later in this chapter, we discuss the sound reasons for including some stock options in CEO compensation. The extremely large size of many awards is driven by current accounting rules that do not require firms to report stock options as a business expense until the options are exercised. As the economists Brian J. Hall and Jeffrey B. Liebman write, "CEO consultants also say that stock options are attractive because they are 'free.' Since there is no current accounting charge from granting stock options, consultants and boards view options as costless."[40] Put differently, the market that evaluates CEO talent is not some process of nature but operates within man-made rules. If the cost of CEO stock options had been subject to shareholder scrutiny, CEO compensation would have grown more slowly, but this would not have meant CEO's were any less intelligent.*

Even with the economy's growing skill bias, the greatest part of income inequality cannot be explained by genetically inherited intel-

---

* The accounting treatment of these options has gone through a number of changes. In the early 1990s, the Federal Accounting Standards Board recommended that firms be required to count the estimated value of options as a business expense at the time they were granted. Congress defeated this recommendation. More recently, firms have been required to list the options granted in the footnotes on income statements, and they have been required to adjust the traditional profit measure of earnings per share in terms of the number of shares that will exist when previously awarded options are exercised.

ligence. Like the hero of the movie *Good Will Hunting,* most true ge-
niuses among us will be discovered, while people with truly weak
mental ability will not do well. Between these extremes—the place
where most of us sit—luck, family income, educational quality,* and
the nation's other equalizing institutions come into play, and it is in
this area that policy has a role. We return to this role in chapter 8.

The Growth of Very High Incomes

To this point, we have focused on inequality in the broad middle of
the earnings distribution. A different aspect of inequality—one that
has received much media attention—is the growing share of all income at the very top of the distribution.

U.S. census data provide little guidance here. To preserve confidentiality and elicit the public's cooperation, the census imposes upper
limits on the income data it records, and even stricter limits on the
income data it releases for research analysis (see the appendix).

To examine very high incomes, the best data come from the U.S. Treasury's *Statistics of Income,* which annually reports adjusted gross incomes
(AGIs) from a sample of tax returns. The Treasury maintains confidentiality by recording no information about the tax filers' personal characteristics—where they live, their gender or age, or education.† Each obser-
vation does include the tax return's AGI and the sources of that income:
wages and salaries, interest and dividends, capital gains, and so on.

The most thorough analyses of these data have been performed by
Daniel Feenberg and James Poterba. Feenberg and Poterba estimate
that in 1994 that the top .5 percent of tax returns reported 10.7 percent
of all AGI.‡ The share is quite large and represents a sharp increase
from the 6 percent of AGI reported by the top .5 percent of all tax

---

* The efficacy of education has been demonstrated in a number of ingenious studies
looking at the earnings of identical twins who have gone on to receive different
amounts of schooling. Because the twins are identical, they share the same genetic
endowment and family backgrounds and so differences in their amounts of schooling
are not surrogates for these background variables. See Ashenfelter and Krueger (1994)
and Miller, Mulvey, and Martin (1995).

† A few characteristics, however, can be gleaned from knowing income sources—for
example, receipt of Social Security benefits may say something about a person's age.

‡ Jim Poterba 1998, personal communication. Feenberg and Poterba look at the top .5
percent of taxpayers in 1989 and then define equivalent fractions of the population in
other years. They do this because tax law changes over time have changed the proportion of the population who owe federal taxes and so the top .5 percent of taxpayers
represents a different fraction of the population in different years. Since individuals can
file separately or jointly, there is no neat correspondence between tax-filing units and
households. In the mid 1990s, there were about 116 million tax-filing units compared to
about 100 million households. Since many of these households had too little income to
file taxes, the incongruence between tax filers and households is larger than these numbers suggest. See Feenberg and Poterba (1993).

returns in 1979. In 1994 the top .5 percent totaled 558,000 tax filers (out of 116 million) with income of at least $282,000 (in 1994 dollars, equivalent to $302,000 in 1997 dollars). Average income within the group was $718,000 and about 69,000 tax-filing units—one return out of every 1,700—had 1994 AGI over $1 million. Since the treasury data represents a fresh sample each year, it is possible that the top income recipients change substantially from year to year and so inequality is less than single-year statistics suggest. The economist Joel Slemrod has examined this question and finds that while there is turnover at the very top of the distribution, few persons who leave the very top fall very far.[41]

The political scientist Andrew Hacker has written a good book examining the people who earn this kind of money—athletes, CEOs, doctors, lawyers (Sam Levinson would be proud), and persons with very large inheritances.[42] Some of these people are well known—Michael Jordan, Warren Buffet, Oprah Winfrey. Some we know by the businesses they have founded—Frederick Smith's Federal Express, for example. Many others are totally unfamiliar to most of us.*

Why has the income share of such people increased so much?†
Hacker provides one starting point by using the *Forbes* list of the four hundred wealthiest Americans[43] to construct a list of the twenty wealthiest Americans whose fortunes are largely self-made. Among these twenty fortunes, six were made in computers and computer software, a seventh was made in computer services (Ross Perot, formerly of Electronic Data Systems), four were made in media (for example, Rupert Murdoch and Ted Turner), four were made in investing and buyouts (Warren Buffet, George Soros, Ronald Perelman, and Kirk Kerkorian), and one was made in athletic shoes (Phil Knight of Nike). The remaining fortunes arose out of oil and chemicals (one each) and direct sales (Richard de DeVos and Jan Van Andel of Amway).

There are different stories here, but one economic factor—the

---

* The best-selling book *The Millionaire Next Door* by Thomas J. Stanley and William D. Danko is about persons whose accumulated wealth, rather than income, is at least $1 million. In 1995, approximately 2.9 million households (out of about 99 million) had net worth over $1,000,000 where net worth is defined to include liquid assets and home equity but not the value of pensions. See the appendix for more details.

† Income concentration may have been higher in the late 1970s than the numbers suggest. High-income individuals often have flexibility in determining when to declare income—for example, when to exercise stock options. As Feenberg and Poterba (1993) write, the federal income tax reforms of 1986 reduced the tax rates on the top incomes (while eliminating many loopholes). It is plausible that the lower rates encouraged some persons to realize capital gains and in other ways report income to which they were previously entitled. See also Gordon and Slemrod (n.d.).

growth of winner-take-all markets—helps explain the prominence of high technology on Hacker's list, as well as a growing number of very high-income surgeons, lawyers, athletes, and other professionals.

In a winner-take-all market, the best performers earn far more money than the runners-up, thereby increasing income concentration. These markets were first discussed at the beginning of this century by the economist Alfred Marshall, who was examining the effect of reputations on income.[44] An example of what Marshall had in mind is the difference between shopping for a banana and shopping for a surgeon to do a delicate eye operation. A person buying a banana usually looks for a low price. She would not be worried about buying a bad banana, both because she knows what a good banana looks like and because the consequences of a mistake are small. If the banana is bad, she can throw it away and buy another from a different store. Because most consumers think this way, no store can maintain banana prices far above the competition's prices.

A person requiring delicate eye surgery faces a different decision. She is purchasing a high-stakes, complicated service that can be done only once. As a nonsurgeon, she does not know how to judge a doctor's surgical ability. Therefore, she looks for an eye doctor with an outstanding reputation. Because most consumers think this way, a doctor who has a strong reputation does not face much price competition from a new doctor who says: "I have not done this operation before, but I received really good grades in medical school and I'll give you a great price." A celebrated defense attorney like Johnnie Cochran is in a similar position.

For winner-take-all theory to explain any *growth* in income concentration, winner-take-all markets must be growing as well. One source of growth was the high-stakes financial transactions that were part of the industrial restructuring that began in the 1980s. Corporate takeovers and mergers put strong investment banking houses in the same position as doctors and lawyers—they became producers of complex, onetime transactions that had to be done right the first time. The compensation of investment bankers rose correspondingly.*

As Robert Frank and Philip Cook describe it, technology—particularly the media—gave a winner-take-all dimension to traditional occupations in other parts of the economy.[45] Consider professional tennis. Forty years ago, even the best tennis players spent much of

---

* Beyond this, of course, was the whole expansion of the financial sector during the 1980s. For example, between 1985 and 1990, net U.S. borrowing per year was nearly three times as great as it had been in 1981. The increase in bond transactions helped expand opportunities for successful bond traders to earn very high incomes.

their time playing in local tournaments before relatively small, live audiences. The modest size of these audiences set limits on what tennis players could earn. Today people interested in professional tennis can bypass local tournaments because television allows them to watch world-class players like Pete Sampras and Martina Hingis. As a result, Sampras and Hingis can command enormous earnings, and the earnings gap between the best and the near-best has grown much larger. In a similar example close to every author's heart, any book now featured on Oprah Winfrey's Book Club sells far more copies than the runner-up books that did not quite make the cut to be on her show.

Winner-take-all theory affects computers and high technology through what economists call network externalities. Word-processing programs provide one example. Suppose we each had a computer, and it was the only computer we used for our written work. Each of us could use a different word-processing program and nobody would notice. But, of course, we do not work in this way. We work on projects with other people with whom we exchange disks (and viruses). We use each other's machines. Because of these exchanges, we put a premium on compatibility among word processors: the more widely a word-processing program is used, the more new users are compelled to buy it. One program can become a standard—the technology most people choose. If a few people can control that technology, they become very rich.

Controlling technology is not easy. The original standard for electronic spreadsheets, Visicalc, was displaced by Lotus 123, which was largely displaced by Microsoft's Excel. IBM developed the dominant technology for personal computers but then lost control of the technology to Microsoft, which developed IBM's operating system, and to Intel, which developed the central processing units that now run most PCs. Bill Gates, Paul Allen,[46] and Steve Ballmer, all of Microsoft, and Gordon Moore of Intel are on Andrew Hacker's list of the top twenty.

Winner-take-all theory can explain part of the increased concentration of income, but it obviously cannot account for it all. For example, most CEOs run corporations that do not compete in winner-take-all markets, and yet many have also done very well. *Forbes* also publishes a list of the eight hundred best-compensated CEO's. An executive near the bottom of this list, Raymond A. Johnson of Nordstrom, had 1996 compensation of $419,000—potentially well above the Feenberg-Poterba cutoff for the top .5 percent of taxpayers.*

---

* We say "potentially" because some part of CEO compensation comes in the form of stock options (which *Forbes* values at the 1996 stock price), but the options do not appear as income until the executive exercises them. See Kichen (1997).

Similarly, Paul Joskow, Nancy Rose, and Andrea Sheppard tracked CEO compensation using a sample of about eight hundred firms per year from 1973 through 1991. Over the 1980s, average real compensation (including stock options) grew at 5.2 percent per year; by 1991 compensation in the sample averaged $2.25 million (in 1997 dollars).[47]

In other words, the average CEO now earns about seventy times as much as the average adult male, a ratio that has grown substantially over the 1980s. An explanation of this growing gap begins with the economy. We have seen how deregulation, technology, and trade create an increasingly competitive environment. In this environment, a CEO has to move more quickly to avoid being overtaken. Technology and trade have also given the CEO new strategic tools, and he is expected to use them. In the 1970s, financial markets would have viewed a firm's downsizing as a sign of trouble. Markets today view the absence of downsizing as a sign of potentially weak management.

A corporate board can argue that in this environment the CEO's job requires extraordinary talent, and talent costs money. The CEO himself can argue that in this environment his position is risky—he could be fired in a moment—so he needs high compensation for financial security.

As in most markets, however, these forces operate within man-made institutions. One institution is the corporate board's composition in which board members who approve the CEO's compensation are often beholden to the CEO for their appointment. A second we have already seen—the accounting standards that govern stock options. The awarding of stock options to a CEO addresses an important issue: A CEO paid only by salary may have weak incentives to maximize shareholder return (chapter 3). The awards' size has been magnified by the accounting standard in which options are not charged against the corporation's current income. Both institutions raise CEO compensation above its free-market level.

The result is a dynamic that has gone beyond the strategy of any individual firm and now prevails in the whole economy. Financial markets expect a firm's CEO to pursue cost reduction vigorously, often relying on downsizing and layoffs. The CEO's action not only affects his own firm but contributes to a general climate in which employees are cautious about pushing for higher wages. Low wage demands in the current recovery have raised the rate of corporate profit, higher profits have contributed to the stock market's remarkable recent performance, and until the summer of 1998 the stock market rise had substantially increased the value of most outstanding stock options.

We should not overstate the argument. The share of profits in gross domestic product has risen in recent years, but it remains lower today than it was in the 1950s and 1960s. Moreover, for any single corporation the immediate impact of downsizing may be to lower profits by incurring severance packages and related charges. Each firm's well-publicized downsizing, however, serves as a caution to workers in other firms and so helps to suppress wage demands throughout the economy.

In our discussion of these high incomes, we have assumed that those with market power—a CEO or a Barbra Streisand or a Henry Kravis—will use that power to maximize their income. This need not be true. Most of us are concerned about making money, but most of us are also concerned about our reputation, which depends in part on our conformance to community norms. A person who makes "too much money" runs a reputational risk, particularly when the money appears to be redistributed from others.* Our definition of "too much money" rose considerably during the 1980s, and increased reliance on the market was one cause. Just as Schumpeter suggested, increased competition leads to more firms rising and falling and less stability of employment at all levels. When jobs no longer provide financial security, people see a greater need for financial assets, and reaching for the highest possible compensation becomes more socially acceptable.

In these ways, increased competition adds to economy-wide inequality. We can see why people who do well under these arrangements argue for even less government intervention in markets on the grounds that "everyone" will benefit. We can also see why people will try to bend the economy's rules to further enhance their position.

As we suggested in chapter 1, however, it is important to separate the self-interest from the science. Government, in its stewardship role, must be concerned with the distribution of the benefits of growth as well as the rate of growth per se. At a time when technology and global trade are both shifting power away from the typical worker, it makes no sense for government to change institutions in ways that accelerate that process. We return to this point in chapter 8.

The Shape of the Future

Having experienced the terrors of the Great Depression and World War II, the men and women of Sam Levinson's generation had already lived through a lot by the 1950s. But in those postwar years

---

* As the management consultant Peter Drucker says, "In the next economic downturn there will be an outbreak of bitterness and contempt for the corporate chieftains who pay themselves millions. . . . Few top executives can even imagine the hatred, contempt and fury that has been created—not primarily among blue-collar workers, who never had an exalted opinion of the 'bosses'—but among the middle management and professional people." See Lenzner and Johnson (1997).

when Levinson's career was taking off, the U.S. economy was in an exceptionally strong position. American consumers had lots of unfilled demands and lots of money. Since foreign competition was weak, domestic producers could supply those demands, improving their productivity and wages as they grew, maintaining generally stable employment.

Today the situation is quite different. Partly in an effort to revive slow-growing productivity, we have increasingly turned to a deregulated, highly competitive environment. Compared to Levinson's time, competition, technology, and global markets have caused small but real reductions in job security. Because of the heightened competition, wages continue to grow slowly, in part because many workers see that they have less power to bargain for a piece of the economic gains. One by-product of these changes, the growing economic premium on education and skills, has slowed the assimilation of some minorities and increased inequality more generally.*

The news is not all bad. Wages are higher now than in Levinson's time. Work itself is cleaner and less dangerous today. The lack of wage pressure has permitted the economy to sustain very low unemployment rates without succumbing to inflation. Nevertheless, some characteristics of a good job, as Sam Levinson would have defined the term, are gone for the foreseeable future. Both college freshmen and CEOs feel that they need the kind of money that offers financial security, but providing a large fraction of citizens with this kind of security will be an enormous challenge.

---

* Obvious exceptions are some groups of Asian immigrants who have benefited from the emphasis on skills. Since the census contains relatively few observations on the incomes of Asians, we do not discuss them in this chapter, but we present a limited number of statistics in the appendix.

CHAPTER 6

The Geography of Income

IN THE spring of 1986, the Massachusetts unemployment rate averaged 3.8 percent. "Things were so tight," recalled one bank administrator, "that we were negotiating educational benefits for the *spouses* of people we were recruiting." In the same year, New York City regained its fiscal autonomy from the state-created Municipal Assistance Corporation. Nevertheless, it was not spring everywhere. In the center of the country, the Great Lakes states had suddenly become "the Rust Belt." In Texas, the governor required state agencies to cut budgets as an austerity measure. In Lafayette, Louisiana, families, suddenly unemployed, walked away from recently purchased homes.

Little of this would have been predicted ten years earlier. Then the United States was in a "rural renaissance," with the most vigorous economic activity concentrated in the nation's center. Texas and Louisiana were riding the crest of an energy boom, and the two coasts were hurting; Massachusetts was most noted for the industry it had lost, and New York City was threatening bankruptcy.

The Role of Migration

The evolution of the nation's industrial structure has a geographic dimension. Economic restructuring and the varying college–high school wage gap have their counterpart in the fortunes of regions, states, and cities. One clue to these fortunes is migration. In the 1940 census, 5.4 percent of the population reported that they had been living in a different state in 1935, a mass movement that included the large Dust Bowl migration from Oklahoma and Texas to California. Postwar migration would become much larger still. In the 1960 census, 9.3 percent of the population reported living in a different state five years earlier. Even today, about 3 percent of all households report living in a different state in the previous year, while about 1 percent report living in a different country.[1]

Most people, of course, were following jobs, and jobs showed similar movement. Between 1960 and 1970, U.S. manufacturing employment increased by 2.6 million. In Texas, however, it increased by 247,000, while it declined by 50,000 in Massachusetts, 120,000 in New York State, and 60,000 in Philadelphia.[2]

These movements had consequences for both the people involved and the income distribution. A 1947 map of U.S. incomes had one principal distinction: family incomes in much of the South were 40 percent less than incomes in other regions (chapter 2). Some of this difference reflected the extremely low incomes of rural black families, but the South was really a nation apart. Black Alabama families averaged $5,400 a year and white Alabama families averaged $12,600, while all families in New York averaged $21,800. (All incomes are in 1997 dollars.) Absent from the map was the income gap between central cities and the small suburbs that surrounded them. Central cities still held much of the urban middle class, and so city-suburban income differences were modest.

The migration of people and jobs over almost five decades reversed this pattern. The process was erratic as regions rose and fell and rose again. Over time, however, regional differences in family incomes narrowed as southern incomes gained substantial parity with those in the rest of the country. Now the biggest income distinctions were within regions as central cities increasingly lagged behind suburbs.[3] City-suburban distinctions did not reflect city-suburban wage differences (many central-city workers were commuters) so much as the increasing number of central-city families headed by women and the growing skills mismatch between central-city residents and central-city jobs.

Taken together, these movements changed the nature of inequality more than its statistical level. In the late 1940s, the poorest quintile of the family income distribution contained a significant number of farmers and farm laborers—many from the South—whose cash incomes were very low (table 2.4). In a mobile country like ours, however, people could move out of depressed regions and so had some control over their situation. By the 1990s, the bottom of the distribution was increasingly occupied by female-headed households, many with limited educations, often living in central cities. To be sure, people have some control over whether they get an education or whether they form a female-headed family. Nevertheless, when they find themselves on the wrong side of these problems, the solutions are usually more difficult than simply moving away.

The Convergence of Incomes Across Regions

The nation's 1947 economic map was dominated by two groups of states: the Mid-Atlantic states (New York through Pennsylvania) and the Great Lakes states (Ohio through Wisconsin) (chapter 2). Together, these states accounted for about two-fifths of the nation's population and about three-fifths of all manufacturing jobs. In this pre-computer age, service-sector jobs often had to locate near their customers, and so there were many service-sector jobs in these states as well.[4]

Like most maps, this point-in-time picture obscured the number of people on the move. Retired whites from the North were moving south, primarily to Florida. Whites from the North and much of the South were moving to California. Blacks from the South were moving to eastern, midwestern, and western cities.

With the exception of the retirees, most of these migrants were looking for better jobs, and in the early postwar years better jobs usually meant manufacturing jobs. Manufacturing could provide good wages for men with limited education (chapter 4). Men leaving agriculture typically had little education, and so the availability of manufacturing work was particularly important. By this measure, some places were ripe for sending immigrants and others were ripe for receiving them.

The Great Plains states—Minnesota and the Dakotas through Missouri and Kansas—were ripe for sending. Their economies were heavily dependent on agriculture, which was becoming increasingly mechanized. Between higher farm productivity and slow-growing demand for food, there were fewer opportunities at home. People—particularly young people—began to look elsewhere.*

The Pacific Coast was an obvious place to look (figure 6.1). During World War II, the West Coast had taken the lead in the fast-growing aircraft industry and was now becoming a manufacturing power. In fostering this industry, California in particular had the advantage of a good climate, but climate was reinforced by the policies of an aggressive state government and a high-quality university system. Between 1929 and 1947, California's manufacturing employment had grown from 350,000 to 660,000.† This *rate* of growth was twice the national average, and in absolute terms the number of new jobs in California

---

* As demographer Larry Long points out, interstate migration is usually concentrated in two age ranges: younger persons age twenty-five to thirty-five who are just starting out, and older persons age sixty-five to seventy who are moving for retirement reasons. See Long (1987).

† For an analysis of regional patterns of manufacturing growth in the post-1929 period, see Fuchs (1962) and Crandall (1993).

Figure 6.1   Major U.S. Migration Routes in the Late 1940s and 1950s

Source: Long (1987).

equaled the number added by such traditional manufacturing states as Ohio and Illinois. As the aircraft industry grew, other industries grew around it, both to support aircraft production and to serve the growing number of aircraft workers.

The Southeast and East-South-Central regions (Delaware and Maryland and everywhere south through Mississippi) comprised three economic areas: Delaware and Maryland, Florida, and all the other states. As postwar incomes rose and more families could afford retirement, many people found Florida's climate and living costs attractive, and the state's economy did well. The other states (excluding Delaware and Maryland) remained far more depressed—in part by their own doing, since many of them regarded manufacturing with ambivalence. Manufacturing might create jobs that paid well (vis-à-vis agriculture), but it might also bring in unions and other pressures that would undermine segregation. There had been some growth of manufacturing in the South, predominantly in textiles; indeed, some mills had relocated from New England. Other manufacturers, however, were put off by the poorly educated labor force, the segregated life, and the abundance of hot weather. In 1947 these states accounted for 24 percent of the U.S. population, but only 11 percent of all manufacturing jobs. The lack of manufacturing jobs in the South was compounded by the loss of farm jobs due to the continued mechanization of agriculture. With its surplus labor, the region was a ready source of out-migration.

Even the economy of New England, while not as weak as many southern states, was not strong. Agriculture had long since ceased to be competitive, and the region was steadily losing textile manufacturing jobs to the South. Between 1929 and 1947, New England's manufacturing employment grew by 18 percent, about half as fast as the rate in the rest of the nation. Except for lower Connecticut—a suburb of New York City—New England was also a source of out-migration.

In the early postwar years, then, significant numbers of people had reason to move, and the resulting flows were large. Over the 1950s, the Great Plains states had *net* out-migration (persons moving out minus persons moving in) equal to 5 percent of their 1950 population. New England (excluding Connecticut) experienced a similar loss. The southeastern states (excluding Florida) lost a net of 1.2 million whites and 1.6 million blacks—almost 10 percent of their 1950 population.

The migrants' destinations varied by race. Among whites, the largest numbers moved to California (net in-migration of 2.8 million) and Florida (1.6 million). Black migration had three main destinations: the Ohio-Michigan industrial belt (504,000), the New York-New Jersey metropolitan area (362,000), and California (255,000) (see figure 6.1). Blacks, far more than whites, migrated to central cities. Over the 1950s, the proportion of *all* blacks living in central cities rose from 41 percent to 51 percent.[5]

People were moving for better opportunities, and in the process they were reducing regional income differences. When poor families (black and white) left the South, they raised the average income of the region. When they moved to northern states, they typically lowered, ceteris paribus, average incomes in that region.

In a stagnant economy, migration flows of the magnitude that prevailed in the 1950s would have led to charges of exporting the poor. Some politicians made such charges, but in most areas the number of migrants led to a *relative* increase or decrease around a rising trend. New York State, for example, had net out-migration of 72,000 whites over the 1950s and net in-migration of 255,000 blacks, a net increase of 180,000 persons. This in-migration, however, was dwarfed by the state's fertility rate. In the baby-boom decade, New York's population, exclusive of migration, increased by 1.8 million persons. It was also a decade of growing wages, and the median family income of New Yorkers grew from $21,800 to $31,500. Migration did have some effect: average income over the decade grew more slowly in New York (44 percent) than in, say, Alabama (73 percent). Nevertheless, incomes were growing fast enough in all regions to keep in-migration from becoming an issue (figure 6.2).

Rising incomes and growing population also helped cushion the western shift of the nation's industrial base. During the 1950s, employment in durable goods manufacturing increased by 1.2 million (14 percent), but three-quarters of this increase came from new industries: aircraft, aircraft parts, electronic equipment, and industrial instruments.[6] Employment in the steel industry actually declined. The implications for the different regions were obvious. From 1949 through 1959, the Pacific Coast added 400,000 new manufacturing jobs, while the Mid-Atlantic region added none. Since World War II, the industrial growth of the Pacific Coast had become self-reinforcing. As the region's population grew, it became more efficient for manufacturers to move production there rather than, for example, to produce California's automobiles in Michigan. These new jobs, in turn, attracted further in-migration from other states, but rapid productivity growth and the baby boom were sufficient to keep population and income growing everywhere.

The Late 1960s Boom

During the 1960s boom, even more than in the 1950s, rapid economic growth obscured regional weaknesses. Over the decade, average family incomes rose sharply in all states: from $31,500 to $42,500 in New York, from $19,500 to $28,900 in Alabama, from $33,200 to $43,000 in California, and from $32,400 to $43,900 in Illinois. These increases, as we have seen, reflected both strong real wage growth and significant declines in unemployment.

Beneath these growing incomes, the industrial base continued to

Figure 6.2 Average Family Incomes for Broadly Defined Regions, 1953 to 1996

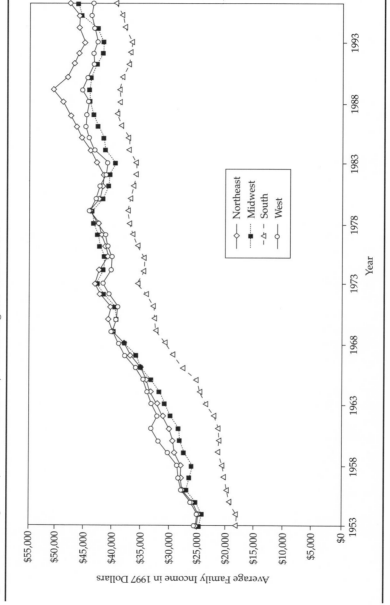

Sources: U.S. Department of Commerce, Bureau of the Census, *Current Population Reports* (various years).

move south and west. During the 1960s boom, *national* manufacturing employment increased by 20 percent, but in the Mid-Atlantic states it again failed to increase; in the Great Lakes states, it increased by only 12 percent. Gains in manufacturing were concentrated in the Pacific Coast. In 1963 California passed New York to become the most populous state in the nation.

It was also in the 1960s that the South—the Southeast, East South Central, and Southwestern regions—began to join the nation. The success of the initial civil rights battles eliminated much of the legal segregation and reduced the region's ambivalence toward new industry. The interstate highway system (begun under Eisenhower) and network television were linking the three regions to the rest of the nation, while the spread of air conditioning was making southern amenities more accessible to the climatically challenged. With these obstacles removed, the region looked more attractive to industry as a place of cheap land, low wages, and few unions.[7] Over the decade, total nonagricultural employment (even excluding booming Florida) grew by three and a half million persons; this increase of 45 percent was significantly higher than the rate in the rest of the economy. Through the development of new industries, southern income levels moved closer to the national average.

Migration statistics continued to track shifting job opportunities. Over the 1960s, the Great Lakes and Mid-Atlantic regions each had net out-migration of 550,000 whites and an approximately equal in-migration of blacks. In each region, high birth rates and the economic boom kept both population and income growing. Through migration flows, however, incomes across regions were becoming more equal.

The Short-Lived Rural Renaissance

The baby boom ended in 1964, and the growth of wages ended in 1973. By themselves, these factors would have heightened inter-regional competition for growth, but they were overshadowed by another development—the rural renaissance of the late 1960s and mid-1970s. During the renaissance, rural and small metropolitan areas—many in the nation's heartland—grew more rapidly than large metropolitan areas on either coast.* The renaissance was driven by the set of macroeconomic factors described in chapter 3. When the 1972 to 1973 worldwide food shortage created a boom in agricultural commodities, migration out of farming areas was slowed. The 1973–1974 OPEC oil price rise created an energy boom in Texas, Louisiana,

---

* Large metropolitan areas are defined as having populations of one million or more at the beginning of the period.

and Oklahoma. The steadily falling dollar helped to limit change in older, durable-goods firms—what would soon become Rust Belt firms. All of these factors increased the demand for blue-collar labor. The rural renaissance was the geographic equivalent of the 1970s fall in the college–high school earnings gap (chapters 3 and 4).* Since the East and West Coasts had generally higher incomes than interior areas, this blue-collar boom—a force for individual earnings equality—also accelerated the convergence of regional incomes.

Although the rural renaissance attracted substantial media attention, it was over by the mid-1970s.[8] By the early 1980s, food and oil were in surplus, with falling prices, while the recession and fast-rising dollar were triggering the process of restructuring in manufacturing. Now regional weaknesses—for example, the weakness in the Great Lakes states' old, durable-goods manufacturing plants—were exposed clearly.

Between 1970 and 1984, Pennsylvania lost one manufacturing job in four—400,000 jobs in all, mostly from the western part of the state. New York also lost 400,000 (23 percent); Ohio lost 300,000 (21 percent), Michigan 228,000 (18 percent), and Illinois 228,000 (17 percent). By contrast, manufacturing employment in the Southeast and Pacific Coast continued to grow moderately.

At the same time, the newer, expanding industries—finance, real estate, defense manufacturing, computers and software—were both more intensive in their use of college-educated labor and more concentrated on the East and West Coasts. The result was the "bicoastal economy" of the early 1980s, the geographic equivalent of the growing college–high school earnings gap. It increased income inequality both within the earnings distribution and among regions.[9]

Again, migration followed the new opportunities. When numbers for the 1970s and early 1980s are combined, the Mid-Atlantic and Great Lakes regions each had a net out-migration (including all races) of 1.8 million persons. The Southeast and East-South-Central regions, excluding Florida, had net *in*-migration of 2.9 million persons. The shift in opportunities was such that the traditional routes of black migration reversed during this period: blacks, on net, were leaving the North to go to the South.[10]

Unlike the 1950s and 1960s, the 1970s had no high birth rates or rising wages to give all regions a cushion; by the 1970s, it was common to see low-level regional warfare—states competing hard for government contracts and new plant locations.[11] And in some states, a new element was influencing growth: immigrants from abroad.

---

* All the more so because the interior states contained relatively low concentrations of college graduates. In coastal states like California, New York, Washington, and Connecticut, 23 to 28 percent of adults were college graduates, compared to 14 to 23 percent in interior states like Iowa, Texas, Illinois, Indiana, and Oklahoma (U.S. Department of Commerce, Bureau of the Census [1996b], table 245).

In chapter 5, we noted that the 1965 amendments to the Immigration and Naturalization Act stimulated large flows of foreign migrants, who focused on a few destinations. In 1990 California and five other states—New York, New Jersey, Illinois, Florida, and Texas—contained about 40 percent of the nation's population, but three-quarters of all immigrants. California alone was home to 12 percent of the nation's population (as tabulated by the census) and one-third of the nation's immigrants.[12]

The growing presence of immigrants, many with little education, created another dimension of interstate competition. Many of the destination states argued that immigrants' use of medical care, education, and other state and local services was a national problem and should be paid for by the federal government. Precisely because so few states had large immigrant populations, it was a hard argument to win. Most senators and congressmen represented areas that were totally unaffected. Over time, the immigration debate turned from demands for more money to restrictive legislation. In 1996 California voters passed Proposition 187, which denies schooling and other public services to illegal immigrants. In the same year, Congress responded by prohibiting legal immigrants (persons who have entered the country legally but have not yet become citizens) from receiving welfare benefits, a policy partially rescinded a year later.

The alarm about immigrants arose out of concern not just over government expenditures but over job competition—in particular, competition with semiskilled native-born workers. At first glance, it seemed possible to examine this competition by comparing the wages of semiskilled workers across states with high- and low-immigrant populations. As George Borjas, Richard Freeman, and Lawrence Katz have noted, however, the comparison is misleading because native-born workers were avoiding immigrant concentrations by moving elsewhere, and so immigrants were indirectly affecting wages beyond the areas in which they were locating. As an example, the authors point out that between 1970 and 1990 California's share of the total U.S. population rose from 10.2 percent to 12.4 percent. California's share of the U.S. native-born population, however, rose only from 9.6 percent to 10 percent, suggesting that immigrants were deterring native-born migrants from moving to the state. Correcting for these movements, Borjas, Freeman, and Katz estimate that foreign immigrants had their largest competitive impact on the earnings of native-born high school dropouts. For dropouts, the presence of immigrants caused earnings declines of 3 to 5 percent—less than one-quarter of the total earnings declines that dropouts had experienced since the late 1970s. Immigrant competition had a much smaller effect on the earnings of high school graduates and workers with some college.

More generally, migratory movements by both native- and foreign-born workers helped to shape the distribution of education across states. Earlier, we saw that the bicoastal economy of the mid-1980s was the geographic equivalent of the widening college–high school earnings gap. By the mid-1990s, most regions had returned to low unemployment, but the industries at the center of the 1980s recovery—finance, electronics, software—continued to attract large numbers of college graduates to coastal areas. The result is a national map with several different educational regions (figure 6.3).

- A coastal crescent, running from Texas west through California and up to Washington, where 20 to 25 percent of adults have at least a bachelor's degree

- A coastal band, running from New Hampshire through Virginia, where 20 to 25 percent of most states' adult population have at least a bachelor's degree and where, in a few states, the percentage exceeds 25 percent

- The remainder of the country, where the proportion of adults with a college degree usually falls below 20 percent and, in some southern states, below 15 percent

These patterns reflect some simple ideas: most people like warmer climates; better educated workers are the most likely to move; better educated workers need to locate near other better educated workers for the best opportunites. By expanding the discussion to industry, however, we can appreciate the impact of events that this simple explanation overlooks: the 1980s collapse of the oil patch states, and the Texas revival thanks to electronics and trade; the 1980s New England resurgence in electronics, biotechnology, and mutual funds; the 1980s recovery of New York City as a financial center; the 1990s collapse of the California economy as defense budgets shrank, and the state's subsequent revival due to strong showings in the entertainment, computer, software, and tourism industries and in foreign trade.*

Beneath the regional busts and booms, the single most important fact over fifty years was the narrowing of regional income differences. Recall that in 1949 family incomes in the Southeast were 40 percent lower than in the rest of the country. By the early 1990s, German automobile manufacturers were locating in South Carolina and Alabama, and the broad regional income gaps had closed to about 20 percent (figure 6.2). The unequal geographic distribution of college graduates imposed some limits on this convergence, but the market and migration had made the regional landscape much more equal.

---

* On the 1980s dependence of Texas on oil, see Maraniss (1986). When Maraniss was writing, every one-dollar fall in the price of a barrel of oil cost the state of Texas $100 million in tax revenues, 25,000 jobs, and $3 billion in total economic activity. On the 1990s California revival, see Cassidy (1998).

Figure 6.3   The Geographic Distribution of College Graduates, 1990

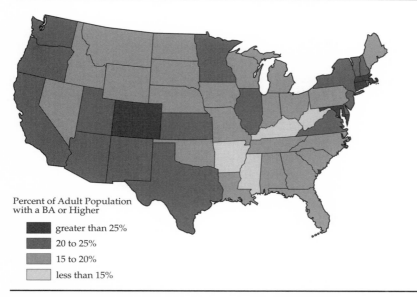

Percent of Adult Population
with a BA or Higher

greater than 25%
20 to 25%
15 to 20%
less than 15%

Source: U.S. Department of Commerce, Bureau of the Census (1996b) table 245.

The Decline of Central Cities

As regional incomes became more equal, *intraregional* inequality grew. The major dimension of inequality was the widening income gap between central cities and suburbs, but over time suburbs, too, were becoming more differentiated by income.

In one sense, the cities' decline was an unintended by-product of economic growth. Historically, cities had been places where producers could be close to cheap transportation and close to each other, while workers could live close to their jobs. Economic growth undermined these functions. After World War II, the mass availability of automobiles and the improved highway system made it possible for plants and workers, pursuing their best interests, to locate further from city centers.* Their dispersal was reinforced by the changing nature of the country's output. Where transportation had been an important cost element in food or steel, it was far less important in distributing many services or computer chips. Some southern and western cities like Houston could capture the dispersal by continually

---

* This process of dispersal is almost as old as cities themselves. See, for example, Vernon (1959).

annexing new territory. By the 1930s, however, most older cities had fixed boundaries and so faced the problem of continually replenishing their economies.

At the close of World War II, these problems had not yet surfaced. Central cities still dominated their metropolitan areas (chapter 2). They housed the middle class as well as the poor, and they contained enough manufacturing to provide rural in-migrants with jobs. This domination had been heavily subsidized, however, by the Great Depression and World War II.

The depression and the war had slowed the production of new cars and houses and so slowed suburban growth. In addition, the needs of war production had kept central-city manufacturing plants in use beyond their normal life spans.[13] All of this made central cities stronger than they otherwise would have been, but even during the depression the underlying trends were apparent. The demographer Larry Long shows that between 1935 and 1940 the second largest migration between two states was the move from New York to New Jersey. It was largely a move to the suburbs, and it involved almost as many people as the move from the Oklahoma Dust Bowl to California.[14]

When the war ended, the sudden availability of automobiles and the low price of housing made it possible for many more families to buy their own homes in the suburbs (chapter 3). Almost all these families were white, and they were joined by other white families moving from rural areas. The rate of suburbanization was remarkable. Over the 1950s, the population of the suburbs grew by twenty million, while the population of the entire United States grew by only thirty million. By 1960 the proportion of the population living in the suburbs had climbed from 23 percent to 31 percent.[15]

During the 1950s, the suburbs' gain was not the cities' loss. The same factors that had sustained older industrial regions—high birth rates and rapid wage growth—also helped central cities. New York City is a case in point. Between 1950 and 1960, New York's suburban ring grew from 1.7 million to 2.9 million persons, but through high birth rates and significant in-migration from rural areas, the city's own population held steady at 7.8 million persons. Many of the in-migrants were black, and over the decade the proportion of blacks in the city's population rose from 10 percent to 15 percent. Chicago, Philadelphia, and other older cities had similar experiences.

The in-migrants were coming in search of higher incomes, and in the early postwar years the cities could accommodate them. Cities had both cheap housing and, most important, manufacturing jobs. In part because of war production, manufacturing was still a central-city activity. In 1947 the ten largest central cities contained two and a half million manufacturing production jobs, one-fifth of all such jobs in the nation.[16] Cities, in addition, had large municipal payrolls including clerk jobs and public works jobs, which required little education.

Because of these jobs, cities were still the place where rural migrants could get a start. By 1959 cities had seen large out-migration of middle-class families to the suburbs and large in-migration from rural areas. Nevertheless, median income among central-city families was $29,100, only $4,000 lower (12 percent) than median income in the suburbs, and well above median family income outside metropolitan areas.[17]

The economic position of cities, however, was tenuous. Central-city manufacturing jobs were largely located in old plants. When firms considered new investment, improved transportation often led them to build new plants outside the city rather than retool the old ones. Similarly, city plants produced "old" products like garments and tires. The growth of the aircraft industry did a great deal for a few Pacific Coast cities—Seattle, Los Angeles, Long Beach—but it helped Pittsburgh and other older cities very little (table 6.1). The resulting loss of manufacturing jobs was striking. Between 1947 and 1963, manufacturing production jobs in the United States grew slightly, from 11.9 million to 12.2 million, but among the ten largest central cities in 1947, only Los Angeles gained manufacturing jobs over the period (113,000). The other nine cities lost a total of 680,000 production jobs.

During this period, *total* city employment declined less dramatically as losses in production jobs were offset by growing employment in services, including an expansion of local governments. Many of the new jobs were in teaching, medicine, financial operations, and other white-collar occupations that required substantial education. Other service jobs with lower skill requirements were often, as we have seen, "women's work"—sales clerks, clerical workers, waitresses, nurse's assistants, and other jobs that required soft skills that less-educated men were not supposed to have. Central cities were the first to experience what the entire nation would experience in the 1980s: the loss of jobs that paid good wages to men with limited education. This particular shift in demand would come to be known as a "skills mismatch" between central-city jobs and central-city residents. In 1985, Samuel Ehrenhalt, then commissioner of labor statistics for the New York region, summarized the problem well:

> A very basic difference [in today's job market] is that the lower level job entrant of yesterday did not have to possess the basic literacy, numeracy, interaction and communication skills needed today.
>
> Increasingly, workers need to be able to successfully function in a word-oriented, information-intensive work environment such as the modern office. They need to be able to learn on a continuing basis, to

Table 6.1   Retail Employment and Manufacturing Employment for Selected Central Cities, 1947 and 1963.

	Retail Employment	Manufacturing Employment
New York		
1947	438,365	940,235
1963	410,174	927,413
Chicago		
1947	259,396	667,407
1963	210,964	508,797
Detroit		
1947	114,915	338,373
1963	72,149	200,586
Los Angeles		
1947	131,311	167,156
1963	148,442	280,221
Philadelphia		
1947	124,258	328,630
1963	100,681	264,893

Sources: U.S. Department of Commerce, Bureau of the Census (1952a).

have a foundation of fundamental knowledge, to reason, draw conclusions, and express ideas. The demands of the New York City job market of today simply do not match up well with a 38 percent high school dropout rate and 40 percent of the resident population age 25 and over without a high school diploma. These groups will face a difficult and increasingly uphill battle in gaining a foothold in today's economy.[18]

From a mayor's perspective, the lack of good jobs for less-educated men could easily feed on itself. In the early 1960s, the cities continued to lose middle-class families and manufacturing jobs, but city economies were still stronger than in many rural southern areas, and so cities continued to attract rural migrants. If a city lacked jobs to raise migrants' incomes, it was left with a growing low-income population and an increasingly stagnant tax base. A weak tax base logically requires reduced expenses, but as the economist George Peterson argued, this was not easy to do. More than in most businesses, city budgets represent ongoing capital commitments: the maintenance of roads, sewers, bridges, hospitals, and schools. As this capital stock ages, it becomes increasingly expensive to maintain. A city's largest element of variable cost is its labor force, and as Peterson wrote:

> in terms of budget expense, a city's labor force tends to act as another fixed overhead item whose cost must be spread over fewer taxpayers once net out-migration commences. It is difficult to reduce public employment under the best of circumstances, but the pressure to retain public sector jobs is doubly great when a city is suffering private sector job loss.[19]

Few public employees would vote for a mayoral candidate who proposed job cuts, and few low-income families, already dependent on public services, would vote for a candidate who wanted service cuts. The result of these pressures was often higher expenditures, higher taxes, and an even greater incentive for the out-migration of jobs and middle-income families.

Earlier we noted that the late 1960s economic boom helped to hide the weaknesses of older industrial regions. The boom's effect on central cities was more ambiguous. Cities shared in low unemployment rates, but as discussed in chapter 5, the boom did not reach a significant fraction of black men who reported low or no earnings. At the same time, the proportion of black families headed by women rose from 22 percent in 1960 to 31 percent in 1970, with many of these female-headed families residing in central cities.[20]

Black male joblessness cannot explain the breakdown in the black family in any simple sense, a point established by the work of Robert Mare and Christopher Winship.* The growth of welfare programs during this period cannot explain much either, a point we establish in chapter 7. A century ago, the relationship between black male joblessness and female-headed families, as W. E. B. Du Bois described it (see chapter 2), may have been more direct. Since that time, the increase in female-headed families has developed a momentum of its own, but continued male joblessness could not have helped. In Du Bois's time, black men's incomes were kept low by discrimination, which excluded them from good jobs. In the postwar period, the changing nature of central-city employment added to this effect.†

By the late 1960s, the breakdown of the black family was compounded in some urban areas by what William Julius Wilson calls the isolation of the ghetto.[21] The problem began as the economic boom

---

* Mare and Winship (1989) show that city-to-city variations in black male joblessness explain only a part of city-to-city variation in the proportion of black families headed by women.

† William Julius Wilson is a major elaborator of Du Bois's ideas. See *The Truly Disadvantaged* (1987).

and the civil rights revolution focused increasing attention on the urban poor. That attention led to increased federal aid to cities (the Great Society), but it also led to an enormous rise in expectations among the poor themselves—and ultimately to a series of major riots in black neighborhoods, including New York City's Harlem and Bedford-Stuyvesant (1964), Cleveland's Hough (1964), Los Angeles' Watts (1965), and Detroit's 12th Street (1967), in which forty-three persons were killed.

One response to the riots was the decision by some local governments to make welfare benefits more accessible to pacify the population (see chapter 7).[22] An equally important response was the conclusion by many black middle- and working-class families that the time had come to leave.

For much of the century, racial segregation kept black neighborhoods integrated by social class. Horace Cayton and St. Clair Drake discuss this integration in describing the black lower class of Chicago:

> Its people are the large mass of poorly schooled and the economically insecure who cluster in the "worst" areas or nestle in the interstices of middle-class communities. The lower-class world is complex. Basic to it is a large group of disorganized and broken families, whose style of life differs from that of other social classes, but who are by no means "criminal" except so far as the children swell the ranks of the delinquents, or the elders occasionally run afoul of the law. Existing side by side with these people is a smaller, more stable group made up of "church folks" and those families (church and non-church) who are trying to "advance themselves." In close contact with both these groups are the denizens of the underworld—the pimps and prostitutes, the thieves and pickpockets, the dope addicts and reefer smokers, the professional gamblers, cutthroats, and murderers. The lines separating these three basic groups are fluid and shifting and a given household may incorporate individuals of all three types, since, restricted by low incomes and inadequate housing, the so-called "respectable" lowers find it impossible to seal themselves off from "shady" neighbors among whom they find themselves. The "church folks," despite their verbal protests, must live in close contact with the world of "sin."[23]

By the late 1960s, residential discrimination was declining. In the aftermath of the riots, many middle-class and working-class families moved away from historically black neighborhoods, often to other parts of the city.[24] For some of those who stayed, the results were disastrous. In the worst cases, older neighborhoods became "underclass areas": neighborhoods with high concentrations of female-headed families, persons who had not finished high school, young persons neither employed nor in school, high rates of drug addiction, persons dependent on welfare, and so on. But while these areas received substantial attention, they represented only a small part of the problem. The most careful estimates suggest that underclass areas accounted for only 10 to 12 percent of all the poor and perhaps one-quarter of the urban poor.[25]

Politically, underclass areas were a devastating problem, but the more serious problem was accelerated black and white migration, not just out of poor neighborhoods but out of cities altogether. The migration was particularly important because, with the end of the baby boom, migration, for cities as for regions, was becoming an important determinant of population. Of the sixty cities with 1960 populations of 200,000 or more, nearly half experienced absolute population declines from 1960 to 1970.[26]

After 1973, the process accelerated, particularly in older cities. Recession and high energy prices accelerated the loss of what manufacturing jobs remained. Inflation put additional pressure on city budgets, which, in turn, caused a reduction in municipal jobs. Many of the lost jobs in manufacturing and city government had been held by low-skilled workers. New York City was a dramatic case. Between 1969 and 1977, the city's employment declined by 700,000 (18 percent), and in 1975 its government almost declared bankruptcy.* Other cities may have had more stable employment, but most cities continued to lose population. In the 1960s, central cities as a group had net out-migration of 345,000 persons per year. In the 1970s, central cities' net out-migration averaged 1.3 million persons per year. The loss over the decade—13 million people—was equivalent to one-fifth of their 1970 population.[27] By the mid-1980s, about half of the U.S. population lived in suburbs, while a few major cities—Detroit is a vivid example—would develop shockingly large expanses of totally vacant land.

Since moving to the suburbs required a decent income, these population movements had consequences for incomes as well as population. In 1970, 41 percent of the population of large metropolitan areas lived in central cities.† By 1990 the cities' share of area population had fallen moderately to 35 percent, but residents increasingly had lower incomes. Recall that as late as 1959 the gap between city and suburban family incomes was $4,000, or 12 percent. By 1985 it had widened to 21 percent—$37,600 in central cities versus $48,000 in suburbs.[28]

---

* On New York City employment declines, see Ehrenhalt (1985). Ehrenhalt shows that over the 1970s employment grew by 24 percent in Los Angeles–Long Beach and by 6 percent in Chicago, but declined by 15 percent in Philadelphia.
† That is, metropolitan areas with populations over one million in 1970.

Figure 6.4   Median Family Income in U.S. Central Cities and Suburbs 1959 to 1996 (in 1997 Dollars)

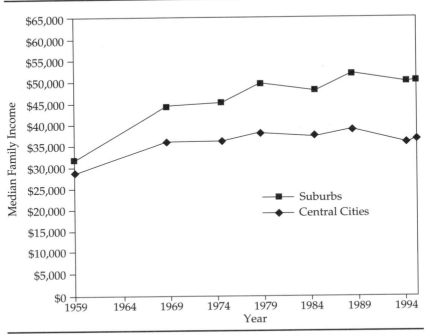

Sources: Author's tabulations of the 1960 and 1970 Decennial Census Public Use Microdata Sample files and the Current Population Survey (various years).

Much of the gap reflected the one-quarter of all central-city families headed by women (figure 6.4).

Through the 1980s and 1990s, this income gap continued to grow even as many central cities experienced a degree of revival. New York City regained most of the employment it had lost from 1969 to 1977; Boston emerged as a center of the finance industry; Pittsburgh was reborn as a technology and medical center; Houston grew in technology and natural resources. As Sam Ehrenhalt had noted in 1985, however, the new city jobs increasingly required skills that the poorest city residents did not have. By 1996, median family income within large central cities averaged $36,700, while median income in their suburbs stood at $50,600, a gap of 27 percent. Beneath these numbers lay two stories.

One story was the changing nature of U.S. poverty. As late as 1970, poverty was still a rural problem: almost half of all the poor lived outside a metropolitan area. Poverty in central cities was real, but manageable. One in seven central-city residents was poor, and the central-city poor (in all cities)* accounted for about one-third of all the poor in the nation.

By the 1990s, poverty was much more of an urban problem. About four-fifths of the poor now live in metropolitan areas. Central cities contain 30 percent of the U.S. population and 45 percent of the U.S. poor, with a poverty rate of about one in five. Among children, the situation is sharper: central cities contain 47 percent of all poor children and one in three central-city children is poor.[29]

The second story was a growing income segmentation among suburbs themselves. In U.S. census publications, metropolitan areas are divided into "central cities" and "outside central cities" rather than "central cities" and "suburbs." It is a useful correction, since many suburbs are actually older industrial cities, like Yonkers, New York, that share many central-city problems. These older, industrial suburbs are now home to about one-third of the poor.

Income differences among suburbs are part of a more general pattern of income-clustering identified by the demographer Paul Jargowsky. U.S. residential areas have always been heavily divided along racial lines, but, as Jargowsky notes, people of the same racial group have increasingly begun to cluster together along income lines. Communities are more homogeneous by income and income inequality involves a growing jurisdictional dimension.[30]

Geography and Family

We began this chapter by arguing that the various migrations around the United States have changed the *nature* of income inequality more than its *level*. Fifty years ago, the bottom quintile of the income distribution contained disproportionate numbers of elderly families from the South and, more generally, families who worked in agriculture. Today the bottom quintile of the income distribution contains disproportionate numbers of central-city families, many of whom are headed by women (tables 2.4 and 2.5).

In the future, these patterns may affect the level of inequality as well. In preceding chapters, we have traced the growing importance of education as a determinant of earnings. In the United States, education is provided as a highly decentralized service: local communities set educational expectations and local governments play a major role in curriculum and educational finance. This way of delivering

---

* That is, not just the central cities of metropolitan areas with over one million persons.

educational services has combined with current residential patterns to create a situation in which the jurisdictions hit hardest by industrial restructuring—cities such as Pittsburgh, Pennsylvania; Gary, Indiana; Oakland, California—are also the jurisdictions being asked to make the biggest improvements in their school systems. Without these improvements, the economic shocks of restructuring (and the poverty of central cities) may well be passed from one generation to the next. Whereas the old regional income differences were eroded by migration and industrial change, the new intraregional differences, based on family structure and education, risk becoming much more durable.[31]

CHAPTER 7

Households, Families, and the Welfare State

IN EARLIER chapters, we discussed the variation in incomes across regions, educational levels, race, and industry. Income differences across family types—two-earner families, elderly families, female-headed families—are often larger and they raise a note of caution in our analysis. We are using the family income distribution as one way to summarize the economy's performance. In reality, however, the distribution is being reshaped by changing living arrangements as well as by the economy, and we have to take that fact into consideration. The same caution applies to the *household* income distribution, which accounts for both families and all other living units—persons who live alone, persons who live with roommates, and so on.*

At the end of World War II, such attention to living arrangements would have been superfluous. Ninety-four percent of the population lived in families (chapter 2). Of those families, almost four-fifths had a husband and a wife under age sixty-five, and in most families of any age the wife did not work. Today young men and women marry later, often living on their own while single. Married women are more likely to work, older men and women retire earlier, and more families are headed by unmarried women. Consider some 1996 average incomes (in 1997 dollars):

- Husband-wife families age forty-five to fifty-four, with both spouses working: $71,200

- Husband-wife families age twenty-five to thirty-four, with only the husband working: $30,000

---

* The census defines a family as two or more persons related by birth, marriage, or adoption.

- Families headed by women age twenty-five or under: $9,200
- Husband-wife families age sixty-five or over: $29,000[1]

As the mix of U.S. families changes, family income inequality will almost surely change as well. At the same time, more families rely on the government for income. Over the post–World War II period, government payments to individuals—the welfare state—have grown from 5 percent to 14 percent of gross domestic product and totaled $1 trillion in 1996. One-quarter of this sum (about $250 billion) is paid out through means-tested programs aimed specifically at the poor. The remainder covers social insurance expenditures—for example, Social Security benefits, Medicare, unemployment benefits, pensions for retired government workers—for which eligibility is established through taxpayer contributions.[2]

The welfare state is one of the nation's major equalizing institutions, designed to protect individuals against the poverty of old age, unemployment, broken families, and similar conditions. In the last two decades, the welfare state has been heavily criticized on two related grounds. One is its total cost. The other is the problem of moral hazard in which a government benefit may undercut individual responsibility thereby worsening the problem the benefit was supposed to solve.*

We know, for example, that in the 1940s, half of all men over age sixty-four worked. Today about 16 percent of such men work while most of the rest are retired and rely heavily on Social Security benefits. To many people, this is the result Social Security was supposed to produce. To others, the existence of Social Security has undermined incentives for individuals to save for retirement. The lack of savings, in this argument, has made the elderly excessively dependent on public funds.† Similarly, Aid to Families with Dependent Children (AFDC) was designed to protect children against a father's death or desertion. Viewed in a different light, this protection becomes an incentive to form female-headed families—again, exacerbating the problem it is supposed to solve.

These and similar critiques often contain elements of the truth. They reflect the fact that many of the welfare state's underlying assumptions are sixty years old: that most single mothers with young

---

* More generally, moral hazard refers to a situation where insuring against a risk (house burglary) reduces the individual's incentives to take normal precautions against the risk (checking that the front door is locked).

† The argument is most associated with the writings of economist Martin Feldstein who adds that by reducing personal savings, Social Security also deprived the nation of substantial savings for investment purposes. See Feldstein (1996).

children had been widowed; a growing economy would raise all workers' incomes and would make the welfare state increasingly affordable; most work is too physically demanding for persons over age sixty-five. If we view the welfare state as part of post-World War II economic history, we can see how a fairly constant welfare state combined with a changing economy and population to create many of today's problems.

The solutions to these problems are not as neat as some would have it. The welfare state must balance two goals: fostering individual responsibility and providing a decent safety net. Those most concerned with individual responsibility propose shrinking the welfare state and requiring individuals to rely more on their own efforts. This was the logic of the Personal Responsibility and Work Opportunity Reconciliation Act of 1996, the reform of AFDC that sharply reduced guarantees of governmental aid to poor families with children. Similar logic underlies proposals to replace Social Security with individual retirement accounts that would cut the redistribution of the current system.* In a different labor market—say the market of the 1950s— these proposals would be consistent with both responsibility and self-sufficiency in all but the poorest areas. In today's labor market, wages for unskilled workers do not guarantee self-sufficiency even for the most responsible.† This points to the need to move to a safety net for work—not simply to cut the current safety net away.‡ We return to the point later in the chapter.

The Growth of Independent Households

Most of us know someone who lives alone—a divorced man, a younger woman who has not yet married. At the close of World War II, this would not have been the case. Together, thirty-six million families and nine million unrelated individuals constituted only thirty-nine million households. The housing shortage of the Great Depression and World War II had forced people to double up. Specifically:

- One family in fourteen (in 1950) was living in a household headed by another person or family, typically a relative.

- Seven unmarried adults in ten lived with other adults or families.

---

* It is important to distinguish between the ideas that some fraction of Social Security funds be invested in stocks (which could be done under the current trust fund program) and that the current trust fund be replaced by individual accounts.
† Implicit in this statement is the idea that average living standards have risen since the 1950s, and a socially acceptable minimum income in the 1950s would not be socially acceptable today.
‡ The phrase "safety net for work" was suggested to me by Gordon Berlin.

- About one-quarter of the population age sixty-five and over (2.8 million persons) lived in households headed by their children.[3]

Privacy is expensive. The Bureau of Labor Statistics estimates that if a young adult moves out of her parents' home, minimum living expenditures for all persons involved increase by one-quarter.* Nevertheless, as postwar incomes rose, people purchased privacy in abundance. The move to the suburbs and the move of northern retired persons to Florida were both part of the breakup of the extended family. By 1970 the extent of doubling-up had declined substantially:

- The proportion of families living in a household headed by another person had declined from one in fourteen to one in forty.
- Among unmarried adults, the proportion who lived alone had risen from three in ten (in 1950) to six in ten.
- The number of persons age sixty-five or over increased from 13 million to 20 million, but the number of elderly parents who lived in their children's households declined from 2.8 million to 2.3 million.[4]

Through the late 1960s, this quest for privacy stopped at the edge of the nuclear family.† The same rising incomes that undermined the extended family permitted young men and women to marry at earlier ages and to have relatively large families. This was the baby boom; in historical terms, it came as a great surprise. Since the beginning of the nineteenth century, the fertility rate had been falling steadily. In 1800 there were approximately 280 births per year for every 1,000 women age fifteen to forty-four, or seven to eight children for the average mother over her lifetime. For more than a century, the fertility rate fell steadily, reaching 103 in the mid-1920s (figure 7.1). Its drop to about 77 during the 1930s reflected the Great Depression's hardship, and some postwar rebound was expected. In fact, the postwar rebound

---

* For example, in 1995 the federal poverty standard for a four-person family, including one child over age eighteen, was $15,569. But the sum of the poverty standards for a three-person family and a fourth person living alone totaled $20,087, a 29 percent increase. See U.S. Bureau of the Census, *Current Population Reports*, series P-60, no. 194 (1996) table A-2.

† Eugene Smolensky reminds me that this is not quite correct. The quest for privacy within the nuclear family took the form of increasingly large homes. Smolensky suggests (and I agree) that the development of multiple-bathroom homes has substantially reduced the level of violent conflict between the hours of 7:00 and 9:00 A.M.

Figure 7.1 The United States Fertility Rate, 1900 to 1997

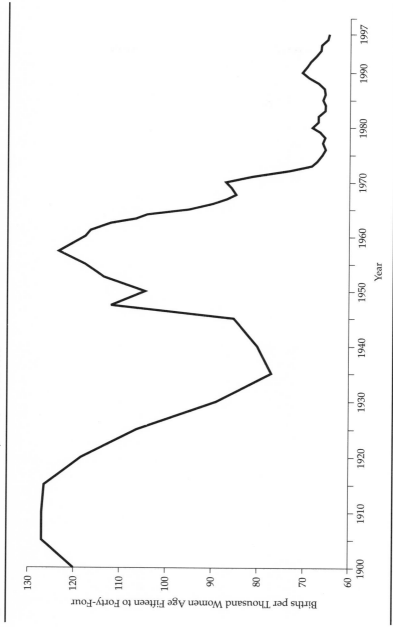

Sources: U.S. Department of Commerce, Bureau of the Census, *Statistical Abstract of the United States* (various years).

Figure 7.2   Average Household Size and Average Family Size, 1947 to 1994

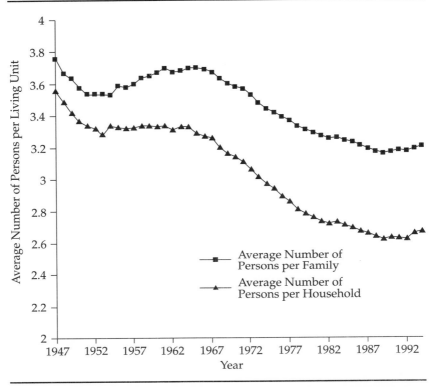

Sources: Author's tabulations of the March 1974 and March 1996 Current Population Surveys.

was enormous. The fertility rate climbed to 107 in 1950 and to 123 in 1957, as high as it had been in the early 1900s.[5]

As the demographer Andrew Cherlin writes, these high fertility rates did not translate into a great number of five- and six-children families but rather into a growing number of women having two or three children rather than one.[6] Many of the women had been raised in the Great Depression and were beginning their families in the mid-1940s, at a time of rapidly expanding opportunity.

These opposing trends—the shrinking extended family and the growing nuclear family—are plotted in figure 7.2. During the 1950s and mid-1960s, average *household* size was flat, but average *family* size continued to grow. The missing link was the increasing number of elderly persons and younger adults who moved out of extended families to form small households of their own.

There was one exception to the flourishing nuclear family—the growing number of black families headed by women. Over the 1950s, the proportion of black families headed by women increased from 15 percent to 22 percent (chapter 3).

The baby boom continued through the early 1960s and then abruptly ended. The fertility rate declined from 123 in 1957 to 109 in 1963 and then fell to 88 in 1967 (figure 7.1). Young men and women continued to marry early, but they postponed childbearing and reduced the number of children they eventually had. Some of the drop was predictable. If fertility rates of the 1930s had been below long-run trends, the birth rates of the 1950s had been far above trend, and some decline seemed likely. The speed of the decline was surprising, however, particularly since the economy in the late 1960s was so good.

Until the 1960s, rapid falls in the fertility rate had been associated with bad times like the Great Depression, when money was scarce. In the late 1960s, this pattern changed. The strong economy expanded women's options. While women's earnings were not improving vis-à-vis men's (chapter 5), they were improving in absolute terms, and we can assume that declining fertility rates partly reflected women's increased interest in pursuing careers.[7]

After 1973, the collapse of wage growth changed the economic context of family formation. Prior to 1973, rapid wage growth had helped young people get off to a quick start. Suppose that an eighteen- or nineteen-year-old man was preparing to leave home. As he left, he took a look at his father's salary and what it would buy, and he kept the memory as a personal yardstick. In the 1950s and 1960s, he would have measured up quickly. By the time the young man was thirty years old, he would have been earning about 15 percent more than his father had earned when the young man was leaving home. The young man knew early in his career that he could live as well as he had seen his parents live.*

As wage growth stagnated, intergenerational progress came much more slowly and young people became more cautious. Women's labor-force participation continued to increase, while fertility rates continued to decline. The baby boomers who were coming of age began to postpone marriage as well. Between 1970 and 1990, the median age of first marriage for both men and women rose by three and a half years (to 25.9 and 24 years, respectively), the highest they had been since about 1900. Through the late 1970s and on into the 1980s, the nuclear family and the average household both shrank in size. In the late 1980s, the fertility rate staged a small rebound, briefly topping

---

* Richard Easterlin (1980) develops similar comparisons for points in time, rather than over time.

100 again. The high number of births reflected both a growing immigrant population and the large number of thirty-something women in the baby-boom cohorts facing the now-or-never decision. Even so, the largest number of births in recent years—4.1 million in 1991—was below the 4.3 million births recorded in 1957, when the number of women of childbearing age was 40 percent smaller.

Slow-growing wages were one factor in the increasing number of later marriages, families with fewer children, and working women. The contraceptive revolution was clearly another factor, as was the willingness of some people to declare their homosexuality. Younger baby boomers may have taken caution from the growing divorce rates among their parents. These various motivations summed to one economic outcome: despite the post-1973 slowdown in wage growth, consumption per capita could continue to rise because there were more workers and fewer children in each household.

Changing living arrangements raised consumption in several ways. Among younger persons, the rising age of first marriage created a large group of young singles—precursors to Seinfeld—who ate out regularly, despite low earnings, because they did not have a family to support. Among married, well-educated couples—DINKS* — the switch to two incomes really did mean high incomes. Until the late 1970s, working wives were more common in families in which the husband had low earnings. During the 1980s, however, most wives started working outside the home, and the greatest gains in the labor-force participation of married women came from those with high-earning husbands (figure 7.3). This shift took place as the large, well-educated baby-boom cohorts were entering middle age. As a result, the number of prime-age couples with incomes above $80,000 grew from 4.3 million in 1973 to 9.4 million in 1996 (in 1997 dollars)—a growing market for sport utility vehicles, specialty food stores, personal bankers, health clubs, and other high-end goods and services.†

Among couples with less education, the switch to two incomes barely offset post-1979 wage declines. In 1996 a thirty-year-old husband with a high school diploma earned considerably less than his 1979 counterpart: $26,900 versus $33,820. The 1996 family had a

---

* DINK, a now dated term, stands for Dual Incomes, No Kids. The paradigmatic treatment of the closely related Yuppie was the December 31, 1985, cover story in *Newsweek*, which proclaimed 1986 "the Year of the Yuppie." An early paper questioning some of the media hype was Levy and Michel (1985).

† For example, a Mercedes-Benz of North America spokesman says that the median income of households buying the ML320 V6 sport utility vehicle is about $120,000 while the new ML430 V8 sport utility vehicle is being targeted at households with a median income of about $150,000. See White (1998) and Hallberg (1995).

Figure 7.3 Average Women's Earnings by Husband's Earnings, 1973 and 1995

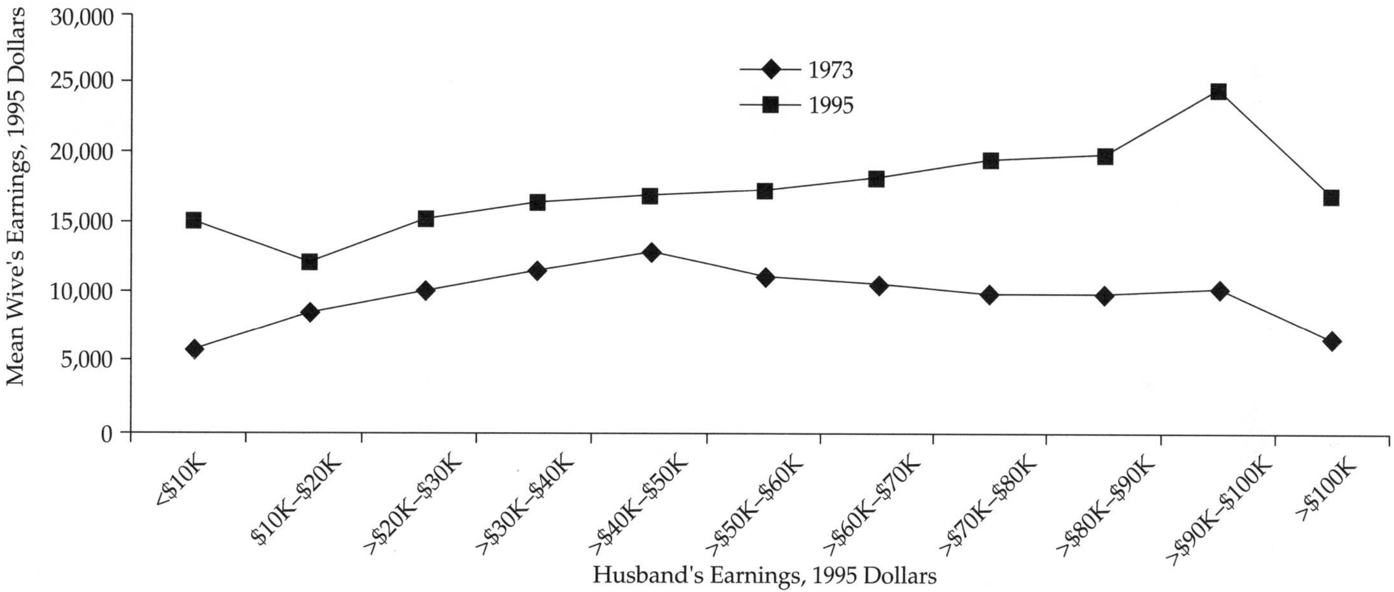

Sources: Author's tabulation of the March 1974 and March 1996 Current Population Survey.

slightly higher income ($43,100 versus $42,000) because the 1996 wife was working about two-thirds time, a level that the 1979 wives would not reach until they were in their late thirties. In fact, increased wives' work was the major reason the 1979 families saw their incomes grow over the 1980s. Among 1996 families, that card had been largely played, and sources of future income growth were unclear.

At all income levels, then, husband-wife families were relying more and more on two incomes. The two incomes sharpened the economic contrast with families headed by women. Recall from chapter 3 that despite the 1960s economic boom the proportion of black families headed by women grew from 22 percent in 1960 to 31 percent in 1970. The proportion continued to increase, so that by 1996, 46 percent of all black families were headed by a woman. Similarly, between 1970 and 1996, the proportion of Hispanic families headed by a single woman rose from 15 percent to 24 percent, while among non-Hispanic whites, the proportion rose from 8 percent to 13 percent.

The growing number of female-headed families had a second dimension. In earlier decades, female-headed families were typically the product of desertion or divorce. Now an increasing proportion were headed by women who had never married and who often had their first child as a teenager.* As a result, at a time when the labor market was increasingly sorting on education, female household heads averaged about one year less of schooling than married women. In 1996, about one-fifth had not finished high school.

Family and Household Structure: The Impact on Inequality

The trends we have described—falling birth rates, more two-income families, more female-headed families, more people living alone—have the potential to reshape both the family and household income distributions. Table 7.1 summarizes postwar changes in both families and other households—households occupied by single individuals or unrelated roommates. While these changes would not make for dramatic headlines—the Ozzie and Harriet family is not exactly dead—the changes are real enough.†

Common sense suggests several different channels by which these trends might have affected the current level of income inequality:

---

* Among female-family heads in 1996, two-fifths of black women, one-third of Hispanic women and one-fifth of white women had never been married.

† More precisely, the prime-age husband-wife family is not dead. If we define an Ozzie and Harriet family as a prime-age husband-wife family in which the wife does not work, the decline is much more dramatic. In fairness, however, the real Harriet Nelson worked—as the actress who played Harriet on the television show.

Table 7.1 Characteristics of Families and Other Households 1949, 1984, and 1996

	1949	1984	1996
Total number of families (millions)	39.9	62.7	70.2
Total number of persons in families (millions)	142.6	202.5	224.1
Head aged sixty-five or over, male or female	12%	16%	17%
Husband-wife family aged sixty-four or under			
Wife works	18%	40%	48%
Wife does not work[a]	60%	30%	18%
Female head aged sixty-four or under	10%	14%	17%
Total	100%	100%	100%
Total number of non-family households (millions)	9.0	24.1	30.8
Persons in non-family households (millions)	9.7	33.8	41.3
Persons aged sixty-five or over	23%	30%	33%
Males aged sixty-four or under			
Aged thirty-five to sixty-four	21%	14%	21%
Aged thirty-four or under	21%	23%	15%
Females aged sixty-four or under			
Aged thirty-five to sixty-four	22%	16%	20%
Aged thirty-four or under	13%	17%	10%
Total	100%	100%	100%

Sources: Author's tabulations of the 1950 Decennial Census Public Use Microdata Sample files and the March 1985 and March 1997 Current Population Surveys.
Notes: Each year's data is collected in March of the following year.
[a]Includes families with only the father present.

- *Female-Headed Households* On average, female-headed families have very low incomes. Other things being equal, we would expect the growing fraction of female-headed families to increase inequality.

- *Two-Earner Couples* The story here is complex. When most working women had low-earning husbands, wives' earnings equalized incomes among husband-wife families. During the 1980s, however, rising earnings among wives with high-earning husbands reduced this equalizing effect (figure 7.3). Thus, the net impact of wives' earnings on current inequality is not obvious.

- *More Prime-Age Persons Living Alone* Fifty years ago, persons living alone were usually elderly or disabled—persons with very low incomes. Since then, the growing number of prime-age persons who live alone should have increased the number of middle-income households and so should have lowered household income inequality.

- *More Elderly Families*   Fifty years ago, if the number of elderly families had been growing, the number of poor families and income inequality would have been increasing as well. Since the early 1970s, however, incomes among elderly families have grown faster than the income of the average family, a story to which we return shortly. Thus, the greater number of elderly families, combined with their rising incomes, have made them a force for greater income equality.

What is the net result of these changes? A number of economists have answered this question by statistically separating living arrangements from trends in wages and other income. These are accounting exercises—not life—since different living arrangements would have required a different economy. A representative study by Paul Ryscavage et al.[8] undertook this analysis for the period 1969 to 1989 by first distinguishing three factors:

1.   Changes in the distribution of household types—the mix among female-headed families, husband-wife families, persons living alone, and so on;

2.   Changes in wage patterns and other income sources, such as Social Security and welfare payments, except for changes in wives' hours of work;

3.   Changes in wives' hours of work.

Ryscavage and his colleagues begin from the fact that the gini coefficient of household income inequality, as measured by the census, rose from .391 in 1969 to .431 in 1989. By varying these three factors, they reach the following conclusions:

- Suppose that the mix of different household types had stayed at its 1969 level, and that, among these households, wages, other income sources, and wives' hours of work all followed their actual paths. The 1989 gini coefficient would have risen to .411 rather than its actual value of .431.

- Alternatively, suppose that hours of wives' work had stayed at 1969 levels, but that the mix of household types and trends in wages and other income sources all followed their actual paths. The 1989 gini coefficient would have risen to .420 rather than .431.

Based on these calculations and the work of other authors, changes in living arrangements account for roughly two-fifths of the increase in household income inequality since 1969, while changes in wages and other income sources, including wives' earnings, account for the remaining three-fifths.[9] While few authors have applied these methods to the family income distribution (as opposed to the household income distribution), we can assume that living arrangements and economic factors within the family income distribution would divide in a similar way.

Using calculations like these, we can see that living arrangements and economic trends reinforced each other over the last fifty years. Recall that from 1947 to 1969 family incomes were becoming more equal. In earlier chapters, we reviewed the economic forces that contributed to this equality: the movement of labor from low-wage agriculture to higher-wage manufacturing jobs; the low levels of education required by many good jobs; the very low unemployment rates of the late 1960s Vietnam War boom. We can now see that living arrangements during this period favored equality as well. For much of the time, female-headed families were not numerically important. When wives worked, it was usually to supplement a husband's low earnings, resulting in more middle-income families.

After the mid-1970s, and particular in the 1980s, economics and demography again worked together, but this time to increase inequality (figures 3.2 and 7.4). We have seen that during this period earnings inequality grew as a consequence of both increasing educational requirements and the growing number of very high earners. Living arrangements reinforced these trends both through the growth of female-headed families and increased work among wives of high-income husbands.[10] Two other trends in this period, however, moderated the trend in inequality: the growing number of middle-income singles and rising incomes among elderly families. Without these two trends, both family and household income inequality would be even larger now than they are.

These trends are connected to popular discussion through the issue of the vanishing middle class. There is no official definition of a middle-class income, but suppose we say that a middle-class family has income between $30,000 and $80,000 (in 1997 dollars).* Suppose further that this definition refers to families in their prime earning years—ages twenty-five to fifty-four—because the incomes of the very young and the retired are not good clues to their "class." When

---

* Note that this definition excludes individuals living alone and other non-family households.

Figure 7.4 The Household Income Distribution, 1973 and 1996

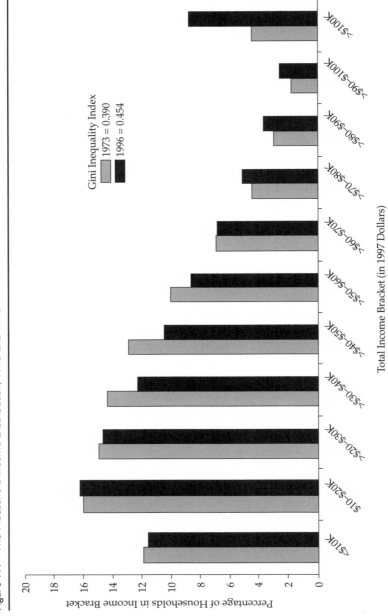

Percentage of Households in Income Bracket

Gini Inequality Index
1973 = 0.390
1996 = 0.454

Total Income Bracket (in 1997 Dollars)

Sources: Author's tabulation of the March 1974 and March 1997 Current Population Survey.

Table 7.2   The "Middle Class" and Other Classes: Income Distribution of Families, Head
Aged Twenty-Five to Fifty-Four

	In Poverty	Poverty to $30,000	("Middle Class") $30,000 to $80,000	>$80,000
Numbers of families (1,000s)				
1973				
Husband-wife	1,215	3,743	19,953	4,825
Female head	1,388	1,538	1,072	52
All other	49	166	427	82
Total	2,652	5,447	21,452	4,419
1996				
Husband-wife	2,000	4,238	20,303	9,384
Female head	2,989	3,036	2,748	265
All other	375	875	1,316	209
Total	5,365	8,149	24,368	9,859
Percent distribution[a]				
All families				
1973	7.8%	16.0%	63.2%	13.0%
1996	11.2	17.1	51.0	20.7
White, non-Hispanic families				
1973	5.1	13.9	66.4	14.7
1996	6.7	14.2	54.9	24.2
Black, non-Hispanic families				
1973	25.6	27.6	42.9	4.0
1996	24.2	26.0	40.9	8.9
Hispanic families				
1973	18.1	27.3	50.8	3.7
1996	26.4	26.6	39.1	8.0

Sources: Author's tabulations of the March 1974 and March 1997 Current Population Survey.
Note: Excludes related subfamilies sharing a household.
[a]Rows sum to 100 percent across columns.

we apply this definition to family incomes in 1973 (when average wage growth slowed) and 1996, we see the same mix of economics and living arrangements at work (table 7.2).

In 1973, almost two-thirds of prime-age families had middle-class incomes (by our definition). At the extremes of the distribution, there was (roughly) a two-to-one ratio on the up-side: 13 percent of families had incomes above $80,000, and 8 percent of families were poor. By

Figure 7.5   Changes in the American Middle Class, 1973 to 1996 (1997 Dollars)

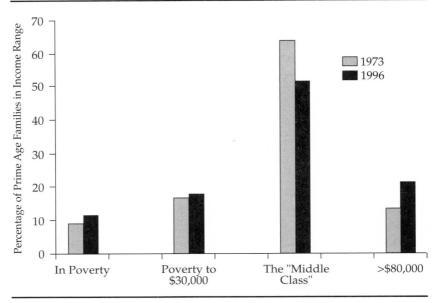

Sources: Author's tabulations of the March 1974 and March 1997 Current Population Survey.

1996, most of the 1973 families had passed beyond age of fifty-four and so the 1996 distribution largely represents a new and different group of families. These 1996 families had more education than their 1973 counterparts. Among men and women who were married, a greater fraction were in two-paycheck families. At the same time, a growing fraction of women were unmarried and in female-headed families. Finally these 1996 families functioned in a different economy where wages for less-educated workers had fallen. Together, these factors spread the distribution out (figure 7.5). The middle class was smaller (51 percent down from 63 percent). The fraction of families with over $80,000 grew (21 percent up from 13 percent). The fraction of poor families grew as well (11 percent up from 8 percent).

   Since the definition of middle class is arbitrary, one can reasonably ask if this spreading out makes any difference. I believe it does make a difference on two grounds. The first is in the reduction of common interests. The spreading distribution represents families with increasingly different incomes, prospects, and expectations of what government should do. The welfare state rests on enlightened self-interest in which people can look at beneficiaries and reasonably say, "There but for the grace of God. . . ." As income differences widen, this statement rings less true.*

The spreading out also has implications for future inequality that work through the lives of children. The fertility rate declined sharply after 1964, but the decline was concentrated among married women. Between 1970 and 1990, the fertility rate per 1,000 women (married or not) declined from 88 to 79, but the fertility rate per 1,000 unmarried women rose from 26 to 45. The rising fertility rate among unmarried women was compounded by a *growing number* of unmarried women, a product of the rising age of first marriage. In the early 1970s, about one child in nine lived in a mother-only family. By 1996, the fraction was one child in four.

Living in a female-headed family usually means living in a low-income family. More female-headed families combined with lower wages for less-educated males meant that in 1996, 28 percent of all children lived in families with income below $20,000 (in 1997 dollars—figure 7.6). Among the heads of these families (male and female) one-third had not finished high school. In today's labor market these children begin life at an enormous disadvantage.

The spreading of the family income distribution varied by race and ethnicity, but not to the extent one might suppose (table 7.2). Hispanic family incomes spread out most sharply, but this reflects the large numbers of immigrants who arrived over the last twenty-five years. Black family incomes showed moderate improvement with a slight decline in the fraction of prime-age families in poverty and a moderate increase in the proportion with incomes over $80,000. The figures support the picture of a growing black middle class, but that picture needs to be qualified. The numbers in table 7.2 describe families and many of the black men who report little or no earnings (for example, figure 5.5) are not married, and so do not appear in these statistics. In addition, middle- and upper-income black families are typically married couples. Since black married couples have particularly low fertility rates, something over half of all black children live in female-headed families while 54 percent live in families with incomes below $20,000.

---

* One can also argue that the definition of the middle class does not mean much if there is substantial income mobility and large numbers of families are constantly moving in and out of the middle class. Greg Duncan and his colleagues have examined income mobility using a similar definition of middle class and found it to be both modest and declining over time. See Duncan et al. (1993).

Figure 7.6 Family Income Distribution of Children Under Age Eighteen, 1973 and 1996

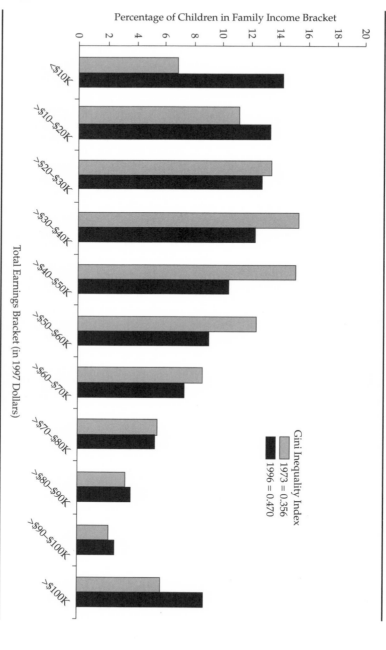

Percentage of Children in Family Income Bracket

Total Earnings Bracket (in 1997 Dollars)

Gini Inequality Index
1973 = 0.356
1996 = 0.470

Sources: Author's tabulation of the March 1974 and March 1997 Current Population Survey.

Families and Government

The large fraction of children in low-income families suggests the possibility of government intervention—an expansion of the welfare state. Yet the issue comes at a time when the welfare state itself and government's ability to promote equality have become suspect.

The roots of the welfare state lie in the Social Security Act of 1935. The act was passed in the teeth of the Great Depression and consolidated disparate state programs to form two kinds of federal programs: social insurance programs, and means-tested programs. Social Security—a program to provide retirement income—was an example of a social insurance program in which people established eligibility by paying into the program's trust fund over their careers. Aid to Dependent Children (ADC) was a means-tested program in which single mothers—presumably widows—established eligibility by having income below certain limits. ADC would become Aid to Families with Dependent Children (AFDC) or, simply, "welfare." It was funded from general tax revenues rather than from a separate trust fund. Over time, both programs and, in fact, the entire welfare state would become subjects of growing controversy. A look at the numbers begins to explain why.

Among government statistics, the most comprehensive definition of income comes from the Department of Commerce's National Income and Product Accounts, which include both money payments and non-money benefits like food stamps and Medicare.* The accounts show that government transfer payments to individuals rose from 5.4 percent to 14 percent of gross domestic product (figure 7.7), and from 21 percent to 46 percent of all government spending.[11] This growth in spending raises an obvious question: how could government benefits more than double as a percentage of GDP without *reducing* income inequality? Put differently, the census reports that the poorest one-fifth of families have received 4.4 to 5.6 percent of all family income in every year since 1946. The census data for households available since 1967 show a similarly stable inequality (appendix). Why did increased government payments fail to increase the bottom's share?

The question has three answers, beginning with definitions. Census statistics define income as pretax money payments. This definition of income understates redistribution by not subtracting taxes at the top of the distribution and by not adding non-money benefits at

---

* Because the National Income and Product Accounts are based on reports of economic activity rather than on household surveys, they contain national aggregate figures with no distributional information across households and thus cannot be used in most parts of our story.

Figure 7.7   Government Payments to Individuals as a Percentage of GDP, 1949 to
1995

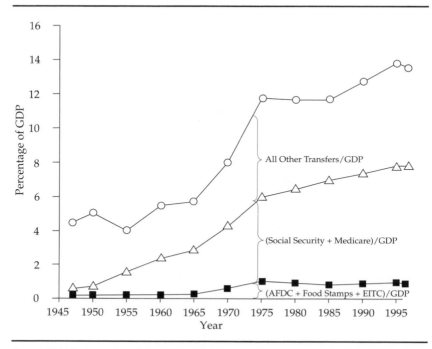

Source: U.S. Department of Commerce, Bureau of Economic Analysis, *National Income
and Product Accounts* (various years).

the bottom. It also misses the value of employer fringe benefits like
health insurance.* For recent years, the census has estimated the impact of these omissions on the household income distribution. If
household income is measured after taxes are deducted and includes
the money value of all government benefits and employer fringe benefits, the 1995 gini coefficient is .409 rather than the official .444. Under the revised definition, income inequality has grown over the last
fifteen years just as it has grown under the standard definition.

The second answer points up the difference between Social Security and AFDC—or, more generally, the difference between social insurance programs and means-tested programs. Both kinds of programs were designed to keep people from becoming economically

---

* While this definition is crude, it has a practical basis. When the census first began
collecting this information, non-money benefits like Medicare and food stamps did not
exist. At the same time, few people know their federal, state, and local tax payments
well enough to recount them to a census interviewer.

distressed, but only means-tested programs like AFDC or food stamps are restricted to people with low incomes. The remaining functions of today's welfare state are social insurance programs, whose benefits go to persons who have established their eligibility through prior contributions. While some recipients of social insurance benefits have low incomes, others do not; these benefits are not limited to the bottom of the income distribution.*

The third and most important answer is that growing government payments did not just go to a constant fraction of the population— they went to a growing fraction of the population. Increased government benefits were part and parcel of the growing number of households without a working member: more female-headed families, a growing number of retired people, a growing number of men who stopped working and collected disability insurance. It is this fact that leads to the question of moral hazard. Where did government benefits compensate for changed living arrangements (including retirement), and where did they exacerbate the problems they were supposed to solve?

We can answer this question by returning to the economic history of previous chapters. Through the history, we can see the problems that arose when government addressed a changing economy with a welfare state of relatively fixed design.

Aid to Families with Dependent Children Through 1973

ADC was President Franklin Roosevelt's attempt to put a foundation under state-run widows' and orphans' programs. Initial plans had included a minimum national benefit, but southern legislators were concerned that too generous a national benefit could disrupt the South's low wage structure. The minimum benefit was defeated, and benefit levels and many administrative details were left to state discretion. The federal government would share in program costs.

The legislative record indicates that Congress expected the ADC program to wither away as the Great Depression ended and Social Security (which included survivors' benefits for widows) matured.† In fact, ADC did not wither away but rather grew at a moderate rate. In 1940 it paid benefits to 372,000 families, about one family in

---

* The economist Daniel Weinberg (1985) calculates that in 1979, 64 percent of Social Security and Medicare benefits went to persons who, without them, would have had incomes below the poverty line.
† For a brief history of the early AFDC program and subsequent reform attempts, see Burke and Burke (1974).

eighty-three. By 1960 it was paying benefits to 803,000 families—one family in thirty-eight.*

A look at census statistics suggests that the growth in ADC payments could have been much larger. The 1960 ADC caseload stood at 803,000, but there were 4.6 million female-headed families (of all ages), half of whom had incomes below $15,000 (in 1997 dollars). A good guess is that many of these families were eligible for ADC benefits but the stigma of welfare and restrictive administration kept them from applying.†

As we saw in chapter 3, the United States rediscovered poverty in the 1960s. The discovery built on the civil rights movement and gained momentum from Edward R. Murrow's television documentary on migrant labor, *The Harvest of Shame* (1960) and Michael Harrington's book *The Other America* (1962). Equally important was the population's economic optimism, which encouraged the idea that poverty was a residual, manageable problem.

The optimism was appropriate. The first step taken by the federal government in studying poverty was to define it. The work was directed by Mollie Orshansky, an economist with the Social Security Administration, who settled on a 1963 poverty line of $3,200 (in 1963 dollars; $16,036 in 1996 dollars) for a family of four, with comparable standards for families of other sizes.[12] When this standard was projected backward (with adjustments for inflation), it showed that the proportion of the population in poverty had declined from 32 percent in 1949 to 22 percent in 1960 (see figure 7.8).

Poverty reduction was another virtue of rising average wages. The poverty standard was adjusted for inflation and so was constant in real dollars.‡ In the late 1940s, incomes were still low enough that the standard fell in the second quintile of the family income distribution. As real wages grew, the income distribution shifted to higher levels, and by 1960 only the lowest quintile remained below the poverty line.§ If wages could keep growing in this way, the proportion of

---

* U.S. Department of Commerce, Bureau of the Census, *Historical Statistics* (1975b).

† Income statistics come from the 1960 census. The figure of 4.6 million includes female-headed families who would have been ineligible for ADC because they had no children.

‡ That is, the poverty line was adjusted each year only for inflation as measured by the consumer price index. If real incomes rose enough, the poverty rate would fall close to zero. The economist Victor Fuchs, among others, has argued that poverty should be defined on a *relative* rather than an absolute basis at perhaps one-half of median family income in each year.

§ This description oversimplifies in two ways. First, it ignores the fact that the official poverty standard is different for different family sizes. Thus, some two-person families in the lowest quintile were not poor, while some five- and six-person families in the second quintile were poor. Second, it ignores the companion calculations for single individuals and others living outside of families.

Figure 7.8   The Link Between the Rising Income Distribution and the Falling Poverty
Population, 1949 and 1960

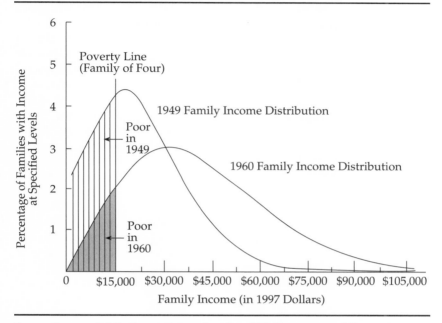

Sources: Income distribution statistics taken from U.S. Department of Commerce,
Bureau of the Census, *Current Population Reports,* series P-60 (various years).
Note: Height of curve at a point describes proportion of families with income within a
$1,000 interval of the point.

families with below-poverty incomes would continue to shrink automatically and government policies could help those persons passed
over by the economy. Lyndon Johnson's War on Poverty was an attempt to establish these policies: expanded manpower training, funding community action programs, offering compensatory education
programs for disadvantaged children, and so on.[13]

How did ADC, renamed AFDC, fit into these anti-poverty efforts?
In a highly ambivalent way. The War on Poverty was waged at least
in part to promote self-sufficiency, and in this sense administrators
continued to hope that the AFDC rolls would wither away. Inevitably,
however, the purpose of a war on poverty was also to raise people's
incomes, and in this AFDC could be a useful tool.

AFDC policies reflected this ambivalence. During the 1960s, the
federal government instructed the states to initiate several AFDC
changes to help states move families off the rolls. The first was an
intensive, federally funded program of social services and counseling
advanced by former Senator Abraham Ribicoff, President Kennedy's

secretary of Health, Education, and Welfare. The AFDC rolls continued to grow, however, and in 1967 Congress tried to increase recipients' incentives to go to work by establishing the "Thirty Dollars Plus One-third Rule," which permitted recipients to keep part of any money they earned rather than have it deducted, dollar for dollar, from their benefits.* In 1968 Congress passed "separation" legislation, which required states to take the jobs of determining eligibility and calculating budgets away from social workers and to give them to eligibility technicians who would presumably administer the program in a less "soft-headed" way.[14]

Simultaneously, other policies made AFDC more attractive. During the 1960s, many states raised AFDC benefits.† In 1965 Congress passed the Medicaid program, medical insurance for low-income persons.‡ Like AFDC, Medicaid was a joint federal-state program with substantial state control. In many states, low-income families with children were eligible for Medicaid only if they were AFDC recipients, a requirement that further increased AFDC's attractiveness.§ After the first big-city riots (chapter 6), many jurisdictions made it easier to apply for welfare, in some cases using a "declaration" AFDC application that required little documentation of an applicant's financial condition. In 1971 Richard Nixon and Congress took the experimental concept of food stamps and expanded it to a full national program. Food stamps were made available to all low-income persons—not just AFDC recipients—but they further increased the income that came with AFDC.

Policy liberalizations reflected the temper of the times. The booming economy and government rhetoric had significantly raised the expectation that poverty would soon be eliminated. At the same time, the Vietnam War and the civil rights revolution had made anti-gov-

---

* Though it was not recognized at the time, the Thirty Dollars Plus One-third Rule had ambiguous effects. By allowing recipients to keep part of their earnings, it gave them an incentive to work, but a by-product of that incentive was to bring AFDC eligibility within the reach of persons with low levels of earnings who had previously been off the rolls. Such persons appear to have been drawn onto the rolls in sufficient numbers to offset the work incentive's purpose. See Levy (1979).

† All states also extended Medicaid benefits to recipients of what is now known as Supplemental Security Income (SSI). SSI was formally created in 1971 and represented a substantially increased federal role in state income programs for the indigent aged, the blind, and the disabled. In addition, some states extended Medicaid benefits to the "medically indigent"—families who received neither AFDC nor SSI but whose income, less medical expenses, fell below an eligibility level.

‡ As distinct from Medicare, which provides health insurance for the elderly.

§ The other major group of Medicaid recipients was the indigent elderly for whom Medicaid paid nursing home bills. (Medicare does not cover nursing homes.) Today nursing home expenses account for about half of all Medicaid expenditures.

ernment protest commonplace, so that the big-city riots were often discussed in political terms. The result was to transform AFDC from a program of emergency assistance into, depending on one's view, either government patronage or an entitlement that all eligible families should receive even if they could make do without it. The political scientists Richard A. Cloward and Frances Fox Piven give a sense of the moment:

> That a demand for information about welfare entitlements had been created is not difficult to show. The Southern California chapter of the ACLU prepared a manual in the summer of 1968, and within a short time, 8,000 copies were sold to many different local organizations which had contact with the poor. Requests for more than one thousand copies were also received from public and private agencies elsewhere in the country. Indeed, even relief officials showed interest for "state welfare departments as far away as South Carolina ordered [sample] copies." After 1964, in other words, there was truly an information explosion, and that had much to do with the explosion of applications for welfare which followed.[15]

The increase in AFDC cases was dramatic and went far beyond the urban black areas. The AFDC caseload grew from 803,000 families in 1960 to 1.3 million in 1967, and to 3.2 million by 1973, with white families comprising half of the increase. In 1973 AFDC was received by one white child in fifteen and by two black children in five nationwide.[16]

Even officials favoring expanded benefits had not expected anything like this growth. Because AFDC was largely limited to mothers and children, officials feared that the program was causing large number of marriages to dissolve, leaving the mother and children eligible for benefits.*

We have seen that this theory, while plausible, was ultimately wrong: significant numbers of low-income, female-headed families—both black and white—had been there all along. What was changing was the willingness of these families to sign up for benefits and the willingness of state programs to accept them (see figure 7.9).[17]

If AFDC did not create female-headed families in the late 1960s, it helped to perpetuate such families during the early 1970s. The effect was clearest among blacks in depressed big-city neighborhoods—underclass areas—where AFDC served as the third leg of a three-legged

---

* In 1960 Congress had permitted states to offer ADC-UP (Unemployed Parent) a program that extended ADC benefits to two-parent families. Only half of the states, however, adopted the program, which contained a number of eligibility restrictions that caused caseloads to be about one-tenth the size of the program for female-headed families.

Figure 7.9   The Number of Female-Headed Families and the Number of Families on AFDC, 1960 to 1995

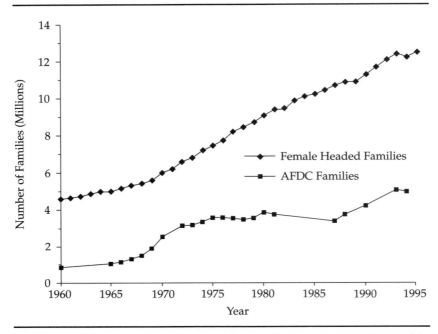

Sources: U.S. Department of Commerce, Bureau of the Census, *Statistical Abstract of the United States* (various years).

stool—jobless men, families headed by women, and income from welfare—and where life was increasingly cut off from the larger economy (chapter 6). But, the total number of families receiving welfare was far larger than residents of underclass areas. Using 1973 census statistics, a good guess at the number of black families with children regardless of where they lived would have been 4 million, comprising 2.1 million husband-wife families; 300,000 female-headed families who were not receiving AFDC; and 1.6 million female-headed families who were receiving AFDC. In the same year, the 27 million white families with children included 23.7 million husband-wife families; 2 million female-headed families who were not receiving AFDC; and 1.6 million female-headed families who were receiving AFDC.[18]

Thus, equal numbers of black and white families were receiving welfare. In relative terms, however, welfare receipt was far more important among blacks, and the near-term prospects of these families were not good. The sociologist Mary Jo Bane and the economist David Ellwood estimate that during the 1970s the average black family enrolling with AFDC would stay on the rolls 5.3 years.* Despite the increased rolls, AFDC was still a small part of welfare state cost: $24 billion in 1973 (1997 dollars) versus $170 billion for Social Security and $33 billion for Medicare. Nonetheless, this was very different than the program envisioned in 1935. A disinterested observer would indeed have to wonder whether AFDC was reducing inequality or making it worse.

Social Security Through 1973

As a social insurance program, Social Security differed fundamentally from the means-tested AFDC program. AFDC was funded by general tax revenues and restricted to low-income families (most headed by women). Social Security was funded by worker and employer contributions, and a recipient could understandably feel that he or she was merely collecting what they had already paid for. If the two funding concepts became blurred, it was because of Social Security's financing.

When Congress created Social Security in 1935, it had two financing options. One was to establish a savings program—a very large accumulated trust fund whose interest would be used to help finance future benefits. The other option was a pay-as-you-go program: today's beneficiaries would be paid directly by today's workers. Social Security initially envisioned the trust fund, but Congress, for a variety of reasons, soon backed into pay-as-you-go.[19]

The economics of a pay-as-you-go system can be summarized in three equations:

(7.1)   Revenues = (Number of Covered Workers) × (Wages per Worker) × (Social Security Tax Rate)

---

* Estimating an individual's duration on AFDC or in poverty is particularly sensitive to the way in which the question is posed. The 5.3-year figure refers to all persons who *begin* to receive AFDC at a particular point in time. This group includes people with temporary problems who get off the rolls quickly and people with serious problems who are on the rolls for a long time. It follows that a second group—all persons who *receive* AFDC at a point in time (including those whose cases started earlier)—will be dominated by families with serious problems. Bane and Ellwood estimate the average duration on welfare for this group to be 10.2 years. See Bane and Ellwood (1983), table 10.

(7.2) Expenditures = (Number of Recipients) × (Benefits per Recipient)

(7.3)   Revenues ≥ Expenditures

> Equation 7.3 is a simplification of the condition that must apply over the life of
> the program. Today, Social Security is building a trust fund to pay future bene-
> fits and so current revenues purposely exceed current expenditures. When the
> baby-boom retires, expenditures in a given year will exceed revenues.

The government is happiest when it can run such a system without
increasing the tax rate, and two conditions facilitate this: the number
of covered workers is growing faster than the number of recipients,
and real earnings per worker are growing faster than real benefits.

If these conditions are not present—if recipients are increasing faster than workers or benefits are growing faster than wages—the government is faced with two choices. It can raise the tax rate on wages,
or it can reduce the growth of benefits. Reducing benefit growth need
not be politically explosive. In the original Social Security program,
recipients' benefits were fixed in dollar terms (rather than real terms)
and subsequently increased only by congressional vote. If Congress
increased dollar benefits more slowly than the rate of inflation, the
program would be brought into balance without actually making dollar reductions.

In the early years of Social Security, the program cost very little.
While it covered a majority of the workforce, few workers had been
in the system long enough to qualify for benefits. In the late 1940s,
there were twelve and a half million persons aged sixty-five or over,
but only three million received Social Security checks. These three
million recipients were being supported by thirty-nine million covered workers—a ratio of thirteen workers per recipient—and so taxes
could remain low.[20]

Through the 1950s and 1960s, the program continued to run
smoothly. Workers' real wages were growing; Congress was steadily
expanding the proportion of workers covered by the program; and
both of these factors increased revenue growth. Whenever this revenue growth was projected forward, the system showed great surpluses and Congress responded by raising benefits. Congress passed
a 14 percent benefit increase in 1952 and a 10 percent increase in 1960,
each with only minor tax increases.[21]

Beginning in 1965, several pieces of legislation placed big bets on
the continued growth of incomes. The first was Medicare, health insurance for the elderly. In one sense, the passage of Medicare simply
redressed a growing imbalance in health care access. Since the end of
World War II, the proportion of all *workers* covered by employer-provided health insurance had grown dramatically. Medicare (and Medi-

caid for certain low-income families) simply put working and non-working families on an equal footing. With the passage of Medicare, however, the demand for health care increased dramatically, while the supply of doctors expanded only slowly. The result was a rapid inflation in medical prices. By 1973 Medicare was costing $33 billion (in 1997 dollars), an amount equal to one-fifth of Social Security itself.

Equally important was the 1972 legislation linking Social Security benefits to the consumer price index. The link was proposed by the Nixon administration as a prudent reform to protect the program's solvency. From 1947 through 1972, the economy had produced twenty-five years of almost unbroken growth in real wages. Since living standards were steadily rising, the indexing of Social Security benefits to keep purchasing power constant seemed an equitable thing to do. Moreover, it undercut election-year pressures to vote even bigger increases. Like the rest of us, Congress had no idea that the nation was about to enter a time of real wage stagnation and decline.

A final program with roots in this period was the Earned Income Tax Credit (EITC). The EITC began life as a wage bonus program developed by Senator Russell Long. Long offered the proposal in 1972 as an alternative to President Nixon's Family Assistance Plan, a program that would have replaced AFDC with a guaranteed minimum income for all families.* Long's plan, by contrast, required all female-family heads who wanted assistance to work in private jobs or in public jobs if private jobs were unavailable. Women in the plan would receive a 10 percent wage bonus to offset their Social Security payroll taxes. In 1972, neither plan passed. In 1975, however, Congress passed a tax stimulus package to deal with the recession following the first OPEC oil price increase. A wage supplement, restricted to families with children and renamed the Earned Income Tax Credit, was included in the package.†

The Welfare State in 1973

By 1973 government payments to individuals had grown to 9.5 percent of gross domestic product (GDP), up from 5 percent in 1947 (see figure 7.7). These payments, together with rising real wages, had reshaped the bottom of the income distribution.

---

* On the family assistance plan, see Burke and Burke (1974) and Moynihan (1973). On the Earned Income Tax Credit, see the excellent paper by Liebman (1997).
† While the EITC did not contain a formal work requirement, a person had to work in order to receive the bonus.

Table 7.3   The Changing Composition of the Family Income Distribution's Lowest
Quintile

	1949	1969	1984	1996
All families over age sixty-five	25%	35%	24%	22%
Husband-wife families under age sixty-five[a]	60	36	41	36
Female-headed families under age sixty-five	15	29	35	42
Total	100%	100%	100%	100%

Sources: Author's tabulation of the 1950 and 1970 Decennial Census Public Use Microdata files and the March 1985 and March 1997 Current Population Survey.
[a]Includes male-headed families with no wife present.

In the late 1940s two-fifths of all families in the bottom quintile
were age sixty-five or over and/or one of the small number of younger, female-headed families. The rest of the quintile were largely
farming families, many from the South. By the early 1970s, the number of farming families at all income levels had declined substantially,
and the elderly and the growing number of female-headed households comprised two-thirds of the quintile (table 7.3). The quintile's
reliance on government benefits grew even more quickly. In the late
1940s, with AFDC and Social Security both small programs, most
families (including many elderly families) had a working member,
and 90 percent of income in the lowest quintile came from earnings.
By 1973 only 55 percent of income in the lowest quintile came from
earnings, a reflection of higher retirement rates, more female-headed
families, and greater AFDC participation.*

Equally sharp changes occurred in the poverty population, which,
unlike the lowest quintile, had no set size but consisted of all persons
in households with incomes below the fixed real poverty standard. As
real wages rose through the 1960s, the proportion of the population in
poverty fell from 22 percent in 1959 to 11 percent in 1973 (table 7.4).[22]

Not surprisingly, the fall in poverty was most rapid among husband-wife families under age sixty-five—the families best able to enter the booming economy. As a result of their success, the composition of the poverty population shifted. Between 1959 and 1973, the
proportion of the poverty population who were elderly stayed constant at about 15 percent, but the proportion who lived in female-
headed families (under age sixty-five) rose from 21 percent to 41 percent in a trend termed the feminization of poverty.†

---

* Author's estimates based on data from the 1950 census and *Current Population Reports*.
† If we add to this figure persons in families headed by a woman over age sixty-five
and female unrelated individuals, the resulting sum of all persons living in households
headed by a woman totals 50.2 percent of the poverty population.

Table 7.4   Composition of the Poverty Population, 1959 to 1996 (in Millions)

Characteristics of Population	1959	1973	1979	1984	1996
All persons aged sixty-five or over	5.5	3.4	3.7	3.3	3.4
Nonelderly persons by living arrangement Persons in husband-wife families aged sixty-four or under	24.5	9.3	9.5	14.3	11.2
Persons in female-headed families aged sixty-four or under	6.4	7.6	9.3	11.6	14.2
Male unrelated individuals aged sixty-four or under	1.2	1.1	1.8	2.2	4.3
Female unrelated individuals aged sixty-four or under	1.9	1.6	1.8	2.3	4.0
Total persons in poverty (millions)	39.5	23.0	26.1	33.7	37.1
Percent of the population in poverty	22.4%	11.1%	11.7%	14.4%	13.9%
Percent of the poverty population who are black	25.1%	32.1%	30.9%	28.2%	26.4%

Sources: Author's tabulation of the 1960 Decennial Census Public Use Microdata Sample files and the Current Population Survey (various years).

The poverty figures seem to say that neither the elderly nor female-headed families were progressing, but that was not the case. The elderly were 15 percent of a *declining* poverty population, and it follows that the number of elderly poor was declining as well (table 7.4). The principal reason was Social Security. Real Social Security benefits had risen over the 1960s, and the proportion of the elderly who qualified for benefits rose as well, from 62 percent in 1960 to 88 percent in 1973.[23] Through these increases and growing private pensions, the proportion of elderly persons in poverty declined from 35 percent in 1959 to 16 percent in 1973.

Even female-headed families made some progress. Recall that before 1973 real wages rose for women as well as for men. Recall also that in the 1960s half of all female family heads worked. As real wages rose over the 1960s, the poverty rate among all female-headed families fell from 50 percent to 36 percent (and from 70 percent to 56 percent for blacks).[24] Thus, any individual female-headed family was less likely to be poor. This progress did not appear in aggregate statistics, however, because the total *number* of female-headed families was increasing rapidly (table 7.4).

As the composition of the poverty population changed, so did its sources of income. By 1973 only half of all families in poverty were headed by an employed person, while 30 percent had no working members at all. In the census definition of income (which excludes the value of Medicare, Medicaid, and food stamps), 50 percent of all income for poor families came from government payments. The welfare state had assumed a big responsibility. It would become even bigger when income growth slowed.

The Welfare State After 1973

By 1973, the welfare state had displayed the problems that would plague it for the next quarter century. As first conceived in 1935, the welfare state was to provide support for persons who could not support themselves through work and wages. Thirty years later, planners of the War on Poverty again looked to work and real wage growth as the major engines of poverty reduction—government benefits would help those whom the economy had missed.

Policy in the late 1960s had been quite different. The late 1960s expansion of AFDC and the passage of Medicaid increasingly rewarded people who did not work. One could imagine an antipoverty strategy centered on work—government subsidies for low wage jobs, the extension of Medicaid benefits to low-wage workers. There was a little of this—the food stamp program was open to low-income families on and off welfare. For the most part, however, government focused benefits on the non-working poor and left the benefits of work to be determined by the economy. This focus made sense (if it made sense at all) only if real wages continued to rise.

Once Social Security benefits were tied to the consumer price index, it too, depended heavily on rising real wages. If real wages kept growing, as Congress had assumed, indexed Social Security benefits could be financed with little strain. If real wages began to stagnate, maintaining indexed benefits would be a financial problem. The problem would be compounded because Medicare costs were rising quickly and because Social Security and Medicare recipients were becoming a strong political constituency.

After 1973, real wages stopped growing and these problems came into sharp relief. In the case of AFDC, the response over the next two decades was to become more restrictive. In the case of Social Security (with its more powerful constituency), the response was largely to pay the bill.

Published data on Social Security benefits per recipient combine two effects: cost-of-living increases and the fact that each year's new recipients retire at higher dollar salaries and so are entitled to higher benefits.[25] With this caveat in mind, the data show that between 1973 and 1984 the average benefits of a retired worker grew from $558 to $722 per month (in 1997 dollars), an increase of 38 percent (figure 7.10). Over this same period, the monthly cost of Medicare per eligible person increased from $91 to $189.[26]

Figure 7.10   Monthly Social Security and AFDC Benefits per Recipient (1997 Dollars)

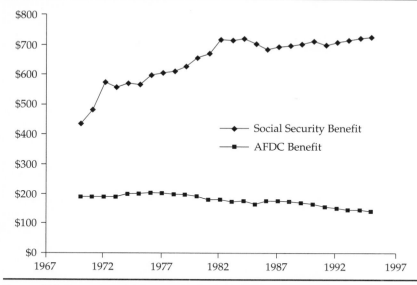

Sources: U.S. Department of Commerce, Bureau of the Census, *Statistical Abstract of the United States* (various years).

By the early 1980s, it was clear that this path could not be sustained. Reacting to the growing program cost and consistent with his goal of shrinking government, President Reagan proposed a broad set of benefit reductions early in his first term. His proposals were met by violent opposition from the elderly, an opposition encouraged by congressional Democrats, who had found no previous issue on which Reagan was vulnerable. In the end, Reagan and the Congress established a commission (headed by Alan Greenspan, the current chairman of the Federal Reserve), which proposed a modest set of reforms—phasing in an increase in the retirement age, treating half of Social Security benefits as taxable income, and briefly postponing cost-of-living adjustments. The episode underlined the point that Social Security and Medicare now served a very potent constituency.*

---

* The temptations of playing to this constituency are illustrated by a 1982 front-page headline in the *New York Daily News* (I cannot determine the precise date). Twice each year, Social Security benefits were raised by a percentage equal to the rate of inflation over the previous six months. Under a Greenspan commission reform, when inflation over a six month period totaled less than .5 percent (one half of one percent), the cost of living adjustment was postponed for six months and made part of the next adjustment. By the second half of 1982, Paul Volcker's tight money policy, supported by President Reagan, had effectively broken inflation (chapter 3) and in one six-month period, inflation fell to below .5 percent. Rather than celebrate the conquering of the 1970s inflation, the *Daily News* bemoaned the news that the Social Security adjustment would be postponed.

AFDC's constituency was much smaller. In the latter half of the 1960s, the National Welfare Rights Organization (NWRO) and similar organizations had achieved modest political power. By 1973, that power was gone. Most state and local administrators agreed that the welfare rolls had expanded too much, and many were tightening eligibility. Their decision was reinforced by the bad economy. Recall that the 1973–1974 OPEC price increase produced both inflation and unemployment. Most states are required to have balanced budgets, and so the economic forces were pulling states in two ways: inflation pointed to higher dollar expenditures, while unemployment led to falling tax revenues and tighter budgets. In the resulting scramble for funds, AFDC received very low priority, and benefits declined in real terms. The 1979–1980 OPEC price increase repeated the process, accentuated this time by new federal eligibility restrictions that were part of the Reagan administration's economic program.* Between 1975 and 1984, real AFDC benefits per recipient declined from $203 to $177 (both in 1997 dollars), or 13 percent.[27] Unlike AFDC, food stamp benefits were indexed to the consumer price index, but when food stamps and AFDC were added together, average benefits still declined in real terms.

AFDC program restrictions limited the number of welfare recipients, but it did little to slow the growth of female-headed families. Between 1973 and 1984—a period containing the blue collar recession—the number of AFDC cases increased from 3.2 million to 3.7 million (figure 7.9), but the number of female-headed families with children, many of them with low incomes, grew from 4.6 million to 6.8 million.

Elderly families did much better, supported by rising Social Security benefits and growing private pension coverage. In essence, elderly incomes rose while the rest of the income distribution was sinking around them. Many elderly families moved up from the bottom to the second quintile. Their vacated places at the bottom were taken by newly formed female-headed families (tables 2.5 and 7.3). Within the bottom quintile, earnings now represented only about two-fifths of all money income.

In many central cities (and for much of the black population), economic restructuring had been accelerating since the first oil price shock in 1973. In the nation as a whole, restructuring began in the blue-collar recession of 1980 to 1982, and it soon began to influence the poverty statistics. For much of the postwar period, recovery

---

* Reagan's AFDC changes were very similar to those made while he was governor of California—the so-called Reagan welfare reforms. See Levy (1978).

from a recession would drive down the poverty rate through falling unemployment and rising real wages. By the time of the 1976 recovery, real wages had stagnated and so the poverty rate stagnated as well, rising from 11.1 percent in 1973 to 11.9 percent in 1979. During the blue-collar recession, the poverty rate had risen sharply, to 15.2 percent in 1983. Unemployment then began to fall, but wages for semiskilled workers were falling as well and so the poverty rate fell slowly.*

Between 1973 and 1984, the number of persons in poverty increased by ten and a half million; the 1984 poverty rate was 14.4 percent. Half of this increase represented newly formed female-headed families (table 7.4). The other half were prime-age husband-wife families, pulled into poverty by the recession and the earnings declines for semiskilled workers. These official statistics overstate poverty because they fail to count nonmoney benefits like food stamps, Medicare, and Medicaid. In 1984, the value of these benefits would have lowered the poverty rate to about 11.5 percent, rather than the official 14.4 percent. But during the economic recovery, this adjusted rate, too, declined only slowly.[28] Through all of this, the number of poor elderly persons increased very little, a tribute to Social Security.

Taken together, these movements reversed traditional economic status across generations. Recall that during this period the proportion of all children in female-headed households was continuing to rise. This increase, combined with falling wages for semiskilled workers and falling AFDC benefits, caused the proportion of all children in poverty to increase sharply (figure 7.11). At the same time, indexed Social Security benefits and private pensions substantially reduced elderly poverty. Since poverty statistics had first been kept, the elderly had been disproportionately poor. By the mid-1980s, however, the overall poverty rate was about 14 percent, the elderly's poverty rate was 12 percent, and the poverty rate for children was 22 percent.[29]

Through the second half of the 1980s, the poverty population continued to stagnate, and by decade's end, AFDC rolls were increasing as well. In the white-collar recession year of 1992, the AFDC caseload stood at 4.9 million families, up from 3.7 million families in 1984. AFDC was paying benefits to one out of every seven U.S. children, and welfare was once again a subject of political debate.

In 1992 Bill Clinton, then a candidate for president, seized this issue by promising to "end welfare as we know it." Clinton's plan would center on a fixed time limit for welfare receipt coupled with child care, medical coverage, and other services to help recipients

---

* In particular, falling semiskilled wages were more important in the slow reduction of poverty than other factors, such as more female-headed families. See Blank (1993).

Figure 7.11 Official Poverty Rates for Children, the Elderly, and the General Population

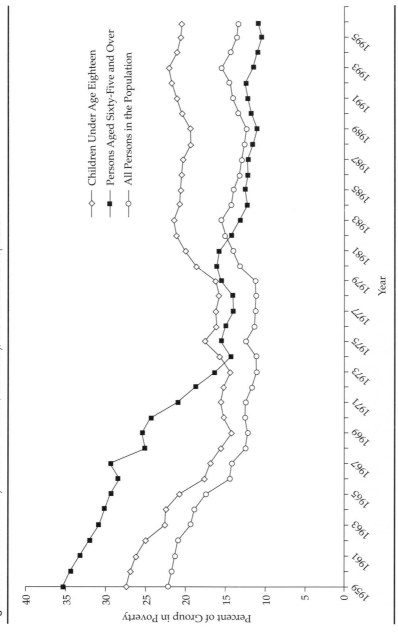

Sources: U.S. Department of Commerce, Bureau of the Census, *Current Population Reports* (various years).

move into work.* Without these supporting services, many recipients would be worse off taking a low-wage job than remaining on welfare, something Clinton wanted to avoid. The plan also provided jobs for persons who could not find private sector work.

Clinton did not introduce his welfare reforms until 1996. By that time, Republicans had gained control of Congress, and they changed Clinton's proposals substantially. The bill that emerged from Congress, the Personal Responsibility and Work Opportunity Reconciliation Act of 1996, terminated AFDC and replaced it with fixed-size block grants to the states along with wide latitude for states to design their own welfare programs. Most of Clinton's supporting services had been removed but states were now required to impose a limit on the total number of years an individual could receive welfare over his or her life.

The welfare reform legislation was one of several changes that modestly reshaped low-wage labor markets in the mid-1990s. Another was a major expansion of the Earned Income Tax Credit proposed by President Clinton and passed by Congress in 1993. Under this expansion—the third expansion since the EITC was passed in 1975—a family with two or more children received a maximum benefit of $3,556.† When this benefit was combined with food stamps and full-time work at the minimum wage, the family's total income now exceeded the poverty line by a small amount, an important symbolic step.

A third change in the low-wage labor market was an increase in the minimum wage itself. The increase, passed by Congress in 1996, raised the minimum wage from $4.25 an hour to $5.15 an hour over a period of two years. Since the early 1980s, increases in the minimum wage had lagged well behind inflation and even this increase did not restore the minimum wage to its 1981 value. Nonetheless, the increase represented a modest counter pressure against falling wages for the least educated workers.‡ The final and most important change, of course, was the strong macroeconomic climate with very low inflation

---

* The plan was based on the work of David Ellwood and is detailed in Ellwood (1989). Both Clinton's proposals and Ronald Reagan's earlier proposals substituted direct pressure on recipients for the 1960s approach of offering them incentives to work.
† A family was eligible for this maximum when its earnings were between $9,140 and $11,930. The family was eligible for a smaller benefit below or above this range. Benefits were adjusted annually for inflation. See Liebman (1997).
‡ Traditionally, economists have argued that a higher minimum wage hurts low-wage workers by causing a loss of employment. More recently, some economists have argued that moderate increases in the minimum wage do not have strong disemployment effects, and erosion of the minimum wage by inflation can be an important element in increased earnings inequality. See Card and Krueger (1995) and DiNardo, Fortin, and Lemieux (1995). In 1996, the strongest argument favoring an increase was the minimum wage's significant decline (in inflation adjusted terms) during the 1980s and 1990s.

and unemployment. Tight labor markets made employers willing to consider potential workers they would have ignored in less buoyant times.

Together these changes began to reverse some of the trends of the previous two decades. Wages at the bottom of the distribution began to rise more rapidly than average wage gains.[30] AFDC caseloads fell by 27 percent—1.8 million persons—between the passage of welfare reform and the spring of 1998.[31] Single women with children entered the labor force in significantly higher numbers.* The black poverty rate fell sharply. At the same time, the EITC became a major anti-poverty program with a total cost of about $23 billion per year. This cost was far smaller than the cost of Social Security ($350 billion per year) or Medicare ($178 billion per year) but the program now cost about as much as AFDC or food stamps.

In essence, current welfare reforms substitute the market for the traditional welfare state. While the reforms are still a work in progress, they give a sense of the benefits and limits of this approach. Earlier we argued that a welfare state has two major goals: to encourage individual responsibility and to provide a safety net. By relying on the market, welfare reform focuses on the first of these goals. Recall that between 1967 and 1975, the number of families on AFDC roughly doubled as a greater fraction of eligible families signed up for benefits. At that time, one could reasonably ask how those families had survived without AFDC, and whether many of the families could not put a member to work. The current welfare reforms are reversing that process by requiring significant numbers of recipients to get jobs or find alternative means of support.

At the same time, market-based welfare reform says little about a safety net. Despite recent gains in the bottom of the wage distribution, the bottom one-fifth of adult wage earners still earn less than $7.25 an hour. Because reform works with two government programs—the expanded EITC and food stamps—a mother and her children can have something like a poverty-level income if she can find full-time work. For many women on welfare, however, obtaining full-time work is not a plausible assumption even in the strong 1998 economy.[32] When the economy enters its next recession, the assumption will be untenable and presages a disaster.

A similar set of issues will confront the reform of Social Security. If productivity and wage growth continue at low levels, the current So-

---

* Liebman (1997) calculates that from 1984 through 1990, the labor force participation rate among single mothers, ages sixteen to forty-five, stood between .73 and .75. By 1996, it had risen to .83. The labor force participation rate among single women of the same age without children is about .95.

cial Security program—the current tax rates, the indexed benefits—is not sustainable. One proposal receiving significant current attention is market-based reform in which the Social Security trust fund is replaced by individual retirement accounts where workers are free to invest their contributions in a variety of financial instruments. Some advocates of this approach argue that the current system is very inefficient and that individual accounts invested in equities* would generate a rate of return perhaps five times as high as the returns projected for today's Social Security contributions.[33]

In reality, the low return on today's Social Security contributions is driven not so much by conservative investments as by two kinds of redistribution. One is the redistribution from current workers to current retirees. Recall that Social Security is largely a pay-as-you-go system. If current workers stopped contributing to the Social Security trust fund and invested only in their own accounts, the trust fund would be quickly exhausted and benefits to retirees and those about to retire would stop. It is inconceivable that Congress would abrogate these benefits, but maintaining the benefits depresses the return that today's workers will see.†

A second redistribution takes place from higher to lower earners. In Social Security, the relationship between benefits and contributions is purposely skewed so low-wage workers receive a larger benefit than their earnings alone imply while high earners receive a smaller benefit than their earnings imply. Abrogating this redistribution would give high earners a higher return on their retirement contribution at the cost of lowering the current system's minimum benefit. Here too, relying heavily on the market would stimulate individual responsibility—in this case, the responsibility to save more for one's own retirement—but it would do little to provide a safety net in very unequal times.

The Welfare State in Perspective

If we think about welfare state expenditure as a fraction of GDP, there is little question that this fraction is higher today than many people had intended. The fraction's increase had two quite different causes. After 1973, GDP—the fraction's denominator—grew much more slowly than people had expected, a product of the sudden slowdown

---

* By law, the Social Security trust fund must be invested in U.S. government securities.

† In essence, today's retirees are underfunded because past presidents and Congresses granted yesterday's retirees higher benefits than their contributions warranted. See Geanakoplos, Mitchell, and Zeldes (1998).

in productivity growth. At the same time, the cost of the welfare state—the fraction's numerator—grew much faster than people had expected and some part of this growth reflected the welfare state's own miscalculations.

The liberalization of AFDC payments in the mid-1960s made it easier for women to raise children on their own at a time when significant number of black males, in particular, were in economic trouble. The indexation of Social Security benefits proved far more expensive than Congress or President Nixon had anticipated. The passage of Medicare expanded demand for medical services and stimulated medical cost inflation. In these and other cases, the welfare state seemed to fight yesterday's war: maintaining a safety net when most people stayed married; when mothers were expected to stay home; when medical costs were low; when rising productivity and wages meant that work translated into self-sufficiency. These were good operating assumptions in the 1950s. They were unrealistic assumptions in the 1970s, 1980s, and 1990s, and they left the welfare state in clear need of reform.

At the same time, reform itself can be predicated on an economy that no longer exists. When we talk about policies for the future, we need to appraise the current economy with a clear eye. We make this appraisal in the final chapter.

CHAPTER 8

What Comes Next?

To this point, our twenty-year experiment with free markets has produced the three economic stories that opened this book: the outstanding performance in inflation and unemployment, the continued slow growth of wages, and high levels of inequality. Through the spring of 1998, the first story dominated public opinion. In one recent national poll, 53 percent of respondents said the nation is generally heading in the right direction. Sixty-four percent of respondents expect their children's generation to enjoy a higher standard of living than the current generation. While 56 percent of respondents said that the rich do not pay their fair share of taxes, only 6 percent said they resent the rich.[1]

When people said "this economy is as good as it gets," they meant it as a compliment. We now know it is also a word of caution. A fifth of all children live in poverty. A fifth of all prime-age black men report no earnings. The current Social Security program is unsustainable. The average wages of adult-male, high school graduates have fallen sharply in the last two decades. In chapter 1, we talked of a shared prosperity, the opportunity to progress over a career, and the opportunity for our children to do better than we have done. When we listed these goals, we had something more than the current economy in mind.

The compliment and the caution coexist because they describe different time frames. Inflation, unemployment, and the current value of the Dow Jones Industrial Index describe the economy's short-run performance. Through a mix of wise policy and luck, these short-run variables were about as good as they could get. By the late summer, the stock market had dropped sharply. But even if the stock market drop were followed by a recession, it would not mean the end of progress because our long-run economic progress depends less on these current conditions than on the three economic

187

variables described in chapter 1: the rate of productivity growth, the economy's level of skill bias, and the quality of our equalizing institutions.

The difference between short and long runs is illustrated by a story my father told me when I was writing *Dollars and Dreams*. When my father was growing up, his family moved several times, and he twice had to repeat the fifth grade. "I always thought," he said, "that the two lost years hurt my early career." I felt confident of all the income numbers I had gathered, and I challenged him on this point. "How much difference could two years make?" I asked. "You don't understand," he said. "I graduated college in 1932. In 1932, you couldn't find a job. The boys who got out in 1930 had a much easier time, and by '32, they were far enough up the ladder to hang on."

My father was right about his early career. Over his whole career, however, he did very well, a success built on his and my mother's initiative and a dose of good luck. Each of my parents were the first in their families to attend a four-year college. They had the bad luck, as my father said, to graduate college in the Great Depression, when neither their education nor their hard work could guarantee much. The twenty-six-year boom after World War II compensated for a lot of the bad luck, and my parents' hard work during that era of rising wages secured them a solid position in the American middle class.

When we compare today's economy to my parents' economy, two differences stand out. In terms of wages or family incomes, the average person's standard of living is about twice as high as my parents' was at the close of World War II. If we talk in terms of per capita income, the increase over fifty years is even higher.* At the same time, upward mobility—the likelihood of big income gains over one's life—is now far less likely than it was in the 1950s. Today's economy offers enormous entrepreneurial opportunities. Most people, however, do not make their living as entrepreneurs and so must rely on general economic trends.

An example illustrates how the trends have changed in fifty years. In 1949, the average thirty-year-old man, a man ten years younger than my father at that time, had an income of about $16,800 (table 4.3). This was not a great deal of money—a little more than the poverty standard for a family of four.† Twenty years later, however, this

---

* See chapter 3 for a discussion of the different trends in family income (and wages) and income per capita.

† Recall from chapter 7 that if poverty standard had been applied to 1949 incomes, about one-third of the population would have been counted as poor.

average man, now fifty, was making almost $40,000. His income had more than doubled in twenty years. An average income can obscure large underlying variations, but in those years, many people experienced big income gains: the rural migrant moved to an urban job, the unionized factory worker saw steady gains in pay, the white collar professional watched his earnings rise even through middle age. Rapid productivity and wage growth were strokes of good luck that helped us achieve many things: an expansion of the American middle class, a reduction in poverty, progress in assimilating minorities, and funding of the welfare state. Growing wages were also a de facto safety net for economic change.

Jump ahead to 1976. The average thirty-year-old wage and salary worker earned $31,100, close to twice as much as his 1949 counterpart. Over the next twenty years, however, his earnings would grow to $37,800, a gain of 22 percent spread over two decades. This slower average growth obscured big differences. Some men beat the average by substantial amounts. Among thirty-year-old male high school graduates, however, average wage and salary income rose modestly and then fell, ultimately moving from $27,600 at age thirty to $28,400 at age fifty.*

In preceding chapters, we have discussed the factors that account for this weak wage growth. First, of course, was the post-1973 slowdown in productivity growth. During much of my father's career, labor productivity grew at 2.5 to 3 percent per year. From 1973 to 1996, labor productivity has averaged about 1 percent per year. Second was the post-1979 surge in skill bias. In the 1950s and 1960s, the principal obstacle to high wages was working in the South or in other rural areas. Today education, far more than region, is the determinant of doing well, and the bottom of the family income distribution is increasingly populated by female-headed families, whose heads have not had any education beyond high school (table 2.4).

The final factor is the shift of power away from the average worker and toward a firm's shareholders. Deregulation, globalization, and technology have reduced the typical employee's bargaining power, and no countervailing institution has arisen to exert an opposite force. A few economists claim that despite these factors, almost all workers still experience substantial income mobility over their careers. Upon

---

* In interpreting these results, recall that we are adjusting for inflation using the Department of Commerce chain-weighted, personal consumption expenditure deflator, a fairly conservative measure of inflation. Standard measures like the consumer price index would show an earnings decline for high school graduates.

inspection, this claim is as overblown as the claim that IQ is the dominant determinant of earnings.*

Because the economy is constantly evolving, these three factors could reverse in a moment. Over 1996 and 1997, productivity growth averaged 1.6 percent per year. As we learn how to better integrate computers into the workplace, this higher rate of productivity growth could continue. If technology begins to replace workers in higher, as well as lower-skilled occupations, the economy's degree of skill bias could moderate, and the relative demand for less-educated workers would strengthen. If both reversals took place, many of the economy's current problems would disappear.[2] Most workers would see rising incomes without the need for big improvements in our schools. The Social Security program would return to solvency without benefit reductions or tax increases. Current welfare reforms could proceed in the knowledge that a working female high school graduate or dropout could earn a wage that was the starting point for a decent living.

If current trends do not reverse, we will face two substantial problems. One is that as much as a fifth of the population will increasingly fall behind the rest of the country, excluded from the economy's growth. The other is that a majority of the population will reject pro-growth policies and will turn the nation toward prolonged stagnation. This is an economic history book—not a book recommending detailed policies. Drawing on the work of others, however, I can sketch the kinds of policies that would give us a chance to avoid these problems.

Class and Opportunity

To rephrase Benjamin DeMott, America is a country where an opportunity society and a class society coexist within the same bor-

---

* In a widely cited 1994 study, W. Michael Cox and Richard Alm, economists at the Dallas Federal Reserve Bank, argue that income mobility is far more extensive than most persons believe. Writing in *The New York Times*, Cox described their study as giving "a startlingly optimistic picture of economic mobility. Take those who were in the bottom fifth of all earners in 1975. The conventional view would lead us to believe that these people were probably worse off in the 1990's. But the [data] found that only 5 percent were still in the bottom fifth in 1991." This result is indeed startling and it reflects the fact that Cox and Alm constructed a sample that included persons as young as age sixteen and that made no distinction between part-time and full-time workers. In this sample, the bottom fifth of all earners in 1975 was heavily weighted toward teenagers and wives with part-time jobs. Their upward mobility reflected the fact that they subsequently joined the full-time labor force. A more sensible measure of upward mobility examines the progress of adults who we expect to be working full time. Using the same data, Peter Gottschalk estimates the mobility of men, ages twenty to fifty-nine, in 1975. Among the bottom fifth of earners in 1975, 36 percent were in the bottom fifth in 1991; 24 percent were in the second fifth, and 40 percent had moved higher in the distribution. See Cox (1996), Cox and Alm (1996), and Gottschalk (1996).

ders.* Since 1979 and the blue-collar recession, economic change has sharpened the class structure along educational lines. Thirty years ago, this book about incomes would have described the rich, the poor, and a broad middle class containing high school and college graduates, most of whom had good prospects. Today's class structure is murkier. More institutions—clubs, neighborhoods, colleges—are now open to those who can afford them, but growing access has been offset by widening income differences. As a result, the 45 percent of the workforce who have not gone beyond high school are frequently viewed as downscale in both commercial and social terms.[3] The trick is to keep these lines from hardening further.

At the end of World War II, one dimension of downscale status was living in a rural area. Faced with poor prospects, rural residents migrated to urban areas. Getting an education, as we have noted, is harder than getting on a bus. Education is a cumulative process involving parental and peer attitudes toward learning as well as school quality. If attitudes are not established in the first twenty years of life, it is hard to get an education later. The growing number of community colleges serve an important purpose here, offering a second chance to people whose initial education was weak.[4] If education is to retain its role as a major equalizing institution, however, we must address the problem described in chapter 6: the communities most hurt by the post-1979 surge in skill bias are the communities now expected to make the biggest improvements in their schools.

Many states' agendas already include plans to improve schools at least in a general way. It is when we get to specifics that disagreements arise. In education as in other areas of social policy, some of the most discussed reforms have a strong market flavor: charter schools, public school choice, vouchers or tax credits that could be applied to any school. As with other market-based solutions, the problem is to expand individual choice while maintaining a safety net. In striking this balance, a plan's details are crucial. A choice plan can require a participating school to accept the plan's voucher as full tuition and to admit some fraction of its student body from a lottery of applicants. Alternatively, a choice plan can permit a school to hand pick every student and to require parents to pay a substantial surcharge on top of the voucher.† The first design may help to raise the achievement of

---

* DeMott, writing about race, actually referred to the "double truth that within our borders, an opportunity society and a *caste* society coexist" (italics added). See DeMott (1995) p. 59.

† See Murnane and Levy (1996) chapter 8, for a description of California's Proposition 189, which, before it appeared on the ballot, had metamorphosized from the first description to the second.

low-income students; the second design almost surely will not. To be effective, even a well-designed choice program must work in conjunction with academic standards. Such standards are important because they give parents something most parents now lack—information on how the schools are preparing their children for the labor market. Without this information, a parent's choice among schools will be made on other grounds—discipline, teacher enthusiasm, and other readily observable factors. These characteristics are important, but they do not directly address the causes of the widening earnings distribution.* Better U.S. schools are attainable—in 1940, three quarters of the adult population had not graduated from high school[5]—but based on past experience, these changes will take time.

As we move toward the bottom of the income distribution, educational issues merge with more immediate problems. Any teacher in a low-income school will attest that enthusiasm and a good curriculum mean little when a child's family is in chaos, and the child passes through two or three different schools in a year. Families in chaos are not a new problem. What is new is the growing penalty for receiving a bad education and that many family problems are being compounded by current welfare reforms. It is one thing to argue in favor of work requirements; in today's economy, however, work is not a guarantee of self-sufficiency. It follows that beyond better education, a second item on the nation's agenda must be a better safety net for workers. Rebecca Blank has outlined one version of such a safety net including the Earned Income Tax Credit, a second refundable child credit for low-income families, the enforcement of child support from absent fathers, and the broader availability of medical care for low-income persons not on welfare.[6] In today's economy, some program along these lines—safety net benefits conditioned on work—is part of a sensible definition of equal opportunity. Within this program, one critical piece is the ability to create public employment during a recession. In the spring of 1998—"an economy as good as it gets"—surveys indicated that at most one-half of women who have left the welfare rolls in the last year had found work. When a recession eventually comes and AFDC no longer exists as a safety net, the consequences are potentially severe.

An obstacle to strong equalizing institutions is the tendency of some groups to "pile on"—to reduce spending on these institutions so as to enhance their own position. The politics of piling on begins with various myths, some of which we have examined: that earnings

---

* Because parental information is weak, opinion polls suggest parents believe that U.S. public schools are seriously deficient but the public schools attended by their own children are fine. This satisfaction weakens the pressure for serious reform. See Murnane and Levy (1996) chapter 1, for an explanation of this view.

are tightly tied to genetic inheritance, or that almost all people still experience substantial economic mobility within the income distribution. While these myths sometimes contradict each other, they serve to justify the currently high level of inequality, which includes very low incomes at the bottom of the distribution. It is a short step to argue that the market's domain should be expanded to further improve economic performance.

A case in point was the unsuccessful 1997 attempt by congressional Republicans to sharply reduce the size of the Earned Income Tax Credit. The budgetary savings would have been used to fund tax cuts for families further up in the income distribution. Proponents of this plan described the EITC as "welfare," a category that made it a legitimate target for reduction.[7] The Earned Income Tax Credit is far from perfect—fraud, while declining, continues to be a problem.[8] At this time, however, when technology and trade have undercut wages for less educated workers, proposing sharp reductions in the EITC is flirting with social Darwinism.

Other examples of piling on are not so blatant.* Rather, they emerge from what we accept as our normal way of doing business. Consider the case of imported shrimp. In the spring of 1998, the World Trade Organization (WTO) invalidated the U.S. ban on shrimp imported from four countries: India, Pakistan, Malaysia, and Thailand.[9] The United States had imposed the restriction under the 1973 Endangered Species Act because the four countries caught shrimp with nets that could also snare giant sea turtles. Other countries fished for shrimp using nets with safety hatches that allowed the turtles to escape.

The WTO based its rejection of the ban on the General Agreement on Tariffs and Trade (GATT), the legal structure that governs world trade. Under GATT, a country cannot discriminate against a good based on the process by which it was made if the regulation has the effect of discriminating against specific importers.† This broad anti-process principle is relevant to our story because it covers not only shrimp caught with suspect nets but products produced with child labor.

The principle is in line with the economic logic of international trade theory. The exporting nation should produce a good any way it

---

* Another potentially blatant case is California's Proposition 229, a state constitutional amendment which would have required California unions to obtain annual approval from their members for using union dues in political campaigns. The proposition contained no symmetrical requirement for corporations to obtain shareholder approval for corporate political donations. As Jack Citrin points out, the thrust of the campaign was not so much aimed against low-wage workers as against the powerful California teachers union. At the same time, the proposition (and similar propositions in other states) had a reach that was potentially broader. Proposition 229 was defeated in June 1998.

† The only exception mentioned in the GATT are goods made with prison labor.

chooses, and the importing nation should let consumers decide whether or not to buy the good—the government per se should not restrict imports. The problem is that this economic theory is concerned only with maximizing economic growth and not with the distribution of that growth. As the economist Dani Rodrik[10] argues, U.S. citizens might object to imports made with child labor, not because they want to dictate the policies of other countries, but because they fear that such imports might undermine child-labor laws and other labor protections in our own country.

The appropriate role of child-labor restrictions in trade agreements is not an easy thing to decide.[11] Less-developed countries argue that any restriction on child labor is simply a way to limit their exports and retard their development, leaving their children even deeper in poverty. Based on past experience, we know that these disputes will be negotiated by neutral, well-educated experts, few of whose jobs will be threatened by the importation of child-made baseball caps.

There is a rationale for such neutral experts, and I will return to it shortly. For the present, note that a general lack of focus on equalizing institutions is consistent with the widening family- and household-income distributions (chapter 7). As incomes spread out and lower-income families are increasingly disconnected from the rest of the population, policies that hurt the bottom of the income distribution—policies that reinforce what the market is already doing—lose some of their stigma and inspire less emotion. Building a decent safety net around work requires that we see ourselves as a nation and that some of this emotion return.

The All-Important Caveat

To sustain economic progress, equalizing institutions must include more than just families at the bottom of the income distribution. The inclusion is more than altruism. If markets produce increasingly unequal outcomes, unmoderated by institutions, we can reasonably expect a collapse of popular support for markets and other pro-growth policies.

In political terms, we have justified our growing reliance on markets with two arguments. The first is that free markets enhance individual freedom. The second is that free markets accelerate economic growth, which benefits everyone. In making this second argument, people repeat the phrase often used by John F. Kennedy, "A rising tide lifts all the boats."*

---

* A researcher at the John F. Kennedy Library has told me that Kennedy used this phrase at a number of different times and in slightly different versions. The library's earliest record of the phrase was on October 15, 1960, during Kennedy's presidential campaign.

At the risk of killing poetry, we can see now that Kennedy was describing the skill-neutral growth of the 1950s and 1960s, a time when displaced agricultural workers could move into manufacturing jobs. When economic growth is skill biased, large portions of the population can lose ground even as the economy grows. During Ronald Reagan's eight years in office, the nation's GDP (in constant dollars) grew by 23 percent and earnings of the average thirty-year-old male high school graduate fell by 7 percent.

Economists know that growth does not automatically benefit everyone and so our support for growth rests on a caveat: Since economic growth expands the nation's economic pie, the winners have the extra income to compensate the losers and still be better off themselves. This caveat is the rationale for having trade law disputes decided by neutral experts: The experts will seek to expand trade; more trade means a bigger GDP, and so the potential exists for everyone to be better off.

If the nation forgets the caveat—if winners see no reason to compensate losers in a time of change—popular support for free market policies will decline. In 1997, with the unemployment rate at 4.9 percent, Congress turned back President Clinton's request for fast-track authority to negotiate international trade agreements under NAFTA. That vote had many motivations, but one was the argument that expanded trade was costing the jobs of unionized supporters of the Democratic party.* When the next recession comes, it is easy to imagine a broader reconsideration of the market: new restrictions on international trade; tighter limits on immigration; a much tougher policy on mergers; regulations limiting numbers of layoffs; and congressional investigations of "excessive" executive compensation.†

Opponents will argue that many of these policies smack of "European economics." In Europe, such policies are now blamed, often correctly, for strangling job creation and economic growth. If, however, people come to believe that economic growth is something that benefits a small fraction of the population, stagnation and temporary security will not seem like such bad choices. Even some loss of freedom—for example, the loss of choice that comes from returning to regulated markets—may not look so bad if the free market generates enough insecurity.

A movement down this road is a short-term fix with a very high long-term cost. Avoiding it requires institutions that allow the gains from economic growth to be more equally shared. For example, if

---

* A different motivation among congressional Republicans—normally free-trade supporters—was that President Clinton had successfully stolen much of their agenda, and this was a chance to hand him a defeat.
† Congressional grilling of Microsoft's Bill Gates in the spring of 1998 had a little of this flavor.

current trends continue, it is likely job security will continue to decline at a moderate rate. In such a labor market, employees must have access to health insurance and the ability to save enough money for retirement even if they do not have a long tenure with a single employer. A strong Social Security program is one element here. The growth of 401(k) retirement plans is a second. A third element is the reforms of individual-health-insurance markets now being undertaken in New Jersey and a small number of other states.* These specific changes are likely to be a part of a more general change—some restoration of the balance of power between employees and shareholders, which technology and increased trade have undermined. This will be no easy job. Paul Osterman (forthcoming) is one among a number of persons who is addressing what it involves.

In 1998, with an unemployment rate below 5 percent, an agenda of this kind seems nice but not urgent. The problem, however, is to develop a robust set of economic and political arrangements—arrangements that can continue to support pro-growth policies even when the economy is not as good as it gets.

Unfinished Business

I opened this book by suggesting that an economy was something like a river, always evolving and showing new faces. When we see an economic problem, our impulse is to fix it permanently. The economy's changing nature makes this impulse pure hubris. The best we can do is to try to fix today's problems and get ready for what comes next.

Our current free-market experiment, like the Keynesian experiment before it, has produced a great deal of good as well as some serious problems. The aggregate economy is far stronger today than it was twenty years ago. Increased technology and expanded trade are clearly engines of growth. For the present, however, they are propelling growth in a very unequal way. As in all periods of rapid transition, the demand side of the labor market is changing far more quickly than people can change their skills so many families and individuals are in serious trouble. In this situation, a reliance on markets to the exclusion of all other policies is as unrealistic as was the sublime faith in Keynesian economics thirty years ago.

---

* In the individual-health-insurance market, a single person or family buys insurance directly from an insurance company rather than through an employer's group policy. For a discussion of New Jersey's successful reforms of this market, see B. Katherine Swartz and Deborah Garnik (1998).

There is, of course, an important difference between today's failures and the failures of Keynesian economics. By the early 1970s, the Keynesian experiment had ended in a stubborn inflation that hurt everyone. The current free market creates high-income winners as well as low-income losers. Under our current political system, the winners are in a much stronger position to influence policy. Their first choice, of course, is allow an even greater expansion of the market.

For the good of the nation, we should recognize that as powerful as the market is, it cannot accomplish all of our goals. Almost a half-century ago, the sociologist Robert A. Nisbet showed how freedom can thrive only within a structure of authority.[12] In a similar way, we can see that in a free society, economic progress can thrive only within a structure of fair treatment. This is an easy idea to deny. Most market forces are anonymous—no one to blame—and so it is easy to conclude that all market outcomes are fair. If we choose this denial, we will find we have made both fair treatment and economic progress commodities in short supply.

Appendix

This appendix contains supplementary information on five topics.

1. Official census trends in family and household income inequality including a definition of the gini coefficient, one standard measure of inequality.
2. Official census trends in the level of family and household incomes.
3. The extent to which these trends change when improvements are made to the official census definition of income.
4. Summary statistics on the distribution of household wealth.
5. A comparison of the average incomes of Asian families with other families.

Official Income Inequality

A broad description of family income inequality begins by ranking families in a list from poorest to richest and dividing the list into five groups of equal numbers of families (quintiles). With this information, we then ask the questions: What share of all family income is received by the poorest one-fifth of families? What share of family income is received by the second fifth of families (the "next to poorest")? Table A.1 contains census data on the income shares of each one-fifth of families as well as the richest 5 percent of families (a part of the top one-fifth) for selected years between 1947 and 1996. Table A.2 contains similar income share data for the household income distribution.*

---

* Recall that a family consists of two or more persons in a living unit related by blood, adoption, or marriage. Households include both families and persons who live by themselves or with unrelated roommates. The census did not begin to compile information on household incomes until the late 1960s.

Table A.1 Share of Aggregate Family Income Received by Each Fifth and Top 5 Percent of Families

Year	1st Quintile (Poorest)	2nd Quintile	3rd Quintile	4th Quintile	5th Quintile (Richest)	Top 5 Percent[a]	Gini Coefficient
1947	5.0%	11.9%	17.0%	23.1%	43.0%	17.5%	0.376
1949	4.5	11.9	17.3	23.5	42.7	16.9	0.378
1959	4.9	12.3	17.9	23.8	41.1	15.9	0.361
1969	5.6	12.4	17.7	23.7	40.6	15.6	0.349
1979	5.4	11.6	17.5	24.1	41.4	15.3	0.365
1989	4.6	10.6	16.5	23.7	44.6	17.9	0.401
1996	4.2	10.0	15.8	23.1	46.8	20.3	0.425

Source: U.S. Department of Commerce, Bureau of the Census, *Current Population Reports* (various years).
[a]Top 5 percent is contained in the fifth quintile.

Table A.2 Share of Aggregate Household Income Received by Each Fifth and Top 5 Percent of Households

Year	1st Quintile (Poorest)	2nd Quintile	3rd Quintile	4th Quintile	5th Quintile (Richest)	Top 5 Percent[a]	Gini Coefficient
1969	4.1%	10.9%	17.5%	24.5%	43.0%	16.6%	0.391
1979	4.2	10.3	16.9	24.7	44.0	16.4	0.404
1989	3.8	9.5	15.8	24.0	46.8	18.9	0.431
1996	3.7	9.0	15.1	23.3	49.0	21.4	0.455

Source: U.S. Department of Commerce, Bureau of the Census, *Current Population Reports* (various years).
[a]Top 5 percent is contained in the fifth quintile.

Figure A.1   The Lorenz Curves of the 1973 and 1996 Family Income Distributions

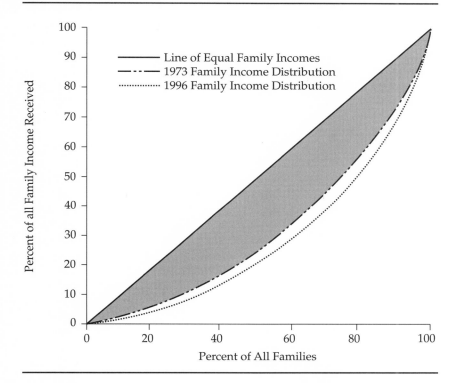

These six figures—the shares of the five quintiles and of the top 5 percent—describe the shape of the distribution, but they are cumbersome and so a variety of measures try to collapse this information into a single inequality statistic. One traditional statistic, used in census publications, is the gini coefficient, a measure best described using a Lorenz curve (figure A.1). The Lorenz curve also begins with a list of families, ranked in ascending income, but then asks a slightly different set of questions:

What percentage of all family income goes to the poorest 1 percent of families?

What percentage of all family income goes to the poorest 5 percent of families?

What percentage of all family income goes to the poorest 10 percent of families?

These questions are repeated until the whole distribution is described.

If all families received equal incomes of, for example, $42,300, the poorest 1 percent of families would receive 1 percent of all family income, the poorest 5 percent of families would receive 5 percent of all family income, and this equality would continue through the distribution. This equal family income distribution is represented by the diagonal line in figure A.1.

In practice, the U.S. income distribution is not equal so that in 1996 census statistics, the poorest one-fifth of families received 4.2 percent of all income, the poorest two-fifths of families received 14.2 percent and so on. This actual distribution is illustrated by the lower of the two curved lines in the figure. This curved line lies below the line of equal incomes because the poorest one-fifth of families receives less than one-fifth of all family income, the poorest two-fifths of families receives less than two-fifths of all family income, and so on up the income scale. The greater the degree of inequality, the lower the curve will be. Thus in the figure, the Lorenz curve for the 1996 family income distribution lies below the Lorenz for 1973 when incomes were moderately more equal.

The gini coefficient for a particular year's distribution is defined as twice the size of the shaded area between the diagonal line and the distribution's Lorenz curve. If income were distributed equally, the curve would *become* the straight line and the gini coefficient would be zero. If all income were received by one family (complete inequality), the "curve" would coincide with the bottom axis of the figure—all families except the richest one would receive nothing while the last family would receive 100 percent of the income. The shaded area would equal .5 (half of a 1.0 x 1.0 square) and the gini coefficient would equal 1.0.* Tables A.1 and A.2 contain gini coefficients along with income share information.

How should we view these data? In 1984, as the United States was rediscovering inequality, a panel of the Conference of Catholic Bishops issued the "First Draft Pastoral Letter on Catholic Social Teaching and the U.S. Economy," a document which noted that the top 20 percent of families received more income that the bottom 70 percent. The panel wrote: "In our judgment, the distribution of income and wealth in the United States is so inequitable that it violates [a] minimum standard of distributive justice."[1]

Media discussion of the bishops' letter implied that the inequality was something new. In fact, family income inequality has been this high throughout the post–World War II period. In 1947, the poorest

---

* Note, however, that collapsing a two-dimensional distribution into a single number loses some information such that many different changes in the distribution's shape can cause the same change in the gini coefficient. For more discussion, see Levy and Murnane (1992) section 2.

one-fifth (quintile) of America's families received 5 percent of all family income while the richest quintile received 43 percent (gini coefficient of .376, table A.1). Inequality declined steadily through the late 1960s, but even in 1969, a low point in family income inequality, the income share of the share of the poorest one-fifth of families had risen to only 5.6 percent of all family income (gini coefficient of .349). Family income inequality stabilized in census measures through the mid-1970s and then began to rise. In 1996, the latest figures available, the share of the poorest one-fifth of families stands at 4.2 percent of all family income, compared to 5 percent in 1947, while the share of the richest fifth stands at 46.8 percent, compared to 43 percent in 1947 (with a gini coefficient of .425, compared to .376 in 1947).

Because household-income statistics mix families and single-person households, their absolute level of inequality is somewhat higher. These statistics trace a similar pattern of rising inequality beginning in the 1970s such that today the top one-fifth of households receive about one-half of all household income. At these levels, U.S. income inequality is higher than income inequality in most other industrialized countries.*

In 1947, the bottom of the income distribution was dominated by farm families (particularly in the South) and elderly families. Over time, the number of farm families declined substantially while the incomes of elderly families improved substantially. These two factors should have caused a steady decline in income inequality, but income inequality only declined until the late 1960s. This is one of the two major stories of the post–World War II period.

Official Income Levels

In assessing official data for average incomes, it is important to recall that the census defines income as pre-tax money receipts excluding capital gains. This definition facilitates data collection, but it differs in several respects from a family's purchasing power. It does not reduce income for taxes paid. Conversely it does not increase income for the receipt of such non-money income as employer-provided health insurance or government-provided Medicare or food stamps.

With this caveat in mind, official census statistics for median family income tell a straightforward story (all figures in 1997 dollars). In

---

* As in the United States, most other industrialized countries have experienced growth in *earnings* inequality, but governmental safety nets have moderated the translation of greater earnings inequality into greater family- and household-income inequality. See Gottschalk and Smeeding (1997).

Figure A.2 Median Incomes 1947 to 1996

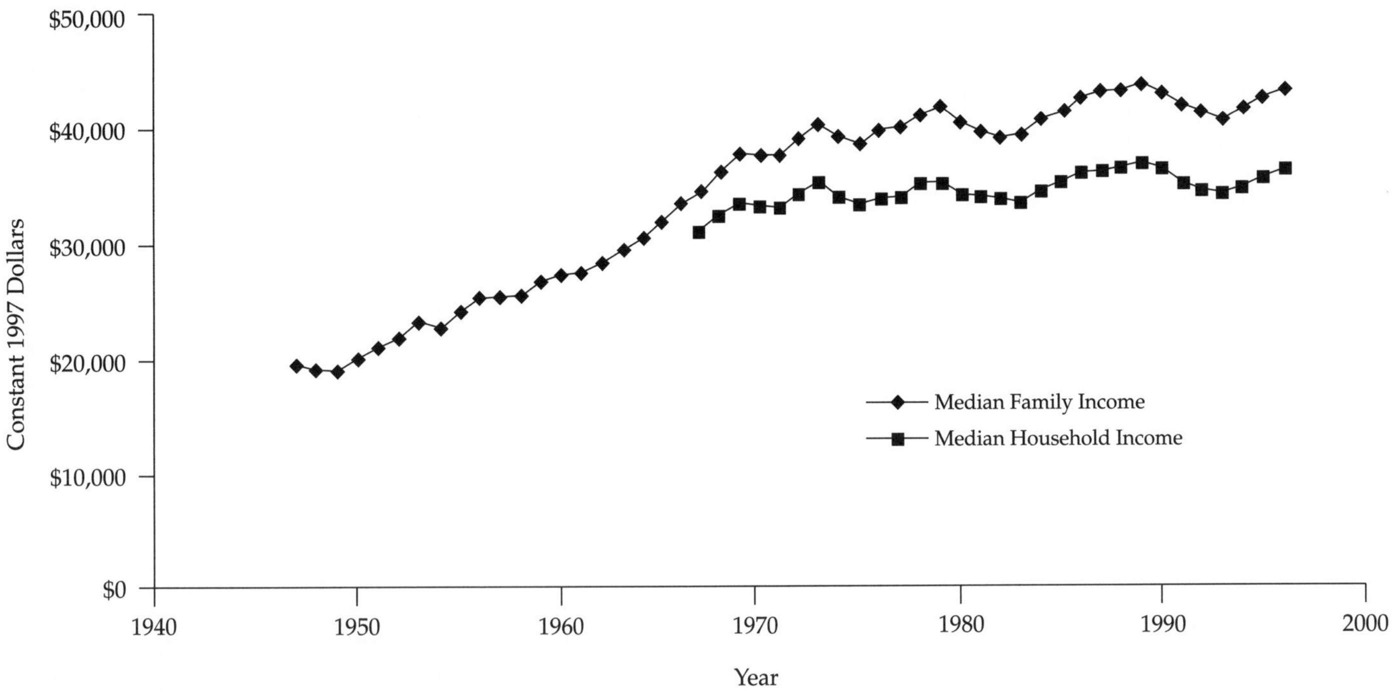

Sources: U.S. Department of Commerce, Bureau of the Census, *Current Population Reports* (various years).

1947, median family income stood at about $19,500 (figure A.2). That was the beginning of a period of substantial growth during which family income (adjusted for inflation) never went more than three years without setting a new record. By the early 1970s, median family income had more than doubled reaching $40,400 in 1973. Growth then slowed substantially and family income peaked at $43,601 in 1989. In 1996, it stood at $42,300.

This sudden break in trend—twenty-six years of strong income growth followed by twenty-three years of much weaker growth—is the other major economic story of the postwar period. The difference between the two periods was the post-1973 collapse of productivity growth. Family incomes also reflect demographic factors—more female-headed families, more two-earner families—but in historical data demographic factors are dominated by the rate of wage growth. For example, in the mid-1960s, Senator Daniel Patrick Moynihan, then an assistant secretary of labor, pointed to the issue of the rapidly growing number of female-headed families.[2] Yet during the 1960s, median family income still grew by more than 40 percent. Median household incomes (available since the late 1960s) trace a similar pattern.

The Effect of Alternative Income Definitions on Historical Trends

As noted above, the census defines income as pre-tax money receipts, excluding capital gains. This focus on money income misses the growing importance of non-money forms of income including employer-provided health insurance, Medicaid, Medicare, and food stamps. The exclusion of capital gains potentially blurs income movements particularly in the upper part of the distribution. The focus on pre-tax income conceals the impact of tax changes upon living standards.

A second set of problems in census numbers involves information on the distribution's upper tail. To preserve confidentiality, census interviewers record incomes only up to fixed limits. In 1996, individual earnings above $1,000,000 were recorded as $1,000,000 or more and the number was treated as $1,000,000 in census inequality calculations.* The problem is compounded by a frequent failure of high-income households to respond to census questions—a problem the census addresses by imputing (estimating) their responses.†

---

* The data tapes released to the researchers for analysis contain substantially lower income caps.

† Imputation is made based on the incomes of persons with generally similar characteristics. See Lillard, Smith, and Welch (1986).

Suppose we could fix these data problems. How would the revised data change our pictures of income growth and inequality? First, we look at income growth. Since 1979, the census has produced two sets of household-income statistics: the official set (described earlier) and a second set, which estimates adjustments for federal and state income taxes, property taxes and the value of non-money income including government- and employer-provided health insurance and food stamps.* The estimates do not address reporting limits on high incomes, but they are suitable for calculating median income and its growth.† In 1995, the official census estimate of median household income was $34,076 (in 1995 dollars). The same estimate adjusted for taxes paid (an income loss) and the value of government programs and employer-provided benefits (an income gain) was $33,306. Under either the standard definition or the adjusted definition, the growth of median household income between 1979 and 1989 was about 4 percent.[3] Thus a more accurate picture of income does not change the picture of slow average income growth in recent years.‡

With respect to inequality, these same census estimates suggest that adjusting for taxes and non-money income—the combination of government benefits and employer-provided benefits—reduces inequality only slightly.§ A complete inequality story, however, requires better information on the upper tail of the income distribution, and this means turning to non-census data.

Statistics on very high incomes (above the census reporting limits) are available annually from the U.S. Treasury's *Statistics of Income*, a summary of the distribution of adjusted gross incomes reported on tax returns. *Statistics of Income* includes detailed information on the size and sources of a representative sample of U.S. tax returns includ-

---

* Most of these adjustments are based on computer simulations rather than direct household responses. In practice, few household members could quickly tell an interviewer the dollar value of the health insurance provided by their employer or the state income taxes they paid last year.

† Median household income is the income level such that half of all households have higher incomes and half have lower incomes. While the census estimates retain reporting limits on the incomes of high-income families, these families remain at the top of the income distribution and so leave the calculation of median income unchanged.

‡ Recall from chapter 3 that income per capita during this period rose more rapidly because household size was declining as more young persons postponed marriage and lived alone.

§ In 1989, for example, census estimates suggest that including the value of employer-provided health insurance in household income would leave the gini coefficient unchanged (since it is received throughout the distribution) while including the value of non-cash government benefits would lower the gini coefficient by .03. See U.S. Bureau of the Census (1992), table 1.

Table A.3   Gini Coefficient Measures of Household Income Inequality Under
Alternative Income Definitions

	1979	1989
a. Standard census definition (pre-tax money income, no capital gains, income reporting limits)	.403	.431
b. CBO definition (pre-tax money income, includes capital gains, no income reporting limits)	.467	.526
c. CBO definition less taxes.	.424	.485

Sources: Line a: U.S. Department of Commerce, Bureau of the Census (1992). Lines b and c: unpublished tabulations of the Congressional Budget Office.

ing returns with very high incomes. To preserve confidentiality, the data contain no information about the person or persons filing the tax return.* Nonetheless, the U.S. Congressional Budget Office (CBO) has constructed a crude merge of census household-income statistics with the treasury data that gives us a better picture of recent inequality trends in money income.†

The first two lines of table A.3 compare official census estimates and comparable CBO estimates of household income inequality over the 1980s. The CBO estimate differs from the census estimate by including income from capital gains and putting no upper limit on reported income.‡ With these additions, it is not a surprise that the CBO estimate of 1979 household-income inequality is higher than the census estimate for the same year (first column, line b versus line a). More important, however, the CBO numbers report a greater increase in inequality over the 1980s than does the census. The faster growth of inequality in the CBO estimate shows that during the 1980s, census-income cutoffs obscured significant income growth at the extreme upper tail of the distribution. This growth is discussed in chapter 5.

The CBO estimates also permit us to see how the tax system affects money-income inequality. In table A.3, lines b and c compare house-

---

* The Treasury excludes personal information for reasons of confidentiality. In addition, since the data is based on tax returns, they exclude any observations of persons too poor to pay taxes.

† Non-money income is not included in the CBO data set.

‡ The two distributions also differ in that CBO weights each household's income by the number of persons in that household while the census counts each household's income only once. This difference may lead to divergent inequality estimates in a single year, but it unlikely to cause significant divergent estimates of the *change* in inequality over the 1980s.

hold-income inequality in the CBO data before and after all taxes are paid. Taken as a whole, the tax system is mildly progressive so that after-tax income is more equal than pre-tax income (first column, line c versus line b). But over the 1980s, inequality in after-tax income grew slightly faster than inequality in pre-tax income.*

The Distribution of Wealth

While income statistics are collected annually by the Census Bureau and the U.S. Treasury, the best wealth data are collected only periodically by the Federal Reserve Board in its *Survey of Consumer Finances* (SCF). These household surveys allow computation of a household's net worth, the value of its assets held—stocks, savings accounts, the value of the principal residence and so on—minus the value of any liabilities including an unpaid mortgage balance, consumer debts. The assets include stock held in 401(k) plans and other retirement accounts, but they do not include the value of employer provided pension plans or the implicit value of Social Security payments since neither of those assets are readily convertible into cash.

Analyses of these data show a distribution of net worth that has been fairly stable over time but is far less equal than the distribution of current income (table A.4). In 1995, the top one-half of 1 percent (.005) of households—about a half-million households out of one hundred million—held 27.5 percent of all household net worth, an average of $11.9 million per household (in 1997 dollars).[4] The bottom 89.9 percent of all households combined held 31.5 percent of all net worth. Within this lower group, net worth averaged $75,800, but there is significant inequality around this average. Among *all* households, half had a net worth below $57,000 including 10 percent of households who had a net worth that was zero or negative.

The Incomes of Asian Families

In 1995, the census counted 1.6 million families of Asian or Pacific Islander decent. This number compared to 8.1 million black families and 58.4 million white families (both groups include families identifying themselves as Hispanics). Like Hispanics, immigration has made Asians an increasingly heterogeneous group ranging from well-educated Japanese and Chinese to rural-born Cambodians.

---

* This is consistent with the analysis of CBO data by Gramlich, Kasten, and Sammartino (1993), which indicates that over the 1980s federal taxes did become somewhat less progressive but that tax changes account for only a small part of the growth in household-income inequality.

Table A.4 Trends in the Distribution of Household Net Worth

Percentile of Households	Share of Net Worth Held by Percentile Groups of Households				
	Bottom 89.9 Percent	90 to 98.9	99 to 99.4	Top .5 Percent	Gini Coefficient
1983	33.4%	35.1%	7.2%	24.3%	n.a.
1989	32.5	37.1	7.3	23.0	0.777
1992	32.9	36.9	7.5	22.7	0.782
1995	31.5	33.2	7.6	27.5	0.788

Percentile of Households	Average Net Worth per Household Within Percentile Group, 1995			
	Bottom 89.9 Percent	90 to 98.9	99 to 99.4	Top .5 Percent
Mean net worth within group (1997 dollars)	$75,844	$807,456	$3,290,140	$11,905,118

Source: Kennickell and Woodburn (1997).
Note: n.a. refers to information that is not available.

The relatively small number of Asian families means that the Current Population Survey contains too few observations of Asian incomes to construct a full income distribution or to create detailed pictures of earnings by age and education. It is, however, possible to compare the median income of all Asian families with the median incomes of other racial groups. In 1995, Asian families had median family income of $48,200 (in 1997 dollars) compared to $42,700 for all white families (including Hispanics) and $25,800 for all black families.[5]

Notes

Chapter 1

1. The most accessible data on income inequality are series developed by the U.S. Census that begin in 1947. For two good recent surveys of inequality trends before 1947, see Ryscavage (1998) and Plotnick et al. (1998).
2. Gray is using the term "liberal" in the 19th century meaning of the term, and he would argue, for example, that broadly distributed economic growth is not an unmitigated good. See Gray (1995) p. 102.
3. Some alternative data sources provide better detail on individual and household incomes for selected years. No other data source provides consistent data going back to World War II.
4. See, for example, Advisory Commission to Study the Consumer Price Index (1995).

Chapter 2

1. See chapter 1 for a discussion of inflation adjustment.
2. For pre-1947 incomes and consumption, see U.S. Bureau of the Census, *Historical Statistics*, series G319–36 and G416–69 (1975b).
3. U.S. Bureau of the Census (1975b).
4. U.S. Bureau of the Census (1975b).
5. See Lampman and Smeeding (1983) pp. 45–66.
6. See Lebergott (1976) and Blinder (1980).
7. Blinder (1980) pp. 428–9.
8. Infant mortality refers to children dying before age one. Infant mortality and life expectancy rates come from U.S. Department of Commerce, Bureau of the Census (1952b) tables 70 and 83; and (1996b) tables 116 and 120.
9. See Converse et al. (1980) table 1.24.
10. See U.S. Department of Commerce, Bureau of the Census (1982) p. 7.
11. See Williamson (1980).
12. See Kain (1968).

13. Author's tabulations from U.S. Department of Commerce, Bureau of the Census (1952a). In 1947 the ten largest cities were, in order, New York, Chicago, Detroit, Philadelphia, Cleveland, St. Louis, Los Angeles, Baltimore, San Francisco, and Washington, D.C.
14. See Long and Dahmann (1980).
15. I discuss the evolution of the Social Security program in chapter 7. On the evolution of private pensions, see Blinder (1982).
16. See, for example, Smith and Welch (1979) pp. 40–73.
17. On the migration of southern blacks, see Lemann (1991).
18. See U.S. Department of Commerce, Bureau of the Census (1985d) table 40. Note that these figures refer to income (from all sources) rather than earnings per se. Comparable historical series restricted to earnings— wages, salaries, and self-employment income—are not available.
19. See O'Neill (1984).
20. See U.S. Department of Commerce, Bureau of the Census (1985d) table 40.
21. See Bianchi and Spain (1986).
22. Du Bois (1899) pp. 67–68.
23. As we noted in chapter 1, the census does not count capital gains in its income statistics.
24. The precise fraction depends on the definition of income. If income includes both money and non-money items, such as Medicare, Medicaid, food stamps, and employer-provided health insurance, the fraction rises to about 20 percent.
25. On the number of Social Security recipients, see U.S. Department of Commerce, Bureau of the Census (1975b), series H125–71.
26. U.S. Department of Commerce, Bureau of the Census, (1975b) series H346–67.
27. Tax estimates by the author are based on U.S. Department of Treasury, Office of Tax Analysis (1998).
28. We choose 1949 rather than 1947 because the detailed breakdowns were published for the 1950 census (covering 1949 incomes) but not for the smaller 1948 Current Population Survey (covering 1947 income).
29. These cash incomes may have understated farmers' living standards, but they are what the census counted.
30. A low current income does not necessarily mean a low standard of living. If the family has saved part of its income over time, withdrawals from those savings do not count as current income since the income was counted when it was first earned. Interest payments on the savings are new income and are counted in the year they accrue.
31. I am indebted to Richard Easterlin for this point.

Chapter 3

1. In this chapter, I have benefited greatly from two superb essays on the early postwar period: Alan S. Blinder, "The Level and Distribution of Economic Well-Being," and Robert J. Gordon, "Postwar Macroeconomics: The Evolution of Events and Ideas," both in Feldstein (1980).

2. See Smith (1980).
3. See Kendrick (1974) pp. 51–59.
4. Stein (1980) p. 173.
5. Barnett and Schorsch (1983) p. 143. Also see Madrick (1995) for an argument linking the exhaustion of economies of scale to the productivity slowdown.
6. Berle and Means (1932). This argument is thoughtfully elaborated, with new evidence, in Mueller (1987).
7. Schumpeter (1942).
8. See chapter 6 for a discussion of both agricultural migrations and the declining number of production jobs in central cities.
9. On Levittown, see Gans (1967) pp. 22, 34. The nationwide figure comes from Levy and Michel (1985).
10. See Blinder (1980) for a similar discussion.
11. On increases in nutrient intake, see U.S. Department of Commerce, Bureau of the Census (1975b), series G849–856. On the continuing Cajun revolution, see the cookbooks of Paul Prudhomme, beginning with *Paul Prudhomme's Louisiana Kitchen* (1984).
12. See White (1961).
13. See, for example, Heller (1960)
14. For an excellent discussion of this period, see Okun (1969).
15. See Sundquist (1968) for the best description of how Democrats built their agenda during the Eisenhower years and then passed much of it when Lyndon Johnson became president.
16. See Levy (1985) for an examination of public opinion polls that showed people in the mid-1960s as both quite optimistic about their economic future and generally agreeable to increased spending for the poor.
17. For a good, if partisan, discussion of this period, see Blinder (1979).
18. Okun (1980) pp. 168–69.
19. The phrase "Quiet Depression" was coined in Levy and Michel (1986a).
20. Though, as illustrated by the quotation by Stein, people were concerned that productivity had slowed moderately after 1966. See Stein (1980).
21. See Hathaway (1974).
22. Landes (1965) p. 275.
23. Council of Economic Advisers (1993) table B-107.
24. See Smith (1980).
25. Council of Economic Advisers (1993) table B-107.
26. See, for example, Cooper (1986) pp. 195–207.
27. I am indebted to the late Eugene Swartz for this story.
28. See Challenger, Gray, and Christmas, press release, July 8, 1996.
29. See Louis Uchitelle and N. R. Kleinfeld, "On the Battlefields of Business, Millions of Casualties," *New York Times*, March 3, 1996. This was the first article in a seven-part series entitled "The Downsizing of America."
30. This agreement was made clear in two papers presented at the 1998 Allied Social Science Association meetings—David Neumark, Daniel Polsky, and Daniel Hansen, "How Has Job Stability Changed? New Evidence and Conflicting Findings," and Henry S. Farber, "Has the Rate of

Job Loss Increased Over Time?"—as well as in the comments by David Marcotte on the Farber and Neumark et al. papers.

Chapter 4

1. See, for example, Bluestone and Harrison (1982); Kuttner (1983), and Steinberg (1983).
2. See Maddison (1987).
3. On the mismeasurement of service sector output, see Slifman and Corrado (1996).
4. Steinberg is currently the chief economist for Merrill Lynch.
5. Steinberg (1983) p. 77.
6. For a fuller exploration of why wages for similar workers might differ across industries, see Fuchs (1968) and Katz and Summers (1989).
7. Clark (1957) p. 176.
8. On the growth of temporary production workers, see Segal and Sullivan (1997).
9. See Fuchs (1981).
10. See Schumpeter (1942) p. 83.
11. Our real interest is not in annual incomes but in hourly or weekly earnings. The census typically does not publish average weekly earnings by age but a reasonable proxy are the annual incomes of prime-age men, most of which come from earnings. The census also publishes annual incomes for women by age, but these statistics confound trends in weekly earnings with rapid increases in the number of women who worked.
12. See Lawrence (1984) p. 21.
13. For example, some older, inefficient eastern steel mills were replaced by newer minimills, many in the southwest. For a good overview of the movement of manufacturing, see Crandall (1993).
14. Estimates of displaced workers by Henry Farber, cited in chapter 5, use a broader definition of displaced worker (for example, the worker does not have to have been on the job three years), which results in larger numbers.
15. See Flaim and Sehgal (1985).
16. For an early article demonstrating how less educated workers lost ground in all parts of the economy, see Bound and Johnson (1992) pp. 371–92.
17. See Marcotte (1994) chapter 4.

Chapter 5

1. Anders (1995).
2. Tabulations by the author of the 1950 and 1980 Census Public Use Microdata Samples.
3. U.S. Department of Labor (1982) table C-5.
4. See Goldin and Margo (1992). The statistics refer to young men of all races, and "young" refers to men with one to five years of work experi-

ence; thus, the high school graduates in this comparison are roughly four years younger than the college graduates.

5. See O'Neill and Sepielli (1985).
6. See Freeman (1976).
7. See American Council on Education (various years).
8. See Converse et al. (1980) table 1.24.
9. Richard Easterlin (1995) argues that this shift into business came from changing preferences (for making more money) as opposed to the weak economy.
10. See Blau (1998) table 1b. The statistics refer to the fraction of white men between twenty-five and fifty-four who were either employed or actively looking for work at a point in time.
11. See, for example, Hecker (1992).
12. For a discussion of this issue see Philip Cook and Robert Frank (1993), and the references cited therein.
13. These figures are based on Farber (1997). The figures refer to all workers in an occupation, not just white males.
14. See Houseman (1997). Also see Segal and Sullivan (1997). In general, post-1980 loss of fringe benefits has been more concentrated among less-educated workers, an aspect of the declining demand and falling wages described earlier.
15. See David (1986).
16. Based on tabulations by the author of the 1960 Census Public Use Microdata Sample files.
17. See U.S. Department of Commerce, Bureau of the Census (1985d) table 40.
18. On the proportion of black men who report no earned income, see Levy (1980). This work is an outgrowth of the work of Butler and Heckman (1977), who argued that traditional comparisons of black-white earnings ratios overstated black progress because published earnings statistics were based on persons who had at least one dollar of earnings. Thus, they potentially obscured the presence of those black men who were out of the labor market altogether. On the distribution of black men's incomes in 1969, see U.S. Department of Commerce, Bureau of the Census (1970a) table 45.
19. See U.S. Department of Commerce, Bureau of the Census (1970a).
20. See Donahue and Heckman (1991).
21. These gains in educational attainment are summarized in Freeman (1973).
22. Bound and Freeman (1992).
23. Moss and Tilly (1996); Kirschenman and Neckerman (1991); Holzer (1997); and the studies in Fix and Struyk (1993).
24. Thernstrom and Thernstrom (1997) and Patterson (1997).
25. See U.S. Department of Commerce, Bureau of the Census (1985d) table 29.
26. For early data on women's labor-force participation, see U.S. Department of Commerce, Bureau of the Census (1975b). For later data, see U.S. Department of Labor (1982) table A-3. For an excellent discussion of trends, see Bianchi and Spain (1986).

27. See U.S. Department of Labor (1982) table A-5.
28. See U.S. Department of Commerce, Bureau of the Census (1983a) table 3.
29. See O'Neill (1984).
30. See O'Neill (1984) and Smith and Ward (1984).
31. See Lerman (1997) and Lee (1998).
32. Blau and Kahn (1992).
33. In the language of income distributions, this reflects the difference between "people distance" and "dollar distance."
34. See U.S. Department of Commerce, Bureau of the Census, (1974).
35. See, for example, Freeman (1973).
36. See Neal and Johnson (1996).
37. See Borjas, Freeman, and Katz (1997).
38. In census data, "Hispanic" is an ethnic rather than racial category. Hispanics can be of any race. Most Hispanics classify themselves as white or "other."
39. DeMuth (1997) p. 24.
40. Hall and Liebman (1997) p. 34.
41. Slemrod (1991).
42. Hacker (1997).
43. See Conlin (1997).
44. Marshall (1961).
45. See Frank and Cook (1995).
46. Allen, who founded Microsoft with Gates, left the firm in 1983 when diagnosed with Hodgkin's disease, but he still owns a substantial amount of Microsoft stock.
47. Joskow, Rose, and Sheppard (1992). I base these calculations on the authors' fixed effects reported in table A.1. The calculations adjust for the changing composition of the sample over time. The $2.26 million figure is somewhat higher than the median 1996 compensation, cited in the *Forbes* list, of Clateo Castellini of the medical products firm Becton Dickinson; his salary plus bonuses came to $1.85 million.

Chapter 6

1. U.S. Department of Commerce, Bureau of the Census (1996b) table no. 33.
2. For trends in jobs by state, see U.S. Department of Labor, (1983). On jobs by industry for big cities, see U.S. Department of Commerce, Bureau of the Census, *County and City Data Book* (published at five-year intervals).
3. For a discussion of this theme from a regional development perspective, see Mieszkowski (1979).
4. Some of the flavor of regional growth—the processes by which concentrations of jobs attract additional jobs—is conveyed in Krugman (1991).
5. On interstate migration flows, see U.S. Department of Commerce, Bureau of the Census, *Historical Statistics,* series C25–75 (1975b). On the proportion of blacks living in central cities, see series A276–87.
6. See Fuchs (1962).

7. For a discussion of the geographic movement of manufacturing over this and subsequent periods, see Crandall (1993).
8. See Forstall (1991) and Long and DeAre (1988).
9. Eberts (1989).
10. On the reversal of black migration to the North, see Long (1973).
11. See, for example, *Business Week* (1976) and Cuciti (1977).
12. See Borjas, Freeman, and Katz (1997), table 8, and Frey (1992). Because both of these articles are based on census statistics, they do not count illegal (uncounted) aliens.
13. See Kain (1968).
14. See Long (1987).
15. See U.S. Department of Commerce, Bureau of the Census (1975b).
16. U.S. Department of Commerce, Bureau of the Census (1952a) table 3.
17. See Long and Dahmann (1980).
18. Ehrenhalt (1985) p. 57.
19. Peterson (1976) p. 45.
20. See, for example, U.S. Department of Commerce, Bureau of the Census, (1970b).
21. See Wilson and Aponte (1985).
22. See Piven and Cloward (1971) chs. 8–10.
23. See Cayton and Drake (1945) p. 600.
24. See Wilson and Aponte (1985), and Lemann (1986). Because much of the movement of blacks took place within cities, it is not easy to trace with published data. Beginning in the 1970s, however, the census began to publish separate data for "poverty areas," also called "low-income areas"—census tracts in which 20 percent or more of the population was poor in the 1970 decennial census. Between 1973 and 1983, the number of blacks living in central-city poverty areas declined from 7.7 million to 7.1 million persons, or from 33 to 25 percent of the black population. Among the blacks who remained in these areas, the poverty rate rose from 39 percent in 1973 to 50 percent in 1983.
25. See, for example, Ricketts and Sawhill (1988), Mincy and Wiener (1993), and Jargowsky and Bane (1991).
26. See Peterson (1976).
27. See U.S. Department of Commerce, Bureau of the Census, *Current Population Reports*, series P-20, no. 368 (1982a).
28. See Long and Dahmann (1980).
29. See, for example, U.S. Department of Commerce, Bureau of the Census, *Current Population Reports*, series P60, no. 194 (1996a).
30. Jargowsky (1996).
31. For a theoretical exploration of this subject, see the work of Benabou (1996).

Chapter 7

1. Author's tabulation of the March 1996 Current Population Survey.
2. See U.S. Bureau of Economic Analysis (1981) table 3.11; (1986) table 3.11.
3. See Lampman and Smeeding (1983).

4. Lampman and Smeeding (1983).
5. See, for example, U.S. Department of Commerce, Bureau of the Census (1975b).
6. See Cherlin (1981) ch. 1.
7. See Butz and Ward (1979).
8. Ryscavage et al. (1992).
9. For another statistical exploration of these points, see Karoly and Burtless (1995).
10. If Karoly and Burtless (1995) or Ryscavage et al. had been able to work with data that captured the actual incomes of the richest households, they presumably would have attributed a higher fraction of inequality to economic factors. See chapter 5 for details on high-income households.
11. See U.S. Department of Commerce, Bureau of Economic Analysis (1998) table 3.11.
12. For a detailed description of the poverty line, see U.S. Department of Health, Education, and Welfare (1976).
13. For a good sense of policy-makers' perceptions of poverty in this period, see Moynihan (1969) and Sundquist (1969).
14. For a good discussion of these policies, see Burke and Burke (1974).
15. Piven and Cloward (1971) p. 302.
16. U.S. Department of Commerce, Bureau of the Census (1978) table 562.
17. Boland (1973).
18. These estimates (which include subfamilies) were obtained through discussions with Patricia Ruggles of the Urban Institute, formerly with the Congressional Budget Office. Ruggles emphasizes the difficulty in meshing data from various sources—in particular, the annual Current Population Survey and the biannual Department of Health and Human Services Survey of AFDC Recipients' Characteristics.
19. For an excellent history of the origins of Social Security, see Derthick (1979).
20. On the number of recipients, see *Historical Statistics of the United States* (1975) series H187, 198, and 199.
21. See Derthick (1979) ch. 17.
22. See, for example, U.S. Department of Commerce, Bureau of the Census, (1985a) table 1.
23. See U.S. Council of Economic Advisers (1985) ch. 5, table 5–6.
24. U.S. Department of Commerce, Bureau of the Census, (1986e) tables 605, 612.
25. Moreover, the initial indexation formula overadjusted benefits for inflation. See Derthick (1979) ch. 19. The overadjustment was subsequently corrected.
26. See U.S. Department of Commerce, Bureau of the Census, *Statistical Abstract* (1986) tables 605, 612.
27. Benefit levels and recipient numbers come from U.S. Department of Commerce, Bureau of the Census, *Statistical Abstract* (various years).
28. See U.S. Bureau of the Census, *Current Population Reports*, series P-60, no. 188 (1995) figure 3.
29. On the poor position of children, see Preston (1984).

30. See, for example, Uchitelle (1998) and Wessel (1998)
31. See *The Wall Street Journal* (1998).
32. On the shortage of low-skill jobs in large cities, see Holzer and Danziger (1998).
33. See, for example, Moore (1997).

Chapter 8

1. *NBC News/Wall Street Journal Poll* (1998) questions 1, 12a, and C14. In the two responses on the rich, I have combined those who say the statement "describes their feelings totally" and those who say the statement "describes their feelings mostly."
2. David Wessel and his colleague, Robert Davis, have written an excellent book about this possibility. See Davis and Wessel (1998).
3. On the changing class structure, see the article by Ralph Whitehead, Jr. (1990).
4. On the important role of community colleges, see Davis and Wessel (1998) chap. 11.
5. U.S. Department of Commerce, Bureau of the Census (1991) table 223.
6. Blank (1997).
7. See for example, *The Washington Post* (1997) and (1998).
8. See Liebman (1996).
9. I am indebted to Dani Rodrik for bringing this example to my attention.
10. See Rodrik (1997).
11. For a good discussion of the issues, see Freeman (1996). In 1997, the U.S. Congress passed the "Sanders Amendment," which banned the importation into the United States of products made with child labor. To this point, the government has not actually banned any imports on these grounds. If the United States does apply the amendment to a particular import, one of several things will happen. The exporting country may be sufficiently embarrassed to change the way it does business or to stop exporting to the United States. Alternatively, the exporting country may bring a case before the World Trade Organization in which, under current law, the United States will almost certainly lose.
12. See Nisbet (1953).

Appendix

1. National Conference of Catholic Bishops (1984) p. 22.
2. See Rainwater and Yancy (1967).
3. See U.S. Department of Commerce, Bureau of the Census (1996) table 12.
4. Calculations based on data contained in Kennickell and Woodburn (1997).
5. See U.S. Department of Commerce, Bureau of the Census (1996b) Table 715, p. 464.

References

Advisory Commission to Study the Consumer Price Index. 1995. "Toward a More Accurate Measure of the Cost of Living." Interim report to the Senate Finance Committee.Washington: U.S. Government Printing Office.

American Council on Education, Cooperative Institutional Research Program. Various years. *The American Freshman: National Norms.* Washington, D.C.: The American Council on Education.

Anders, George. 1995. "Numb and Number: Once a Hot Specialty, Anesthesiology Cools as Insurers Scale Back." *Wall Street Journal,* March 17, 1995, p. 1.

Ashenfelter, Orley, and Alan Krueger. 1994. "Estimates of the Economic Returns to Schooling from a New Sample of Twins." *American Economic Review* 84 (5): 1157–73.

Bailey, Thomas, and Roger Waldinger. 1991, "The Changing Ethnic/Racial Division of Labor." In *Dual City: Restructuring New York,* edited by John Mollenkopf and Manual Castells. New York: Russell Sage Foundation.

Baily, Martin Neil, and Margaret M. Blair. 1988. "Productivity and American Management." In *American Living Standards: Threats and Challenges,* edited by Robert E. Litan, Robert Z. Lawrence, and Charles L. Schultz. Washington: Brookings Institution.

Baily, Martin N., and Alok K. Chabrabarti. 1985. "Innovation and Productivity in U.S. Industry." *Brookings Papers on Economic Activity,* no. 2. Washington, D.C.: The Brookings Institution.

Bane, Mary Jo, and David T. Elwood. 1983. "The Dynamics of Dependence: The Routes to Self-Sufficiency." Report prepared for the U.S. Department of Health and Human Services by Urban System Reseach and Engineering. Table 10.

Barnett, Donald F., and Louis Schorsch. 1983. *Steel: Upheaval in a Basic Industry.* Cambridge, Mass.: Ballinger.

Baumol, William. 1967. "Macroeconomics of Unbalanced Growth: The Anatomy of the Urban Crisis." *American Economic Review* 57 (June): 415–26.

Benabou, Roland. 1996. "Heterogeniety, Stratification, and Growth: Macroeconomic Implications of Community Structure and School Finance." *American Economic Review* 86 (3): 584–609.

Berle, Adolf A., and Gardner G. Means. 1968 [1931]. *The Modern Corporation and Private Property*. Rev. ed. New York: Harcourt Brace Jovanovich.

Bianchi, Suzanne M., and Daphne Spain. 1986. *American Women in Transition. The Population of the United States in the 1980s: A Census Monograph Series*. New York: Russell Sage Foundation.

Blackburn, McKinley L., David E. Bloom, and Richard B. Freeman. 1990. "The Declining Economic Position of Less Skilled American Men." In *A Future of Lousy Jobs*, edited by Gary Burtless. Washington, D.C.: Brookings Institution.

Blair, Margaret M., and Martha A. Schary. 1993. "Industry-Level Pressures to Restructure." In *The Deal Decade*, edited by Margaret M. Blair. Washington, D.C.: Brookings Institution.

Blank, Rebecca M. 1993. "Why were Poverty Rates so High in the 1980s?" In *Poverty and Prosperity in the U.S.A. in the Late Twentieth Century*, edited by Dimitri B. Papadimitriu and Edward N. Wolff. New York: St. Martin's Press.

———. 1997. *It Takes a Nation: A New Agenda for Fighting Poverty*. New York/ Princeton, N.J.: Russell Sage Foundation/Princeton University Press.

Blau, Francine D. 1977. *Equal Pay in the Office*. Lexington, Mass.: Heath.

———. 1998. "Trends in the Well-Being of American Women, 1970–1995." *The Journal of Economic Literature* 36(1): 112–65.

Blau, Francine, and Lawrence Kahn. 1992. "The Gender Earnings Gap: Some International Evidence." *National Bureau of Economic Research Working Paper*, no. 4224. Cambridge, Mass.: National Bureau of Economic Research.

Blinder, Alan S. 1979. *Economic Policy and the Great Stagflation*. New York: Academic Press.

———. 1980. "The Level and Distribution of Economic Well-Being." In Martin Feldstein, ed., *The American Economy in Transition*. Chicago: University of Chicago Press.

———. 1982. "Private Pensions and Public Pensions: Theory and Fact." *National Bureau of Economic Research* Working Paper, no. 902. Cambridge, Mass.: National Bureau of Economic Research.

Bluestone, Barry, and Bennett Harrison. 1982. *The Deindustrialization of America*. New York: Basic Books.

Boland, Barbara. 1973. "Participation in the Aid to Families with Dependent Children Program (AFDC)." In U.S. Congress, Joint Economic Committee, *The Family, Poverty and Welfare Problems: Factors Influencing Family Instability*. Studies in Public Welfare Paper, no. 12 (part 1). Washington: U.S. Government Printing Office.

Borjas, George J. 1990. *Friends or Strangers: The Impact of Immigrants on the U.S. Economy*. New York: Basic Books.

Borjas, George J., Richard B. Freeman, and Lawrence F. Katz. 1997. "How Much do Immigration and Trade Affect Labor Market Outcomes?" *Brookings Papers on Economic Activity*, no. 1. Washington, D.C.: Brookings Institution.

Bound, John, and Richard B. Freeman. 1992. "What Went Wrong? The Erosion of Relative Earnings and Employment Among Young Black Men in the 1980s." *Quarterly Journal of Economics* cvii(1): 201–32.

Bound, John, and George Johnson. 1992. "Changes in the Structure of Wages in the 1980's: An Evaluation of Alternative Explanations." *American Economic Review* 82 (1992): 371–92.

Burke, Vincent J., and Vee Burke. 1974. *Nixon's Good Deed*. New York: Columbia University Press.

Business Week. 1976. "The Second War Between the States." *Business Week* (May 17): 92–114.

Butler, Richard, and James J. Heckman. 1977. "The Government's Impact on the Labor Market Status of Black Americans: A Critical Review." In *Equal Rights and Industrial Relations*, edited by Leonard J. Hausman et al. Ithaca, N.Y.: Industrial Research Association.

Butz, William P., and Michael P. Ward. 1979. "The Emergence of Countercyclical U.S. Fertility." *American Economic Review* 69 (June): 318–28.

Card, David E., and Alan Krueger. 1995. *Myth and Measurement: the New Economics of the Minimum Wage*. Princeton, N.J. : Princeton University Press.

Cassidy, John. 1998. "The Comeback." *The New Yorker* (February 23 and March 2): 122ff.

Cayton, Horace, and St. Clair Drake. 1945. *Black Metropolis*. Chicago, Ill.: University of Chicago Press.

Challenger, Gray, and Christmas, Inc. 1996. Press release. July 8, 1996.

Cherlin, Andrew J. 1981. *Marriage, Divorce, Remarriage*. Cambridge, Mass.: Harvard University Press.

Clark, Colin. 1957. *The Conditions of Economic Progress*. 3rd ed. New York: St. Martin's Press.

Conlin, Michelle. 1997. "When Billionaires Become a Dime a Dozen." *Forbes* (October 13): 148 ff.

Converse, Philip E., Jean Dodson, and Wendy J. Hoag. 1980. *American Social Attitudes Data Sourcebook, 1947–78*. Cambridge, Mass.: Harvard University Press.

Cook, Philip, and Robert Frank. 1993. "The Growing Concentration of Top Students at Elite Schools." In *Studies of Supply and Demand in Higher Education*, edited by C. Clotfelter and M. Rothschild. Chicago: University of Chicago Press.

Cooper, Richard N. 1986. "Dealing with the Trade Deficit in a Floating Rate System." *Brookings Papers on Economic Activity*, no. 1. Washington, D.C.: The Brookings Institution.

Cox, W. Michael. 1996. "It's not a Wage Gap but an Age Gap." *The New York Times*, April 2, 1996, editorial.

Cox, W. Michael, and Richard Alm. 1996. "By Our Own Bootstraps: Economic Opportunity and the Dynamics of Income Distribution." *Federal Reserve Bank of Dallas Annual Report 1995*. Dallas: Federal Reserve Bank of Dallas.

Crandall, Robert. 1993. *Manufacturing on the Move*. Washington, D.C.: The Brookings Institution.

Cuciti, Peggy L. 1977. *Troubled Local Economies and the Distribution of Federal Dollars*. Congressional Budget Office Background Paper (August). Washington, D.C.: U.S. Government Printing Office.

Cyert, Richard M. 1984. "Easing Labor's Trauma." *New York Times*, July 22, 1984, sect. 3, p. 3.

David, Frances. 1986. "The Stories They Can Tell on Philly Joe." *Philadelphia Inquirer*, June 15, 1986, sect. H, p. 1.

Davis, Bob, and David Wessel, 1998. *Prosperity: the Coming 20 Year Boom and What It Means to You.* New York: Times Books/Random House.

DeMott, Benjamin. 1995. *The Trouble with Friendship: Why Americans Can't Think Straight about Race.* Boston: Atlantic Monthly Press.

DeMuth, Christopher C. 1997. "The New Wealth of Nations." *Commentary* (October): 23–28.

Denison, Edward F. 1985. *Trends in American Economic Growth, 1929–82.* Washington, D.C.: Brookings Institution.

Derthick, Martha. 1979. *Policy Making for Social Security.* Washington, D.C.: Brookings Institution.

DiNardo, John, Nicole M. Fortin, and Thomas Lemieux. 1995. "Labor Market Institutions and the Distribution of Wages, 1973–1992: A Semiparametric Approach." National Bureau of Economic Research working paper 5093. Cambridge, Mass.: National Bureau of Economic Research.

Donahue, John J., and James J. Heckman. 1991. "Continuous Versus Episodic Change. The Impact of Affirmative Action Policy on the Economic Status of Blacks." *Journal of Economic Literature* 29(4): 1603–44.

Doyle, Edward. 1996. "Physician Pay: the Bottom Line." *ACP Observer,* April 1996.

Du Bois, W. E. B. 1967 [1899]. *The Philadelphia Negro.* New York: Schocken Books.

Duncan, Greg J., Timothy M. Smeeding, and Willard Rogers. 1993. "W(h)ither the Middle Class? A Dynamic View." In *Poverty and Prosperity in the U.S.A. in the Late Twentieth Century,* edited by Dimitri B. Papadimitriu and Edward N. Wolff. New York: M.E. Sharp.

Easterlin, Richard A. 1974. "Does Economic Growth Improve the Human Lot? Some Empirical Evidence." In *Essays in Honor of Moses Abramovitz,* edited by Paul David and Melvin Reder. New York: Academic Press.

———. 1980. *Birth and Fortune.* New York: Basic Books.

———. 1995. "Preferences and Prices in the Choice of a Career: The Switch to Business, 1972–87." *Journal of Economic Behavior and Organization* 27 (1): 1–34.

Eberts, Randall W. 1989. "Accounting for the Recent Divergence in Regional Wage Differentials." *Economic Review,* 25(3). Cleveland, Ohio: Federal Reserve Bank of Cleveland.

Edin, Katheryn, and Laura Lein. 1997. *Making Ends Meet: How Single Mothers Survive Welfare and Low-Wage Work.* New York: Russell Sage Foundation.

Ehrenhalt, Samuel M. 1985. "Growth in the New York City Economy, Problems and Promise." Paper presented at the eighteenth annual Institute on the Challenges of the Changing Economy of New York City, New York (May 8, 1985).

Ellwood, David. 1989. *Poor Support.* New York: Basic Books.

Farber, Henry S. 1997. "The Changing Face of Job Loss in the United States: 1981–1995." *Brookings Papers in Economic Activity; Microeconomics.* Washington, D.C.: Brookings Institution.

———. 1998. "Has the Rate of Job Loss Increased Over Time?" Paper presented at the Allied Social Science Meetings, Chicago, Illinois (1998)

Feenberg, Daniel R., and James M. Poterba. 1993. "Income Inequality and the

Incomes of Very High Income Taxpayers: Evidence from Tax Returns." In *Tax Policy and the Economy, 7* , edited by James Poterba. Cambridge, Mass: MIT Press.

Feldstein, Martin, ed. 1980. *The American Economy in Transition*. Chicago: The University of Chicago Press.

———. 1996. "The Missing Piece in Policy Analysis: Social Security Reform." *National Bureau of Economic Research Working Paper*, no. 5413. Cambridge, Mass.: National Bureau of Economic Research.

Fischer, Claude S., Michael Hout, Martin Sanchez Jankowski, Samuel R. Locua, Ann Swidler, and Kim Voss. 1996. *Inequality by Design: Cracking the Bell Curve Myth*. Princeton, N.J.: Princeton University Press.

Fix, Michael, and Raymond Struyk, eds. 1993. *Clear and Convincing Evidence: Measurement of Discrimination in America*. Washington, D.C.: The Urban Institute Press.

Flaim, Paul O., and Ellen Sehgal. 1985. "Displaced Workers of 1979–83: How Well Have They Fared?" *Monthly Labor Review* (July): 3–16.

Forstall, Richard L. 1991. "Regional and Metropolitan/Nonmetropolitan Population Trends in the United States, 1980–90," Paper prepared for the Association of American Geographers, Miami, Florida (April 14, 1991), revised November 13, 1991.

Frank, Robert H., and Philip J. Cook. 1995. *The Winner-Take-All Society*. New York: Martin Kessler Books.

Freeman, Richard B. 1973. "Changes in the Labor Market for Black Americans, 1948–72." *Brookings Papers on Economic Activity*, no. 1. Washington, D.C.: The Brookings Institution.

———. 1976. *The Over-Educated American*. New York: Academic Press.

———. 1996. "International Labor Standards and World Trade: Friends or Foes" In *The World Trading System: Challenges Ahead*, edited by Jeffrey J. Schott. Washington, D.C: Institute for International Economics.

Freudenheim, Milt. 1986. "AMA Report Sees Too Many Doctors." *New York Times*, June 14, 1986, p. 1.

Frey, William H. 1992. "Race, Class and Poverty Polarization Across Metro Areas and States: Population Shifts and Migration Dynamics." Research Report 93–293. Ann Arbor, Mich.: Population Studies Center, University of Michigan.

Fuchs, Victor A. 1962. *Changes in the Location of Manufacturing in the United States Since 1929*. New Haven: Yale University Press.

———. 1968. *The Service Economy*. New York: National Bureau of Economic Research and Columbia University Press.

———. 1981. "Economic Growth and the Rise of Service Employment." In *Towards an Explanation of Economic Growth*, edited by Herbert Giersch. Tubingen: Mohr.

Gans, Herbert. 1967. *The Levittowners*. New York: Pantheon Books.

Geanakopolos, John, Olivia S. Mitchell, and Stephen P. Zeldes. 1998. "Would a Privatized Social Security System Really Pay a Higher Rate of Return?" Paper originally prepared for the National Academy on Social Insurance, conference on Social Security reform (January 1998), revised draft, April 2, 1998.

Goldin, Claudia, and Robert Margo. 1992. "The Great Compression." *The Quarterly Journal of Economics* 57 (February): 1–34

Gordon, Roger H., and Joel Slemrod. no date. "Are "Real" Responses to Taxes Simply Income Shifting Between Corporate and Personal Bases?" Mimeo. Ann Arbor, Mich.: University of Michigan, Department of Economics.

Gordon, Robert J. 1980. "Postwar Macroeconomics: The Evolution of Events and Ideas." In *The American Economy in Transition*, edited by Martin Feldstein. Chicago: University of Chicago Press.

———. 1998. "The Great Productivity Speed-Up and Slowdown: How Much Is Mismeasurement?" Paper presented at the Allied Social Science Meetings, Chicago, Ill. (1998).

Gottschalk, Peter. 1996. "Notes on 'By Our Own Bootstraps: Economic Opportunity and the Dynamics of Income Distribution' by Cox and Alm." Working Paper. Chestnut Hill, Mass.: Department of Economics, Boston College.

Gottschalk, Peter, and Timothy Smeeding. 1997. "Cross-National Comparisons of Earnings and Income Inequality." *Journal of Economic Literature* 35(2): 633–87.

Gramlich, Edward M., Richard Kasten, and Frank Sammartino. 1993. "Growing Inequality in the 1980's: The Role of Federal Taxes and Cash Transfers" In *Uneven Tides: Rising Inequality in America*, edited by Sheldon Danziger and Peter Gottschalk. New York: Russell Sage Foundation.

Gray, John. 1995. *Enlightenment's Wake: Politics and Culture at the Close of the Modern Age*. London: Routledge, Inc.

Hacker, Andrew. 1997. *Money: Who Has How Much and Why?* New York: Scribner's.

Hall, Brian J., and Jeffrey B. Liebman. 1997. "Are CEO's Really Paid Like Bureaucrats?" *National Bureau of Economic Research Working Paper*, no. 6213. Cambridge, Mass.: National Bureau of Economic Research.

Hall, Robert E. 1982."The Importance of Lifetime Jobs in the U.S. Economy." *American Economic Review* 72 (September): 716–24.

Hallberg, Garth. 1995. *All Consumers are Not Created Equal*. New York: John Wiley and Sons.

Harrington, Michael. 1962. *The Other America*. New York: Macmillan.

Hathaway, Dale E. 1974. "Food Prices and Inflation." *Brookings Papers on Economic Activity*, no. 1. Washington, D.C.: The Brookings Institution.

Hecker, Daniel E. 1992. "Reconciling Conflicting Data on Jobs for College Graduates." *Monthly Labor Review* (July): 3–12.

Heller, Walter. 1960. *New Dimensions in Political Economy*. Cambridge, Mass.: Harvard University Press.

Herrnstein, Richard J., and Charles Murray. 1994. *The Bell Curve: Intelligence and Class Structure in American Life*. New York: The Free Press.

Hirschman, Albert O. 1982. *Shifting Involvements*. Princeton, N.J.: Princeton University Press.

Holzer, Harry. 1997. *What Employers Want: Job Prospects for Less-Educated Workers*. New York: Russell Sage Foundation.

Holzer, Harry J., and Sheldon Danziger. 1998. "Are Jobs Available for Disadvantaged Workers in Urban Areas." Working paper. East Lansing/Ann Arbor, Mich.: Michigan State University/University of Michigan.

Houseman, Susan N. 1997. "Temporary, Part-Time and Contract Employment in the United States: A Report on the W.E. Upjohn Institute's Employer Survey on Flexible Staffing Policies." Report. Kalamazoo, Mich.: W.E. Upjohn Institute.

Jargowsky, Paul. 1996. "Take the Money and Run: Economic Segregation in U.S. Metropolitan Areas." *American Sociological Review* 61(December): 984–98.

Jargowsky, Paul A., and Mary Jo Bane. 1991. "Ghetto Poverty in the United States: 1970 to 1980." In *The Urban Underclass*, edited by Christopher Jencks and Paul E. Peterson. Washington, D.C.: The Brookings Institution.

Joskow, Paul, Nancy Rose, and Andrea Shepard. 1993. "Regulatory Constraints on CEO Compensation." *Brookings Papers in Economic Activity, 1993*, no. 1. Washington, D.C.: The Brookings Institution.

Kain, John F. 1968. "The Distribution and Movement of Jobs and Industry." In *The Metropolitan Enigma*, edited by James Q. Wilson. Cambridge, Mass.: Harvard University Press.

Kane, Thomas J. 1995. "Rising Public College Tuition and College Entry : How Well Do Public Subsidies Promote Access to College?" *National Bureau of Economic Research Working Paper*, no. 5164. Cambridge, Mass.: National Bureau of Economic Research.

Karoly, Lynn A., and Gary Burtless. 1995. "Demographic Change, Rising Earnings Inequality and the Distribution of Personal Well Being, 1959–89." *Demography* 32(3): 379–405.

Katz, Lawrence F., and Lawrence H. Summers. 1989. "Industry Rents: Evidence and Implications." *Brookings Papers on Economic Activity: Microeconomics*. Washington, D.C.: Brookings Institution.

Kendrick, John W. 1974. *Postwar Productivity Trends in the United States, 1948–69*. New York: National Bureau of Economic Research.

Kennickell, Arthur B., and R. Louise Woodburn. 1997. "Consistent Weight-Design for the 1989, 1992, and 1995 SCFs, and the Distribution of Wealth." *Board of Governors of the Federal Reserve Working Paper*. Washington, D.C.: Board of Governors of the Federal Reserve System.

Kichen, Steve. 1997. "Spoils of Success." *Forbes* (May 19): 172 ff.

Kirkland, Richard I., Jr. 1985. "Are Service Jobs Good Jobs?" *Fortune* (June 10): 38–43.

Kirschenman, Joleen, and Katheryn M. Neckerman. 1991. " 'We'd Love to Hire Them, But . . . ' : The Meaning of Race for Employers." In *The Urban Underclass*, edited by Christopher Jencks and Paul E. Peterson. Washington, D.C.: Brookings Institution.

Korenman, Sanders, and Christopher Winship. 1995. "A Reanalysis of *The Bell Curve*." *National Bureau of Economic Research Working Paper*, no. 5230. Cambridge, Mass.: National Bureau of Economic Research.

Krugman, Paul R. 1991. *Geography and Trade*. Cambridge, Mass.: MIT Press.

Kuttner, Bob. 1983. "The Declining Middle." *Atlantic* (July): 60–72.

Lampman, Robert J., and Timothy M. Smeeding. 1983. "Interfamily Transfers as Alternatives to Government Transfers to Persons." *Review of Income and Wealth*, series 29, 1 (March): 45–66.

Landes, David. 1965. "Technological Change and Development in Western

Europe: 1750–1914." In *Cambridge Economic History of Europe from the Decline of the Roman Empire*, edited by H.J. Habakkuk and M. Postan. New York: Cambridge University Press.

Lawrence, Robert Z. 1984. *Can America Compete?* Washington, D.C.: Brookings Institution.

Lebergott, Stanley. 1976. *The American Economy: Income, Wealth and Want.* Princeton, N.J.: Princeton University Press.

Lee, David S. 1998. "Wage Inequality in the U.S. during the 1980s: Rising Dispersion or Falling Minimum Wage?" Working Paper, no. 399. Princeton, N.J.: Industrial Relations Section, Princeton University.

Lemann, Nicholas. 1986. "The Origins of the Underclass." *Atlantic* (June): 25–31 (part 1); (July): 54–68 (part 2).

———. 1991. *The Promised Land: The Great Black Migration and How It Changed America.* New York: Knopf.

Lenzner, Robert, and Stephen S. Johnson. 1997. "Seeing Things as They Really Are." *Forbes* (March 10): 122 ff.

Lerman, Robert. 1997. "Reassessing Trends in U.S. Earnings Inequality." *Monthly Labor Review* (December): 17–25.

Levy, Frank. 1978. "What Ronald Reagan Can Teach the United States About Welfare Reform." In *American Politics and Public Policy*, edited by Martha Wagner Weinberg and Walter Dean Burham. Cambridge, Mass.: MIT Press, 336–63.

———. 1979. "The Labor Supply of Female Household Heads or AFDC Work Incentives Don't Work Too Well." *Journal of Human Resources* 14: 1 (Winter): 76–97.

———. 1980. "Changes in the Employment Prospects for Black Males." *Brookings Papers in Economic Activity*, no. 2. Washington, D.C.: The Brookings Institution.

———. 1985. "Affluence, Altruism and Happiness in the Postwar Period." In Martin David and Timothy Smeeding, eds. *Horizontal Equity, Uncertainty and Economic Welfare.* Chicago: University of Chicago Press.

———. 1987. *Dollars and Dreams.* New York: Russell Sage Foundation.

Levy, Frank, and Richard C. Michel. 1983. "The Way We'll Be in 1984: Recent Changes in the Level and Distribution of Disposable Income." Working Paper. Washington, D.C.: Urban Institute.

———. 1985. "Are Baby Boomers Selfish?" *American Demographics* 17 (April): 38–41.

Levy, Frank, and Richard J. Murnane. 1992. "U.S. Earnings Levels and Earnings Inequality: A Review of Recent Trends and Proposed Explanations." *Journal of Economic Literature* 30(3): 1333–81.

Liebman, Jeffrey B. 1996. "Who Are the Ineligible EITC Recipients?" Mimeo. Cambridge, Mass.: Harvard University.

———. 1997. "The Impact of the Earned Income Tax Credit on Incentives and Income Distribution." J. F. Kennedy School of Government, Mimeo. Cambridge, Mass.: J. F. Kennedy School of Government.

Lillard, Lee, James P. Smith, and Finis Welch. 1986. "What Do We Really Know About Wages?" *Journal of Political Economy* 94: 3 (June): 489–506.

Long, Larry H. 1973. "Interregional Migration of the Poor: Some Recent

Changes." U.S. Bureau of the Census, *Current Population Reports*, Special Studies Series P-23, no. 73. Washington: U.S. Government Printing Office.

———. 1987. *Migration and Residential Mobility in the United States*. The Population of the United States in the 1980s: A Census Monograph Series. New York: Russell Sage Foundation.

Long, Larry H., and Donald C. Dahmann. 1980. "The City-Suburb Income Gap: Is It Being Narrowed by a Back-to-the City Movement?" U.S. Bureau of the Census, *Special Demographic Analyses*, CDS-80-1. Washington: U.S. Government Printing Office.

Long, Larry, and Diana DeAre. 1988. "U.S. Population Redistribution: A Perspective on the Nonmetropolitan Turnaround." *Population and Development Review* 14(3): 433–50.

Maddison, Angus. 1987. "Growth and Slowdown in Advanced Capitalist Economies: Techniques of Quantitative Assessment." *Journal of Economic Literature* xxv (June) : 649–98.

Madrick, Jeffrey G. 1995. *The End of Affluence : the Causes and Consequences of America's Economic Dilemma*. New York: Random House.

Maraniss, David. 1986. "For West Texans, It's Merely Boom and Bust, as Usual." *Washington Post*, February 11, 1986, p. 1.

Marcotte, David E. 1994. "The Effects of Competition and Technology on Skills, Training, and Employment in the Maryland Banking Industry. " In *Skills, Wages and Careers: Essays on the Emerging Economy and Its Implications for Education and Training Policies*. Unpublished dissertation. College Park, Md.: The University of Maryland School of Public Affairs.

———. 1998. Comments on papers by Henry Farber and David Neumark, Daniel Polsky, and Daniel Hanson. Allied Social Science Meetings, Chicago, Ill. (1998).

Mare, Robert D., and Christopher Winship. 1989. "Socioeconomic Change and the Decline of Marriage for Blacks and Whites." In *The Urban Underclass*, edited by Christopher Jencks and Paul E. Peterson. Washington, D.C.: The Brookings Institution.

Marshall, Alfred, ed. 1961. *Principles of Economics*. 9th (variorum) ed., with annotations by C. W. Guillebaud. New York: Macmillan for the Royal Economic Society.

Miezkowski, Peter. 1979. "Recent Trends in Urban and Regional Development." In *Current Issues in Urban Economics*, edited by Peter Miezkowski and Mahlon Strasheim. Baltimore: Johns Hopkins Press.

Miller, Paul, Charles Mulvey, and Nick Martin. 1995. "What Do Twins Studies Reveal About the Economic Return to Education? A Comparison of Australian and U.S. Findings." *American Economic Review* 85 (3): 586–99.

Mincy, Ronald B., and Susan J. Wiener. 1993. "The Under Class in the 1980's: Changing Concepts, Constant Reality." Working Paper. Washington, D.C.: The Urban Institute.

Moore, Stephen. 1997. "Prepared Testimony on the Future of Social Security for This Generation and the Next." House Ways and Means Committee, Social Security Subcommittee, U.S. Congress, Washington, D.C. (June 24, 1997).

Moss, Phil, and Chris Tilly. 1996. "Soft Skills and Race: An Investigation of Black Males' Employment Problems." *Work and Occupations* 23 (3): 252–76.

Moynihan, Daniel P., ed. 1969. *On Understanding Poverty: Perspectives from the Social Sciences.* New York: Basic Books.

———. 1973. *The Politics of a Guaranteed Income.* New York: Random House.

Mueller, Dennis. 1987. *The Corporation: Growth, Diversification, and Mergers.* London: Gordon and Breach.

Mueller, Dennis C. and Elizabeth A. Reardon. 1993. "Rates of Return on Corporate Investment." *Southern Economic Journal* 60(2): 430–53.

Murnane, Richard J., and Frank Levy. 1996. *Teaching the New Basic Skills.* New York: The Free Press.

Murnane, Richard J., John Willett, and Frank Levy. 1995. "The Growing Importance of Cognitive Skills in Wage Determination." *Review of Economics and Statistics* 77(2): 251–66.

Murray, Charles. 1984. *Losing Ground.* New York: Basic Books.

National Conference of Catholic Bishops, Ad Hoc Committee on Catholic Social Teaching and the U.S. Economy. 1984. "First Draft Pastoral Letter on Catholic Social Teaching and the U.S. Economy." *National Catholic Reporter* (November 23, 1984).

NBC News / Wall Street Journal Poll, Jan. 13–16, 1996.

NBC News / Wall Street Journal Poll, Feb. 26–Mar. 1, 1998.

Neal, Derek A., and William R. Johnson. 1996. "The Role of Premarket Factors in Black-White Wage Differences." *Journal of Political Economy* 5 (104): 869–95.

Neumark, David, Daniel Polsky, and Daniel Hanson. 1998. "How Has Job Stability Changed? New Evidence and Conflicting Findings." Paper presented at the Allied Social Science Meetings, Chicago, Ill. (1998).

Nisbet, Robert A. 1953. *The Quest for Community.* New York: Oxford University Press.

Nixon, Richard. 1962. *Six Crises.* New York: Doubleday.

Okun, Arthur M. 1969. *The Political Economy of Prosperity.* Washington, D.C.: Brookings Institution.

———. 1980. "Postwar Macroeconomic Performance." In *The American Economy in Transition,* edited by Martin Feldstein. Chicago: University of Chicago Press.

———. 1981. *Prices and Quantities.* Washington, D.C.: Brookings Institution.

O'Neill, Dave M., and Peter Sepielli. 1985. *Education in the United States: 1940–1983.* U.S. Bureau of the Census, Special Demographic Analyses, CDS-85-1. Washington: U.S. Government Printing Office.

O'Neill, June. 1984. Rev. ed. "The Trend in the Male-Female Wage Gap in the United States." Mimeo. Washington, D.C.: Urban Institute.

O'Neill, June, and Simon Polacheck. 1993. "Why the Gender Gap in Wages Narrowed in the 1980s." *Journal of Labor Economics* 11(1, pt. 1): 205–28.

Osterman, Paul. Forthcoming. *Making America Work* Princeton, N. J.: Princeton University Press.

Patterson, Orlando. 1997. *The Ordeal of Integration : Progress and Resentment in America's "Racial" Crisis.* Washington, D.C.: Civitas/Counterpoint.

Pear, Robert. 1997. "Doctors Assert There Are Too Many of Them." *The New York Times,* March 1, 1997, p. 9.

Peterson, George E. 1976. "Finance." In *The Urban Predicament,* edited by William Gorham and Nathan Glazer. Washington, D.C.: Urban Institute.

Piven, Frances Fox, and Richard A. Cloward. 1971. *Regulating the Poor.* New York: Pantheon Books.

Plotnick, Robert, Eugene Smolensky, Eirik Evenhouse, and Siobhan Reilly. 1998. "The Twentieth Century Record of Inequality and Poverty in the United States." *Institute for Research on Poverty Discussion Paper*, no. 1166–98. Madison: Institute for Research on Poverty, University of Wisconsin.

Preston, Samuel H. 1984. "Children and the Elderly: Divergent Paths for America's Dependents." *Demography* 21:4 (November): 435–57.

Prudhomme, Paul. 1984. *Paul Prudhomme's Louisiana Kitchen.* New York: Morrow.

Rainwater, Lee, and William L. Yancy. 1967. *The Moynihan Report and the Politics of Controversy.* Cambridge, Mass.: MIT Press.

Ricketts, Erol, and Isabel V. Sawhill. 1988. "Defining and Measuring the Underclass." *Journal of Policy Analysis and Management* 7(2): 316–25.

Rodgers, T.J. 1998. "Give Us Your Tired, Your Poor—and Your Engineers." *The Wall Street Journal*, March 3, 1998, p. A18.

Rodrik, Dani. 1997. *Has Globalization Gone too Far?* Washington D.C.: Institute of International Economics.

Rosenthal, Neal H. 1985. "The Shrinking Middle Class: Myth or Reality?" *Monthly Labor Review* (March): 3–10.

Ryscavage, Paul. 1998. *Income Inequality in America: An Analysis of Trends.* Armonk, N.Y.: M.E. Sharpe, Inc.

Ryscavage, Paul, Gordon Green, and Edward Welniak. 1992. "The Impact of Demographic, Social, and Economic Change on the Distribution of Income." In "Studies in the Distribution of Income," by Paul Ryscavage, Gordon Green, Edward Welniak, and John Coder. *Current Population Reports*, ser. P-60, no. 183. Washington: U.S. Government Printing Office.

Samuelson, Robert J. 1983. "Middle Class Media Myth." *National Journal* (December 31): 2673–78.

Schumpeter, Joseph. 1942. *Capitalism, Socialism, and Democracy.* New York: Harper and Row.

Segal, Lewis M., and Daniel G. Sullivan. 1997. "The Growth of Temporary Services Work." *Journal of Economic Perspectives* 11(2): 117–360.

Slemrod, Joel. 1991. "Taxation and Inequality: A Time- Exposure Perspective." In *Tax Policy and the Economy*, 6, edited by James Poterba. Cambridge, Mass.: MIT Press.

Slifman, L., and C. Corrado. 1996. "Decomposition of Productivity and Unit Costs," *Washington, D.C. Federal Reserve Board of Governors, Occasional Staff Studies*. Washington, D.C.: Federal Reserve Board of Governors.

Smith, James P., and Michael P. Ward. 1984. *Women's Wages and Work in the Twentieth Century.* Santa Monica, Calif.: Rand Corporation.

Smith, James P., and Finis Welch. 1979. "Race Differences in Earnings: A Survey and New Evidence." In *Current Issues in Urban Economics*, edited by Peter Mieszkowski and Mahlon Strasheim. Baltimore: Johns Hopkins University Press.

Smith, Tom W. 1980. "America's Most Important Problem—A Trend Analysis, 1946–76." *Public Opinion Quarterly* 44(2): 164–80.

Stanley, Thomas J., and William D. Danko. 1996. *The Millionaire Next Door.* New York: Longstreet Press.

Stein, Herbert. 1980. "Changes in Macroeconomic Conditions." In *The American Economy in Transition*, edited by Martin Feldstein. Chicago: University of Chicago Press.

Steinberg, Bruce. 1983. "The Mass Market Is Splitting Apart." *Fortune* (November 28): 76–82.

Sundquist, James L. 1968. *Politics and Policy: The Eisenhower, Kennedy, and Johnson Years*. Washington, D.C.: Brookings Institution.

———. ed. 1969. *On Fighting Poverty: Perspectives from Experience*. New York: Basic Books.

Swartz, Katherine, and Deborah Garnick. 1998. "Regulating Markets: Lessons from New Jersey's Individual Health Coverage Program." Draft of working paper, September 17. Boston: Harvard School of Public Health.

Thernstrom, Abigail, and Stephen Thernstrom. 1997. *America in Black and White: One Nation, Indivisible*. New York: Simon and Schuster.

Triplett, Jack. 1998. "The Solow Paradox: What Do Computers Do to Productivity?" Paper presented at the Allied Social Science Meetings, Chicago, Ill. (1998).

Tyler, John, Richard J. Murnane, and Frank Levy. 1995. "College Graduates in High School Jobs? A New Look at the Evidence" *Monthly Labor Review* 118 (12): 18–27.

Uchitelle, Louis. 1998. "The Middle Class: Winning in Politics, Losing in Life." *The New York Times*, July 19, Section 4, p. 1.

Uchitelle, Louis, and N. R. Kleinfeld. 1996. "On the Battlefields of Business, Millions of Casualties." *New York Times*, March 3, 1996, p. 1 ff.

U.S. Council of Economic Advisers. 1982. *Economic Report of the President: 1982*. Washington: U.S. Government Printing Office.

———. 1985. *Economic Report of the President: 1985*. Washington: U.S. Government Printing Office.

———. 1986. *Economic Report of the President: 1986*. Washington: U.S. Government Printing Office.

———. 1993. *Economic Report of the President: 1993*. Washington: U.S. Government Printing Office.

———. 1997. *Economic Report of the President: 1997*. Washington: U.S. Government Printing Office.

U.S. Department of Commerce, Bureau of the Census. 1950. *1950 Census Public Use Microdata Sample*. Washington: U.S. Government Printing Office.

———. 1951. "Income of Families and Persons in the United States: 1949." *Current Population Reports*, ser. P-60, no. 7. Washington: U.S. Government Printing Office.

———. 1952a. *County and City Data Book, 1949*. Washington: U.S. Government Printing Office.

———. 1952b. *Statistical Abstract of the United States: 1952*. Washington: U.S. Government Printing Office.

———. 1961a. "Average Income of Families Up Slightly in 1960." *Current Population Reports*, ser. P-60, no. 36. Washington: U.S. Government Printing Office.

———. 1961b. "Income of Families and Persons in the United States: 1959." *Current Population Reports*, ser. P-60, no. 35. Washington: U.S. Government Printing Office.

———. 1961c. "Occupation by Earnings and Education." *U.S. Census of Population: 1960*. Final Report PC(2)-7B. Washington: U.S. Government Printing Office.

———. 1967. *County and City Data Book: 1967*. Washington: U.S. Government Printing Office.

———. 1970a. "Income in 1969 of Families and Persons in the United States." *Current Population Reports*, ser. P-60, no. 75. Washington: U.S. Government Printing Office.

———. 1970b. "24 Million Americans: Poverty in the United States: 1969." *Current Population Reports*, ser. P-60, no. 76. Washington: U.S. Government Printing Office.

———. 1971. "Income in 1970 of Familes and Persons in the United States." *Current Population Reports*, ser. P-60, no. 80. Washington: U.S. Government Printing Office.

———. 1973. "Earnings by Occupation and Education." *1970 Census of Population*. Subject Report PC(2)-8B.

———. 1974. "Educational Attainment in the United States, March 1973 and March 1974." *Current Population Reports*, ser. P-20 , no. 274. Washington: U.S. Government Printing Office.

———. 1975a. "Characteristics of the Low-Income Population: 1973." *Current Population Reports*, ser. P.-60, no. 98. Washington: U.S. Government Printing Office.

———. 1975b. *Historical Statistics of the United States: Colonial Times to 1970*. Washington: U.S. Government Printing Office.

———. 1975c. "Money Income in 1973 of Families and Persons in the United States." *Current Population Reports*, ser. P-60, no. 97. Washington: U.S. Government Printing Office.

———. 1977. "Money Income in 1975 of Families and Persons in the United States." *Current Population Reports*, ser. P-60, no. 105. Washington: U.S. Government Printing Office.

———. 1978. *Statistical Abstract of the United States: 1978*. Washington: U.S. Government Printing Office.

———. 1981a. "Characteristics of the Population Below the Poverty Level: 1979." *Current Population Reports*, ser. P-60, no. 130. Washington: U.S. Government Printing Office.

———. 1981b. "Geographical Mobility: March 1975 to March 1980." *Current Population Reports*, ser. P-20, no. 368. Washington: U.S. Government Printing Office.

———. 1981c. "Money Income of Families and Persons in the United States: 1979." *Current Population Reports*, ser. P-60, no. 129. Washington: U.S. Government Printing Office.

———. 1982. *Statistical Abstract of the United States: 1982*. Washington: U.S. Government Printing Office.

———. 1983a. *1980 Census of Population and Housing, Earnings by Occupation and Education*, Subject Report PC80-2-8B. Washington: U.S. Government Printing Office.

———. 1983b. *1980 Census of Population and Housing, General Social and Economic Characteristics: United States Summary*. PC80-C1, pt. 1. Washington: U.S. Government Printing Office.

———. 1985a. "Characteristics of the Population Below the Poverty Level: 1983." *Current Population Reports*, ser. P-60, no. 147. Washington: U.S. Government Printing Office.

———. 1985b. "Household and Family Characteristics: March 1984." *Current Population Reports*, ser. P-20, no. 398. Washington: U.S. Government Printing Office.

———. 1985c. "Marital Status and Living Arrangements: 1984." *Current Population Reports*, ser. P-20, no. 399. Washington: U.S. Government Printing Office.

———. 1985d. "Money Income of Households, Families, and Persons in the United States, 1983." *Current Population Reports*, ser. P-60, no. 146. Washington: U.S. Government Printing Office.

———. 1986a. "Characteristics of the Population Below the Poverty Level: 1984." *Current Population Reports,* ser. P-60, no. 152. Washington: U.S. Government Printing Office.

———. 1986b. "Household Wealth and Asset Ownership." *Current Population Reports*, ser. P-70, no. 7. Washington: U.S. Government Printing Office.

———. 1986c. "Money Income of Households, Families, and Persons in the United States, 1984." *Current Population Reports*, ser. P-60, no. 151. Washington: U.S. Government Printing Office.

———. 1986e. *Statistical Abstract of the United States: 1986.* Washington: U.S. Government Printing Office.

———. 1991. *Statistical Abstract of the United States: 1991.* Washington: U.S. Government Printing Office.

———. 1992. "Measuring the Effect of Benefits and Taxes on Income and Poverty: 1979–1991." *Current Population Reports*, ser. P-60, no. 182RD. Washington: U.S. Government Printing Office.

———. 1995. "Income, Poverty and Valuation of Noncash Benefits: 1993." Current Population Reports, ser. P-60, no. 188, Washington: U.S. Government Printing Office.

———. 1996a. "Poverty in the United States: 1995." *March 1996 Current Population Survey*, ser. P-60, no. 194. Washington: U.S. Government Printing Office

———. 1996b. *Statistical Abstract of the United States: 1996.* Washington: U.S. Government Printing Office.

———. 1997. *Statistical Abstract of the United States: 1997.* Washington: U.S. Government Printing Office.

———. U.S. Department of Commerce, Bureau of Economic Analysis. 1981. *The National Income and Product Accounts of the United States, 1929–76.* Washington: U.S. Government Printing Office.

———. Various years. *Survey of Current Business.* Washington: U.S. Government Printing Office.

U.S. Department of Education, National Center for Educational Statistics. 1994. "NAEP Trends in Academic Progress." Report in brief, July. Washington, D.C.: National Center for Educational Statistics.

U.S. Department of Health, Education, and Welfare. 1976. *The Measure of Poverty: A Report to Congress as Mandated by the Education Amendments of 1974* (April). Washington: U.S. Government Printing Office.

U.S. Department of Labor. 1982. *Employment and Training Report of the President: 1982*. Washington: U.S. Government Printing Office.

———. 1983. *Handbook of Labor Statistics* (December). Washington: U.S. Government Printing Office.

U.S. Department of the Treasury, Office of Tax Analysis. 1998. "Average and Marginal Federal Income, Social Security and Medicare, and Combined Tax Rates for Four-Person Families at the Same Relative Positions in the Income Distribution, 1955–1999." Report. Washington, D.C.: U.S. Department of the Treasury, Office of Tax Analysis.

U.S. House of Representatives, Committee on Ways and Means. 1985. *Children in Poverty* (committee print, May 22). Washington: U.S. Government Printing Office.

U.S. Office of Management and Budget. 1981. *America's New Beginning: A Program for Economic Recovery*. Washington: U.S. Government Printing Office.

Vernon, Raymond. 1959. *The Changing Economic Function of the Central City*. New York: Area Development Committee of the Committee for Economic Development.

The Wall Street Journal. 1997. "Rebate Rising." *The Wall Street Journal*, December 1, 1997, editorial, p. A22.

———. 1998. "Welfare Load Falls 27% To 8.9 Million Since '96." *Wall Street Journal*, May 28, 1998, p.A2.

The Washington Post. 1997. "Tax Fraud." *The Washington Post*, June 29, 1997, editorial.

Weinberg, Daniel H. 1985. "Filling the 'Poverty Gap': Multiple Transfer Program Participation." *Journal of Human Resources* 20, 1 (Winter): 64–89.

Wessel, David. 1998. "Inflation Adjusted Wages are on the Rise for Typical U.S. Worker, Shifting Trend." *Wall Street Journal*, July 17, 1998, p. A2

White, Gregory L. 1998. "Mercedes Raises ML320 Price, To Unveil ML430." *The Wall Street Journal*, August 14, 1998, p. B8.

White, Theodore H. 1961. *The Making of the President, 1960*. New York: Atheneum.

Whitehead, Ralph, Jr. 1990. "Class Acts: America's Changing Middle Class Faces Polarization and Problems." *Utne Reader* January/February: 50–53.

Williamson, Jeffrey G. 1980. "Unbalanced Growth, Inequality and Regional Development: Some Lessons from United States History." In Victor L. Arnold, ed., *Alternatives to Confrontation*. Lexington, Mass.: Lexington Books.

Wilson, William Julius. *The Truly Disadvantaged*. Chicago: University of Chicago Press.

Wilson, William Julius, and Robert Aponte. 1985. "Urban Poverty." *Annual Review of Sociology* 11: 231–58.

Index

Numbers in **boldface** refer to figures or tables.

FRANK LEVY is Daniel Rose Professor of Urban Economics at the Massachusetts Institute of Technology.